CHANGE YOUR DIET

and

CHANGE YOUR LIFE

Food Intolerance & Food Allergy Handbook

Sharla Race

Tigmor Press

This book is dedicated to you the reader.
It is my sincere wish that the guidelines in this
book help you find the diet that truly works for
you.

May you find heath, happiness and serenity.
You are unique - never doubt this.

Sharla

For more information on food intolerance please visit
Food Can Make You Ill
http://www.foodcanmakeyouill.co.uk

A Tigmor Press publication

CHANGE YOUR DIET AND CHANGE YOUR LIFE
Food Intolerance and Food Allergy Handbook

First published 2001

Tigmor Press
14 Zetland Terrace, Saltburn by the Sea,
Cleveland, TS12 1BS, UK

Printed and bound by Antony Rowe Ltd

DISCLAIMER

Food Can Make You Ill has been written to provide you with information on food intolerance and related issues. It is not my intention, nor should it be seen as being my intention, to provide medical advice or diagnosis. I am a researcher and a person with severe food intolerance NOT a doctor.

As there are many possible causes of illness, it is essential that at all times you consult with your doctor or medical practitioner. Any proposed changes to your diet should be discussed with your doctor or medical practitioner before being started. Under NO circumstances should you stop taking prescribed medication without the consent of your doctor or medical practitioner.

It is my hope that you will find the information in this book useful and helpful but the responsibility for what you do with the information you read is completely your own.

CONTENTS

1

WELCOME

Are you fed up of being ill?

Have you, for as long as you can remember, been plagued by minor health problems - headaches, skin rashes, constant colds, viruses, fleeting pains, bloating, sleeplessness, stomach upsets?

Have you never had a fully healthy skin?

Have you tried to lose weight and never succeeded, and if you have lost weight have you put it on again?

Do you get recurring problems like joint and muscle pains, restless legs, fatigue, headaches, tics, rashes, depression, anxiety, tinnitus?

Have you had long periods of coping with everything and then suddenly become exhausted and has this happened more than once?

Do you feel tired after a full night's sleep?

Do you feel as if you've never totally been yourself?

Have you felt as if your life goes round in circles? You have periods of feeling okay when you get on with your life, make plans, see friends... Then you find the pace is speeding up, it seems that there's too much to do but you're still okay, coping. Then suddenly, or so it appears, everything seems too much and you descend into feelings of despair and not coping - all you really want to do is withdraw. And when it finally passes do you feel confused and unsure of yourself?

Have you ever made a major change to your diet and, after an initial high, felt worse?

Do you frequently have stomach problems - wind, indigestion, constipation and/or diarrhoea?

Have you had bouts of anxiety, nervousness or depression for no apparent reason?

Has a doctor, more than once, told you he can find nothing wrong or that there's nothing to worry about - it (the rash, pain, whatever) will go away, or has suggested your problem is stress related when you know it isn't?

If you have answered yes to more than one of the above questions then there is a strong likelihood that something you are eating is making you ill. You are in good company!

We change our diets, take supplements, exercise more and still we feel no better. So what is going wrong? It is my belief that the focus of health care is fundamentally flawed. Rather than looking for the cause of our problems, doctors usually focus on treating the symptoms. We have come to accept this approach and to expect it, even demand it. We want the quick fix that will remove the pain, rash or depression but, sadly, without sorting out the cause the symptoms usually return.

If your diet is not the right one for you then you will not be as healthy as you could be both mentally and physically. By finding the diet that works for your body and mind you will change your life - you will experience fewer health problems, have more energy, an increased sense of well being and a return of hope and joy. If this sounds far fetched, I simply ask for your patience and time. Read on and you'll discover for yourself the truth about how food can make you ill. I myself would not have believed the extent to which food can effect us if my own life had not been dramatically changed by eliminating the foods that were making me ill.

Being constantly plagued by minor health problems had become a way of life for me. The crippling joint pain, the yo-yoing weight, the skin rashes, headaches, sinusitis, PMS, and tinnitus had become so usual that I had stopped seeing them as 'illness' and accepted them as normal for me. What else could I do?

My diet was healthy packed full of fruit and vegetables. Visits to doctors invariably resulted in diagnoses of a virus, stress, wear and tear, or tiredness. There was, apparently, nothing wrong with me. I knew I wasn't as healthy as I could be but no matter what I did nothing changed. During this time I pretty much became an expert on relaxation techniques, meditation, healthy eating, stress management, alternative therapies and creative visualisation. Life, at times, did get easier but I was never wholly well.

By the time I was in my late thirties, the problems had become serious. I was constantly ill and began experiencing episodes of severe debilitating tiredness and illness that I now know would have been diagnosed as Chronic Fatigue Syndrome and Fibromyalgia if I'd had a doctor with knowledge and belief in these but according to the medical profession there was nothing wrong with me that some fresh air, exercise and maybe a drop in weight wouldn't cure. I stopped being able to work and my life began to unravel.

Thankfully I am a fighter and thankfully I had helped my husband 'cure' his migraines and depression by an anti-candida regime and elimination diet. Looking back I can only smile at how throughout that process it never once occurred to me that my own problems, mental as well as physical, could have their foundation in the food I was eating. It was on a sunny day out in York that I finally made the connection. Sitting on the steps of the Minster, nursing a migraine, I watched people closely and came to the conclusion that the bloating I was experiencing and the translucent mottled skin I had developed were most definitely not normal. But what was wrong with me?

Biting into an apple my migraine raged even more ferociously and then receded leaving me with a severe low blood sugar problem. It was at that moment that I thought to myself that maybe, just maybe, some of my problems were being caused by food.

Within a few weeks of following an elimination diet I had made enormous progress. The weight began to disappear, the headaches stopped, my skin began to clear, my joints were mobile, no more ringing in my ears and my sinuses were clear. But what surprised me most of all were the changes in my behaviour and feelings.

The manic hyperactive energy followed by extreme fatigue, the mood swings, the inexplicable anxiety, tension, disorientation and confusion, the memory problems, and the extreme need to be alone all began to fade into the background. I had long ago decided that I had a personality defect probably caused by some event that was locked in my memory and I couldn't access. I was wrong, seriously wrong. These psychological and behavioural symptoms were all being caused by the food I was eating.

To cut a very long story short my health improved and I returned to work but a few months later began to re-experience problems. At this point it seemed that I was intolerant of nearly everything I ate and my diet was very restricted. I decided not give in but to carry out more research and eventually I discovered the information on food chemicals, and salicylate in particular, that I needed. At last I had found the cause of my problems. The journey had been long, painful and extremely lonely but at last I had arrived at a reason and a 'cure'. In my forties, I am now far healthier than I have ever been.

My problems are not some medical oddity, quite the opposite. My research has shown me quite clearly that food intolerance can be the cause of many physical and mental health problems. It has also shown me that food as a cause is very rarely explored and so many people go throughout their lives suffering totally unnecessarily.

Life is far too short to have its quality impaired by what we eat and I have written this book and the 'Food Can Make You Ill' web site to help others on their journey towards health. I do not believe that food intolerance is the cause of all problems but I do believe, and know, that for many a change in diet can truly change their lives.

References in the text, of which there are many, are indicated by a bracket containing a number and full details can be found at the end of the book.

I wish you every success.

Sharla Race

2

FOOD INTOLERANCE

You are unique.

Yes, *you* are unique and in more ways than you can probably imagine. We live in an era that accepts differences in height, weight, body shape and personality without question yet assumes that, because we all have bodies, we all need the same type of food and the same amount of nutrients, to be healthy.

Not so. In 1956, Dr Roger Williams, who discovered pantothenic acid (B5) and folic acid, coined the term 'Biochemical Individuality'. Biochemical individuality means that not only do we have a unique physical appearance but that internally we are also very different from each other.

Our internal organs are different sizes and the way they function varies. Some of us are deficient in certain enzymes such as those needed for digestion, others have these in abundance. Our ability to resist and fight disease varies. Some of us require vast amounts of certain nutrients whilst others don't, some feel pain more than others do and some of us are more likely to develop food intolerance and allergy problems than others.

Our genetic inheritance defines not only how we look but also how our bodies function internally at the level of every single cell. Before you start blaming your genes on everything, remember that other factors will also effect how healthy you are - your lifestyle, what you eat, the amount of exercise you take and your environment. But these only strengthen the argument for viewing each individual as exactly that - an individual.

So, although we are able to say that the body requires protein, minerals and vitamins we can not say that you will function well on the same diet as me. Your needs will differ from mine and my needs will differ from yours. It is this fundamental uniqueness that provides the key to unravelling many baffling health problems.

The first step on the road to health is to embrace the idea that *you are unique* and that you may need to be treated differently than others with the same or similar symptoms. My focus in this book is to introduce you to the idea that eating the wrong diet could be impairing your physical and mental health, maybe even both.

The fact that you may have a problem with wheat, milk or a food chemical, such as salicylate, does not mean there is anything 'wrong' with you. It is simply part of who you are - part of your own unique biochemical make-up. You will be unlikely to find a cure but you will be able to find a solution by eliminating the food or reducing the amount that is consumed.

You may be asking yourself why I insist on you involving your doctor when so many have little experience of this field. Quite simply - illness is complex and has many causes and I do not want you to undergo any additional unnecessary suffering. If all other causes of your problem have been eliminated and your doctor does not want you to try dietary changes you can always change doctors.

As awareness increases more help will become available and there are, currently, doctors who are experts in this field and others who have a more open mind than some of their colleagues.

I must stress that involving your doctor is even more important if you are suffering from any mental health problem, whether diagnosed or not, as the reactions that can take place when testing foods can be extreme. In these instances, testing of foods must be done with medical supervision.

If your body cannot tolerate a particular food, or one of its ingredients, then you will experience an unwanted reaction. The type of symptoms that arise are very individual specific and it is not possible to say that, for example, apples will cause headaches or milk will cause stomach problems. They may do, but they may also cause other symptoms. The simple truth is that any reaction can be provoked by any food.

It is also important to understand that food intolerance is not the same as food allergy. In the case of an allergic reaction there is an immunological response that can be measured and 'seen' in the blood. No such method of testing exists for food intolerance.

The safest, and most accurate, way of detecting food intolerance is by using an elimination diet that first removes the suspect food, in all its forms, from your diet and is then reintroduced. If there is a negative reaction that food, for whatever reason, is not safe for you to eat. If, after a period of time, there is no reaction then the food is safe, for you, to eat. Without the aid of an appropriate blood test it is unlikely that you will know if your reaction can be defined as an allergy or intolerance problem.

The situation is further complicated by the fact that reactions caused by allergy and intolerance, with the exception of anaphylaxis, are very similar. The terms 'food intolerance' and 'food sensitivity' are used throughout this book to refer to *any* negative reaction caused by any food, naturally occurring chemical or food additive.

In some instances it is possible to identify the cause of the intolerance. For example, many people cannot tolerate milk because they are lacking in the enzyme lactase which is essential for the digestion of lactose, the sugar found in milk. We also know that some substances, such as caffeine, act like drugs and we can point to a problem of overuse or overdose. Sadly, for most other forms of intolerance the situation is not as clear cut and if you find yourself intolerant of a food the odds are seriously stacked against you knowing the reason for your intolerance. Vatn (425) suggests that the mechanism behind food intolerance is one of the greatest enigmas of modern medicine.

Although this may be cause for concern for doctors and researchers, it need not concern you. Maybe one day they will ascertain the reasons, and maybe even find solutions, but until then you can still get healthier by avoiding the food or foods that cause you a problem. It is after all the case that many drugs have proved effective at removing or relieving symptoms yet little is actually known as to how some of these work - this is especially the case with drugs used to treat so called mental illnesses.

Many people do not suspect food as being part of their problem because of a common myth that a reaction will take place straight away. The following list shows the full range of ways in which food intolerance can manifest:

◆ An immediate reaction such as rash or nasal congestion.
◆ A delayed reaction - anything from a few hours to a few days.
◆ No immediate reaction but episodic bouts of recurring illness - usually focused on one area whether it be the nose, skin or digestive system.
◆ Recurring bouts of general malaise and flu-like or non-specific symptoms.
◆ A general sense of never really feeling well with no noticeable starting point.
◆ A history of recurring illness - specific and non-specific often leading to periods of crisis in health, frequently starting in childhood and continuing into adulthood.
◆ A sudden down turn in health after serious illness, drug treatment, major stress or trauma.

The result of presenting these symptoms to a doctor is often treatment for a viral infection, depression or stress. As the condition progresses a label may be given - irritable bowel syndrome, arthritis, chronic fatigue syndrome etc... At this point the search for answers usually stops and the search for solutions begins. But if the diagnosis is wrong then the solution will never wholly appear.

There may be improvement but the problem never goes away and the patient becomes the label and may, as time progresses, move on to acquiring even more labels. If you have been diagnosed as having a condition your first step on the road to recovery could very well be to throw out the label you have been given.

Still in doubt? In 1976 Dr Richard Mackarness (224), writing of the UK, estimated that "30 per cent of people attending GPs have symptoms traceable exclusively to food and chemical allergy; 30 per cent have symptoms partly traceable to this cause, and the remaining 40 per cent have symptoms that are unrelated to allergy."

Dr Coca (73), in 1945, estimated that as many as 90% of Americans had one or more food allergies. In the 1970s Dr Mandell (250) estimated that fifty to eighty per cent of the daily medical practice of most doctors was the "result of allergy and chemical susceptibility". It is highly unlikely that this has changed.

Some general indicators of food being a problem include:

- Feeling unwell all over.
- Fluctuating weight.
- Occasional swelling of face, hands, feet and more generally.
- Persistent stomach problems.
- Persistent tiredness not helped by sleep or rest.
- Sudden changes from feeling well to unwell.
- Sudden tiredness or chills after eating.

CHANGE YOUR DIET AND CHANGE YOUR LIFE

To give you an idea of the type of problems that food intolerance can cause, lists of symptoms are given below. Each of the symptoms and conditions has been found, in some individuals, to be caused by food. Please do not assume that just because your symptom or condition is listed that food is the cause - check it out with your doctor first. The purpose of these lists is solely to give you an idea of the overwhelming range of symptoms and illness that can be caused by eating food that is not right for you.

Many people are surprised to discover that behaviour, emotions and feelings can be determined by the food we eat but the cells in the brain are just as at risk as any other in the body. Consider how alcohol effects you and how it effects others differently. The same principle applies to food.

The bloodstream carries molecules of chemicals, natural and artificial, throughout the body. In the brain, these chemicals interfere with the chemical and electrical functioning of the brain cells and so effect our thoughts, feelings and behaviour. It can take a very small amount of a chemical, that your body sees as toxic, to produce an unwanted effect. Some additives and natural food chemicals, such as salicylate, are very similar in structure to some of the brain's neurotransmitters and, when these are wrongly identified by the body, internal chaos begins. Emotional factors are, most definitely, not the only explanation for mental disturbances.

Rinkel, Randolph and Zeller (341) showed that removing foods, and then reintroducing them into the diet, could lead to the disappearance and subsequent reappearance of a variety of 'psychological' symptoms including catatonia, delusions, depression, feeling drugged, hallucinations, headaches and paranoia. Dr Mumby (281) writes that he has seen allergy (food and environmental) lead to "heightened sexual feelings, murderous assault, schizophrenic psychosis, woolly thinking, hallucination, hyperactivity, depression, anxiety, learning difficulties, dyslexia and autism."

Mainly physical: Symptom list

Arthritis
Athlete's foot
Bedwetting
Bloating
Blurred vision
Catarrh
Coated tongue
Constant hunger
Crawling sensation on skin
Difficulty in swallowing
Eczema
Excessive or no sweating
Eyes puffy/burning
Feeling drained
Food cravings
Frequent sore throats
Gritty feeling in eyes
Heavy body odour
Hives
Joint pain/stiffness/swelling
Menstrual problems
Migraine
Muscle aches/cramps
Muscle weakness
Palpitations
Poor balance
Pre-menstrual problems
Rashes
Restless legs syndrome
Sensitivity to noise
Sleep disturbances
Stiff neck
Temperature fluctuations
Tics

Asthma
Bad breath
Blackouts
Blood sugar problems
Breast pain
Chronic Fatigue
Colitis
Constipation
Diarrhoea
Dizziness
Excessive thirst
Eyes sore/itchy
Fatigue
Flushes
Frequent need to urinate
Gall bladder problems
Headaches
High/low blood pressure
Itchy and red ears
Lethargy
Metallic taste
Mouth ulcers
Muscle spasm/tremor
Nausea
Persistent cough
Post-nasal drip
Racing pulse
Recurring ear infections
Sensitivity to light
Sinusitis
Sore tongue
Styes
Thrush
Tinnitus

Urticaria   Vertigo
Weight problems   Wheezing

Mind, emotions and behaviour: Symptom list

Accident prone
Anger for no apparent reason
Anxiety   ADD/ADHD
Behavioural problems   Blankness
Brain fogging   Changes in handwriting
Clumsiness   Confusion
Delusions   Depression
Detached or unreal feeling   Difficulty waking up
Disorientation   Dyslexia
Feelings of disassociation   Fidgeting
Hallucinations
Hearing without comprehension
Hyperactivity   Inability to think clearly
Indifference   Irritability
Maths and spelling errors   Memory loss
Mental exhaustion   Mood swings
Panic attacks   Phobias
Poor concentration   Poor self image
Poor memory   Reading problems
Restlessness
Slow processing information
Slurred speech   Stammering
Suicidal Feelings   Tenseness
Uncontrollable rage   Withdrawn
Weepiness

Speer in his book 'Allergy of the Nervous System' (394), published in 1970, presents evidence that shows that emotional and neurological symptoms arising from allergies have been recorded since the 1920s. In fact, in 1905, Francis

Hare, an Australian doctor, wrote 'Food Factor in Disease' in which he gave numerous examples of patients whose symptoms include 'mental problems' that were caused by various foods.

Dr Randolph (327), at the time of writing his book, had treated about 20,000 people for food allergies and related problems having dealt with "every kind of chronic illness on an allergic basis". About 37.5 per cent of these patients were primarily suffering from 'mental problems'; many were helped significantly often when conventional treatments had failed. He says that allergy can be responsible for a "host of so-called mental problems, including some cases of what looks like outright psychoses".

Dr Philpott, in his book on Brain Allergies (321), provides us with numerous examples including: Hyperactivity in a child being caused by string beans; violent anger in a woman that was triggered by oranges; sensitivity to wheat in a seventeen year old who had been classed as mentally ill for three years; watermelons leading to depression and irritability in a twelve year old; manic depression being caused by milk in a thirty year old patient. Dr Philpott cites many other cases where people's 'psychological' problems have in fact turned out to be reactions to food, chemicals in the environment, preservatives and additives, non-caking agents in table salt, and chlorinated water.

What surprises, and saddens, me greatly is that this information is not more widely available and that it is not embraced by the medical profession. You are still more likely to be given pills, hospitalised or told there is nothing wrong with you than have your diet and environment examined for clues to your condition.

There is now an acceptance and understanding that certain drugs will have side-effects that produce a change in behaviour. In fact some drugs are designed to do exactly that - change how you behave and feel. If we accept that drugs do this, often with little understanding of how, why can we not accept that food and the chemicals within food can do the same?

Let's just briefly look at two hypothetical examples. I am taking more time to explore the links between food and the mind because this is a seriously neglected area of study and you need to know that it is not only your body that is at risk from self poisoning by the food you eat.

In our first example, Josh complains of being tired all the time. He is irritable, has no energy and little interest in anything. He is a busy individual with many responsibilities and says he is feeling under stress yet has previously coped quite adequately with far busier and more demanding times in his life. He also has fleeting joint pains, migraines and a recurring rash. A battery of tests show no physical problem and the doctor is likely to agree with the diagnosis of 'stress'. Josh may also be prescribed exercise to help joint mobility, pain killers for the migraine, and ointment for the rash. None of which will help identify and then treat the cause of the problem.

In our second example, 30 year old Carol has developed agoraphobia. Her husband died a year ago and she now finds herself unable to leave the house. Prior to his death and for the first two months after his death she had no symptoms of agoraphobia. The most obvious diagnosis would be that the agoraphobia was brought on by the bereavement and to recommend a course of counselling. But would something different emerge if Carol was asked about any other changes in her life?

In both the above cases it is easy to see how the diagnoses were arrived at but what if Josh had quite simply reached a time in his life when his body just could no longer cope with the diet he was eating - maybe his sensitivity to wheat, which he eats at every meal, had reached crisis point. (This mechanism is explained in more detail in the next section.)

What if Carol's problem was that her husband had been the cook and her diet had changed dramatically from home made meals to take-outs and microwave dinners and she was taking in additives and MSG to such an extent that they were effecting her brain, increasing her anxiety and preventing her from leaving the house. There have been studies (some are mentioned in Martin's (255) book 'The Sickening Mind') that show the immune function of the bereaved partner is diminished in the weeks after the death. This reduction in function could have been the key factor in stopping her body processing the cocktail of chemicals she was now eating. She could in fact always have been sensitive to MSG or an additive. Had she ever in the past experienced a similar problem?

Five, ten or fifteen minute consultations will never provide these answers. If you truly want to get well you need to be an active participant in the process. Your doctor only knows your symptoms not *you*. Food intolerance can cause problems across the behavioural spectrum from manic 'happy' behaviour to severe depression.

We seemed to have reached a point in our history where we too easily blame our mental states on inherent personality flaws or stress. Yet it could just be what you are eating. I had certainly never experienced the calm that I now have until I changed my diet. I thought my anxiety, mood swings and hyperactivity were just part of who I was. They weren't - they were only symptoms arising from substances that my body saw as toxins.

Perhaps the most dangerous diagnosis of the modern age, aside from 'stress' is that of psychosomatic illness. This is when no physical cause can be found for the symptoms you have and the doctor therefore assumes that they must be being induced by your mental state. This assumption becomes a diagnosis that may lead to some form of talking therapy, a suggestion to reduce stress or no action at all. All three of these will be totally ineffective in relieving symptoms in the long term. If your body is being poisoned by the food you eat, or the chemicals in your environment, then you will continue to be ill until these are removed and you begin to recover.

Dr Philpott (321) writes: "According to Randolph - and my experience bears this out - more than half of the so-called psychosomatic reactions are in reality undiagnosed allergic reactions."

Rapaport (328) sums up my own thoughts exactly: "If mental illness caused by allergies were recognised more, and emotional factors not always sought to explain mental disturbances, a great deal of time and money could be saved, and patients' mental conditions eliminated."

Food intolerance does not just lead to physical and mental symptoms. It affects all areas of your life including your appearance, relationships, work, leisure activities, and self-esteem. The ways in which it can effect your appearance include:

1. You can look fatter and flabbier than the 'real' you actually is. Bloating/swelling can occur on your face, legs, ankles and feet, around your abdomen, thighs and buttocks. You could spend a fortune on products trying to clear your cellulite with no success when all you need to is change your diet.
2. Your skin will probably not be at its best. It could be too oily, dry, or covered in a rash or spots that you just cannot clear.
3. Your eyes could have a discharge, be bloodshot or cloudy, seem very small due to puffy eyelids, feel grainy and tired. At times, your vision may be blurred and your eyes could be light sensitive.
4. Your lips could be cracked, sore and swollen. Your tongue may be coated, sore and swollen and your mouth plagued with ulcers. And, regardless of how thorough a dental hygiene programme you have, you could have bad breath.

5. Your nose could be swollen, constantly running, itchy or red in colour.
6. Your hair, no matter what you do with it, could be lank, excessively dry or oily.
7. If you are constantly feeling ill you probably look tired, miserable and, maybe, even sad or anxious.
8. Clothes and shoes won't always fit - one day they'll be fine, the next too tight and uncomfortable.

Some of the other ways in which food intolerance can have an impact on your life include:

♦ Limiting the activities you can do due to, for example, fatigue and joint pain.
♦ Work can become increasingly stressful when you are plagued with problems due to brain fogging that effect your ability to concentrate and lead to memory problems.
♦ You may have been passed over at work because of excessive time away due to sickness. You may even have had to give up your career.
♦ Relationships can be put under serious strain by constantly having to deal with a partner's seemingly unexplainable bouts of low energy, forgetfulness, irritability, depression, mood swings, seeming distant and far away, anxiety, and obsessive behaviour.

If food was my problem surely I'd know, wouldn't I?
How I wish this was could be true. To doubt that there is a link between what you eat and your mental and physical health is a natural response. After all you eat food every day surely you would have noticed if you had a food related problem and surely, if it was a possibility, your doctor would have said something. If only it was so easy...
  You could go throughout your whole life with your health being impaired without knowing that food was your problem or your doctor even suggesting it. The reason for this is the

body's amazing ability to keep on going against the odds. Sadly, when the problem is not identified early on, the symptoms in the long term become more and more debilitating leading to depression, anxiety, fatigue and overall ill health. I shall try explain what happens in a little more depth.

Your immune system is highly complex and amazing. It has many different layers of defence which are all designed to protect your body from harm whether it be from bacteria, viruses, parasites or toxins. It is a system that is spread throughout your body and it serves you well but it can get overworked. An exhausted immune system will not be able to protect you as well as it should.

One of the ways this exhaustion can come about is by a daily assault from food that is not right for you. Hans Selye (371) in his book "The Stress of Life" describes how our bodies deal with prolonged bouts of stress. The description below is based loosely on his ideas.

1. At first when it receives the food you have a problem with, your body will let you know that there is a problem - some symptoms will appear but these are often ignored, not noticed or happened when we were children so we don't remember.
2. The body then goes into an acceptance phase. It adapts to the toxin and does its level best to keep you going. You may not experience very good health but you are managing.
3. Eventually it will reach the point of exhaustion. It can longer deal with the onslaught and your health begins to break down. Mystery viruses, fatigue, minor problems, loss of zest etc... all begin to appear and you just never seem to feel well.

When stage three takes place will vary from individual to individual. For some it will take place in childhood, in others much later in life or as a result of illness or trauma. It is also not a one-off process. You may find that you become so ill that you have to rest for weeks or months and then you seem to be okay but actually you have returned to stage two and sooner or later will revisit stage three again.

The difficulty is that when stage three is reached you are often presenting a puzzling array of seemingly unrelated symptoms and it is not easy for any medical practitioner to recognise that food intolerance may be the root of the problem. This form of delayed hypersensitivity can involve a whole-body response involving several organ systems and leading to a chronic illness with recurring flu like symptoms. The array of resulting symptoms can be extremely puzzling. By my mid thirties I had such a long list of symptoms that I never presented them to a doctor for fear of being labelled a hypochondriac.

This breakdown in health does not takes place overnight but can take a life time to evolve. Usually in childhood there are symptoms of colic, eczema, nasal congestion, recurring ear infections and 'growing' pains. The child seems fully well for only short periods of time. The pattern continues into adulthood with recurring bouts of a variety of symptoms such as nasal congestion, sore throats, generalised muscle aches and stiffness, abdominal pain and bloating, fatigue, weakness, problems concentrating, inability to think clearly etc...

It is often the case that no specific physical cause can be found. Patients at some point acquire a label, either one of a number of syndromes such as chronic fatigue, fibromyalgia, irritable bowel, depression, panic disorder, or a single aspect is identified as the main problem such as migraine, rheumatic disease, asthma, Crohn's disease, urticaria, or arthritis. The presence of the hidden food problem is not identified and the individual continues to suffer.

Doctors, including Rowe and Randolph, have also identified a tension-fatigue syndrome, characterised by sensory and motor hyperactivity and/or sensory and motor fatigue, linked directly with food sensitivities. Once again, this condition does not appear overnight but at first occasionally bothers the individual then increases in occurrence and intensity leading the patient and doctor to a sense of desperation as nothing can be found to be wrong. The symptoms increase - tiredness after a full night's sleep, tiredness when not being particularly active, mental sluggishness, an inability to concentrate or get oneself going, possible depression, aching and sore muscles, bloating and so on. Studies by doctors who have accepted the existence of this syndrome have shown that the symptoms most generally go into remission when the offending foods are removed from the diet.

Food intolerance can occur at any age. It can be a short term problem or a lifelong condition. If not identified early on it can lead to more serious problems in later life: for example, colitis in a child, that is caused by milk intolerance, can lead to Crohn's disease in adulthood.

It is also the case that any food can cause problems. Although some foods, like wheat and milk, have been identified as most likely to cause problems they are not the only culprits. *Any* food can cause your body and mind to be ill. You can be intolerant of any of the following:

1. A complete food such as milk, soya, carrot, egg, pork, wheat, mushroom, chicken, apple.
2. A naturally occurring chemical such as salicylate in many herbs, fruit and vegetables, tyramine in aged meat, cheeses and wine, purines in protein foods, amines in cooked foods, solanine in vegetables, naturally occurring MSG (monosodium glutamate).
3. An added ingredient that does not occur naturally in the food - such as a preservative, artificial sweetener, colouring, flavour or antioxidant.
4. In a complex food, i.e. any processed food, you could be sensitive to any one of the ingredients. For example, in

bread it is possible to react to wheat, preservatives, yeast, or bleaching agents.

The focus of this book is on intolerance rather than allergy although much of the information applies to both. One of the big differences was always thought to be that there have been deaths from anaphylactic shock resulting from exposure to an allergen. But cases of anaphylaxis as a result of sulphite sensitivity have now also been recorded. As far as I am aware, sulphite sensitivity is the only form of food intolerance that has led to sudden death after unexpected ingestion. If you suspect you have an allergy get tested (a referral by your doctor is the safest way). This will save you a lot of potential distress.

Over the last few years more and more information on allergies has become available but information on food intolerance is still sparse - the subject is often covered as part of a discussion on allergy but leaves out vast amounts of information that you need to know. I suspect that part of the reason for this neglect of food intolerance is because of difficulties with definition.

In the late to mid 1920s a more rigid definition of allergy began to appear and although doctors may have found this more 'scientific' it effectively drew boundaries that have led to food intolerance problems often being ignored and, at times, even denied. Older definitions along the lines of allergy is 'an unwanted reaction in the body or mind caused by a food or chemical' quite clearly encompassed what we now know as food intolerance. So don't be fooled - food intolerance is a serious problem.

Soutter et al (389) found that food intolerance is more likely to be a reaction to chemical substances found in many foods rather than the individual foods. Symptoms are dose-related and may be cumulative from eating a range of foods containing the same substance. There can be a single symptom or a combination of a number of symptoms and these can vary over time. Reactions can take place within thirty minutes or up to 48 hours after eating the problem food. They also found that preservatives and salicylates are the most likely to cause reactions but the range of substances that can affect a sensitive person varies from individual to individual.

Other research has found that individuals react to various foods but when tested are not 'allergic' so food intolerance, although often linked with food chemicals, can also be to any individual food. Future research may identify further chemicals that cause problems and clear this issue up but for the moment it is unknown for definite what the actual cause is.

Myth of a Healthy Diet

It is a myth to suppose that there is such a thing as a single healthy diet that works for all. A healthy diet is a diet that works for you. You are unique and if you eat the wrong diet for you, even if it follows all the current healthy diet guidelines, you will not experience good health and you will probably have weight problems.

A case in point is the focus placed on eating diets high in unrefined carbohydrates. The Drs Eades and the Drs Heller, among many others, have found that these diets lead to health and weight problems for many. The ideal diet for these individuals would be one that was high in protein and low in carbohydrate.

The current healthy diet guidelines generally suggest that you:

- Eat a variety of different foods.
- Eat the right amount to be a healthy weight.
- Eat plenty of foods rich in starch and fibre.
- Don't eat too many foods that contain a lot of fat.
- Don't have sugary foods and drinks too often.
- Don't eat too much salt.

- Look after the vitamins and minerals in your food.
- If you drink alcohol, drink within sensible limits.

The guidelines tend to focus around the food pyramid which is briefly as follows.

- At the top oils and fats which should be used sparingly.
- On the next level down are protein and dairy products with suggestions that 2-3 portions of meat, fish and beans are eaten as well as 2-3 times portions of milk and dairy foods.
- Next come the fruit and vegetables with a recommendation that at least 5 portions are eaten each day (ideally 3-5 of vegetables, and 2-4 of fruit).
- And at the bottom of the pyramid, the foundation of the diet, are bread, cereal, rice, pasta and, sometimes, potatoes. Six to eleven servings a day are recommended.

As a general guideline this may be adequate but it can never work for everyone. You could in fact follow these guidelines and be very unhealthy. For example, if you are intolerant of milk, gluten or wheat then you would not be able to eat the portions recommended in the dairy and grains sections. The Health Education Authority in the UK includes breakfast cereals, tea cakes, crumpets and crackers in this category which is of some concern as many of these are high in sugar, salt and refined grains.

Do not see these guidelines, or any others, as being cast in stone. Evidence on dietary fat which has caused so much concern over the last few decades is contradictory. It is now thought that we do actually need fat in the diet and not all fat is bad. Benton (32) took a random sample of 7,076 British people and divided them into three groups depending on the amount of fatty foods that were eaten. The findings showed that reaction times of those eating higher amounts of fatty foods were quicker. The results did not differ across different age, sex or occupation groups.

Dr Ronald Krauss (43), chairman of the American Heart Association said that studies in healthy people show genetic differences in their response to low fat diets. It would seem that two thirds of the population would show only minimal benefit from a low fat diet and that for some it would be harmful. Yet in 1999, led by the American Heart Association, four major health groups agreed on a diet to reduce heart disease, stroke, cancer and diabetes that was low in fat. These were issued as general guidelines for a healthy diet.

There is a further danger in these guidelines with people interpreting 'low fat' as 'no fat' and seriously malnourishing their bodies. We all need protein, energy and nutrients from our food but how we obtain these will vary enormously. No single diet can be right for everyone. Over the last twenty years there has been an explosion in diets not just aimed at slimmers but for general good health. If any of these worked for all of us wouldn't we all be healthier, and slimmer, than we currently are? By all means investigate the different diets on the market but don't see any one of them as the ideal one for you.

Success with some of these diets is often due to finding, by luck, one that excludes the foods that cause you a problem or provides you with the missing foods your body needs. For example, macrobiotic diets have worked wonderfully for some people but this could be because they have a sensitivity to the food chemical 'solanine'. All vegetables in the deadly nightshade family are excluded on a macrobiotic diet and all of these are high in solanine. Also, the diet relies on fresh food and has no preservatives and additives which will invariably remove troublesome elements from the diet.

The raw food diets work well for some because they increase the alkalinity in the body and make you feel great. For many they are a serious problem as most vegetables and fruit contain naturally occurring chemicals that some people are sensitive too. Stone age diets remove grains, and often dairy products, from the diet as do many low carbohydrate diets. Could not the success of these be due to eliminating, two of the most common trouble makers, milk and wheat?

Slimming diets that increase the fibre content of the diet may work because they are helping the individual to balance their blood sugar more and so preventing over eating yet for those with a grain sensitivity they do not work and in some cases lead to weight gain. Some people thrive on vegetarian diets others become ill not because of the lack of meat protein but because they are consuming more dairy products than they can tolerate, have a sensitivity to lectins in beans, or are intolerant of grains or vegetables.

No 'off the shelf' diet is going to work for everyone. Please do not think I am knocking these diets. I think the variety of them is a good thing and they are very useful for the people who can use them. But failing to improve, lose weight or being able to maintain one of these diets is not necessarily a sign that you have done something wrong, it is more likely that you have quite simply been trying to follow the wrong sort of diet for *you*.

It is strange that at this point in history we need guidelines on what to eat. Perhaps the greater choice and greater availability of food have clouded our own innate judgement as to what is healthy for us and what isn't it but sadly guidelines can only ever be part of the story. You are going to have to take responsibility for your own diet. Whilst trying to find the right diet for yourself do be sensible. Eat a variety of foods and use your common sense.

As you will discover, in the next chapter, there is an overwhelming amount of evidence that demonstrates how food can make you ill. So, why is the link between food and health, proven by many doctors, not accepted by the majority? I put forward the following answers not as excuses but as a way of explaining the mechanism at work in traditional western medicine.

+ Accepting food as a cause of illness is seen as too simplistic and would contradict accepted theories of disease causation put forward by highly respected members of the profession.
+ There is always another promised wonder drug around the corner that, with media hype and marketing, overshadows research on links between food and illness.
+ Increasing specialisation means doctors focus on a single set of symptoms rather than on the totality of the person.
+ Treating symptoms rather than looking for causes is what doctors are taught to do.
+ Doctors receive virtually no training in nutrition. The ones that come to accept the links between food and illness have often seen the effects of food intolerance on themselves, a relative or patient.
+ The range of symptoms that can be caused by food intolerance is so vast that food intolerance would nearly always have to be considered and this is not seen as valid use of a doctor's time - it is far easier, and saves time, to treat the symptom than to assist the patient in finding the cause.
+ Assessing food intolerance is not something that can be done solely by the doctor - control must pass to the patient and patients are not generally trusted to take responsibility.
+ There is still little understanding of how food intolerance and allergies can cause so many symptoms and this is unsettling to doctors used to relying on weighty tomes of scientific evidence.
+ Little funding is available for research into the relationship between food and health. Drug research is more readily funded as pharmaceutical companies have a vested interest in the results. There is, quite simply, no profit to be made from understanding food intolerance.

◆ Research that requires the comparison of identical cases is virtually impossible in the area of food intolerance as what effects one individual with, for example, migraine, will not necessarily effect another. Case studies are seen as being to individual specific and often ignored as evidence.

One of the other reasons is that doctors do not learn from their patients. Dr Mansfield (251), an advocate of the link between nutrition and arthritis, states that patients who have had spectacular improvement in their arthritis have been met by disbelief when reporting their success with a change in diet to their GPs and rheumatologists. Their improvement in virtually all cases has been put down to 'spontaneous remission'. Dr Mansfield says: "These physicians, amazingly, seem uninterested by the patient's offer to re-eat the 'bad' foods and demonstrate an abrupt end to this 'spontaneous remission' for a few days."

Other doctors, including Philpott, Mackarness, Mumby, Randolph, and Rowe, have been equally amazed at how findings on links between nutrition and health have, rather than being embraced, been ignored. In 1998 Professor Jonathon Brostoff (56), Professor of Allergy and Environmental Health, University College, London, said that re-education of doctors was essential. "The education system does not even mention nutrition, let alone food intolerance. We do not have a body of doctors who have learned about the role of food and diet in health."

A further reason, and the last one I shall give, is that doctors want scientific evidence which, because of the focus on drugs, has been predominantly laboratory based where the results can be replicated. Food intolerance does not lend itself easily to scientific testing in this way which, for many, questions its validity. Also, much of the research that has identified links between diet and illness has been unable to go a step further and say why this is the case.

This is illustrated in a study carried out by Mullen (280) which identified food allergy as an important factor in irritable bowel syndrome. Although patient improvement was acknowledged, concern was expressed that the underlying mechanism had not been explained on an immunologic basis and remained unknown. Likewise, Merry et al (264) in a study of the links between diet and rheumatic symptoms found that whilst certain substances, such as purines, sodium nitrate, wheat, maize and beef, have been seen to exacerbate arthritis there appeared to be no consistent cause.

During the course of the research for this book, I have come to appreciate the difficulty faced by doctors and researchers in scientifically establishing the role of food in illness. Thankfully, with appropriate tests, allergies can now be more easily recognised but food intolerance continues to cause problems. This will become easier when the various mechanisms by which food affects individuals become known and defined. Research in the area of food additives and the effects of naturally occurring food chemicals is taking place but is fraught with difficulties for the following reasons.

1. Little is still known about why some individuals have problems with eliminating these substances from their bodies.
2. Most of these substances are cumulative in the body and this can make testing extremely difficult.
3. The symptoms produced vary in type and intensity from individual to individual.
4. Tolerance levels are individual specific.
5. Challenging with a single dose often produces a negative result.

This inability to explain why food 'x' causes symptom 'y' and the fact that any food can cause any symptom leaves many doctors sceptical and resistant to exploring food intolerance as the cause of illness. Scepticism is healthy but total dismal is ignorance and the result is that millions of people are denied the help they need. Suffering continues and the cost of health care keeps on rising.

One cannot fault the drive for medical advances to prevent or cure diseases that cause so many deaths such as cancer and heart disease but ignoring the host of more minor complaints that people continuously suffer from is criminally insane. It is time health organisations and professionals recognised that avoiding certain foods and additives can greatly improve a patients condition, improve their quality of life and help prevent more serious illness.

As Gaby (136) in his paper on the role of hidden food allergy and food intolerance in chronic diseases says, "Food allergy is an important and frequently overlooked cause of (or triggering factor for) a wide range of chronic, physical and mental disorders. Routine use of elimination diets in clinical practice can greatly increase the response rate in many difficult-to-treat medical conditions."

Doctors indifference to the role of nutrition in illness is perhaps nowhere best seen than in the disregard for evidence that shows that hospitalised patients are frequently provided with nutritionally deficient diets. A few examples follow:

- Todd et al (415) found that the daily energy, protein, iron and vitamin intake of patients on different wards of an English hospital were less than those recommended for healthy adults.
- Allison (7) found that treatable malnutrition could be occurring in up to 25% of hospital patients and that nutritional status may also deteriorate during a prolonged stay. Suggestions were made that hospital managers had a positive policy towards nutritional care, that catering services recognised and addressed the problem and that, for optimal success, a skilled nutrition team was necessary and cost effective.

- Nevett (287) found that malnutrition is a common problem amongst hospitalised patients and that this leads to an increased risk of mortality and morbidity.
- The development of malnutrition whilst in hospital is the result of changes in diet, nutrition not being seen as a high priority, common hospital practices, and lack of knowledge of patients' previous nutritional state is the conclusion reached by Edwards (104) in a comprehensive overview of malnutrition in hospital patients.
- An assessment of the nutritional status of surgical gastrointestinal and orthopaedic patients by Bruun et al (57) showed that new routines and staff education are needed. Thirty nine per cent of the patients assessed were mildly/borderline to severely malnourished.

I find these type of studies distressing. Surely, during a stay in hospital, a patient should be able to expect the best possible care and that this should include an adequate and nutritious diet. In 1999, a study by the Nuffield Trust in the UK (293), found that 40% of adult hospital patients are undernourished and many others become so during their time in hospital. The report recommends that food provision be considered as part of clinical care rather than a 'hotel' function.

The role of food in health is being overlooked by those very people responsible for our health and who produce the guidelines for healthy eating. Just what message are they sending out if these are not implemented in hospitals?

By ignoring nutrition and the role that food intolerance plays in illness, doctors are closing the door on health for a great many people. If someone presents at a doctor's surgery with a recurring rash and headaches their body is undergoing stress and if it is not dealt with adequately their immune system will suffer. If an ointment and pain relief are prescribed then the symptoms may abate but the problem will still remain. And prescribing a different ointment and higher strength pills will still not solve the problem.

The more stress and damage we do to our finely tuned immune systems the harder it will be for them to deal with an invasive disease or illness. Modern medicine has become focused on signs and symptoms, and drugs and treatments to 'cure' them. The approach by doctors has become standardised and narrow, overlooking (usually not even considering) the unique aspects of an individual's condition.

Finding appropriate help has become expensive and exhausting and it is a tragedy that many people are unable to get the help they need. The food we eat, and the environment we live in, can never be ignored. For many people, an exploration of these would lead to an end to unnecessary suffering. And food intolerance does cause suffering - not just rashes and headaches but, if not identified, a lifetime of chronic ill health can ensue.

If doctors can't help us we need to educate ourselves and force them to 'hear' us. I know you may have great difficulty finding appropriate help but at least through this book, and others, you will have more information to guide you and help you guide your helpers. We need to take more responsibility for our own health. If we are serious about our health we cannot wait for doctors to find the answer for us. We must do some of that work ourselves.

Can I be tested to find out if I am intolerant?

An allergic reaction leads to an immunological response that can be measured and 'seen' in the blood. No such method of identification, and hence testing, exists for food intolerance. The safest and most accurate, way of detecting food intolerance is by using an elimination diet that first removes the food, in all its forms, from your diet and is then reintroduced. The three main types of medically approved allergy testing are:

1. The Skin Prick Test where the suspected allergen is injected just under the surface of the skin and the reaction

is observed. Not all allergies can be identified by this method.

2. Patch Testing where the test substance is applied to the skin, covered with a patch and left in place for a period of time (up to 48 hours). Mainly used to establish if there is a contact allergy leading to some form of skin rash.

3. RAST Testing is used to detect the presence of an antibody called IgE in the blood. IgE is the substance that causes allergic reactions. Different substances produce specific IgEs and this enables the test to identify more than one allergen. Results are expressed on a grade that indicates how much IgE specific to the substance you tested for, is present in your blood. The higher the grade the more likely you are to be allergic.

The RAST test used to only be available through the medical profession but there are some organisations that will now carry out these tests for you. You should note that a negative test does not 100% rule out an allergy. It is, also, possible to have a positive IgE test when you have either outgrown the allergy or not yet developed any symptoms. RAST testing will not identify a food intolerance problem.

Other tests are available and some of these claim to identify food intolerances as well as allergies. The ALCAT test measures platelet aggregation and changes in white blood cells after mixing whole blood with various food extracts. Hoj (176) found it to be fairly reliable for identifying reactions to food additives but Fell et al (124) found it far less successful in the testing of food allergies.

Provocative testing, using dilutions of food extracts are used by some practitioners and a similar procedure is used to 'neutralise' or desensitise allergies. Although the efficacy of food extract injection therapy has been demonstrated in a double-blind study by Miller (268) others including Lehman (227) failed to find a beneficial effect.

What you need to know before parting with your money is that food intolerance does not cause a specific response in the body that can be measured. Yes, it does sometimes cause a fluctuation in the pulse that can be detected and sometimes a measurable IgG but not always. Also, no one substance is produced in the blood that can be used to measure *all* forms of food intolerance. Given that any food can cause any reaction and that your food problems could in fact be being caused by food chemicals these tests need to approached with some degree of caution.

If you have ever suspected that you have an allergy and been sent for tests that have all turned out negative and been told there is nothing wrong with you, when you know there is, then don't despair - you are probably food intolerant. Just because you can't measure it doesn't mean it doesn't exist.

In 1991 Sloper et al (384) presented their findings on the links between eczema and food in children and reported on their immunological findings. Although they were able to observe that eczema, for many of the children, improved significantly during the diet and became worse on food challenges, the clinical outcome of food elimination could not be predicted by the initial skin prick test results, serum immunoglobulins, total or food-specific IgE, or complex IgG or IgE. This study sends a very clear message that allergy tests are not enough.

What you have to understand is that an allergic reaction can be caused by a very small amount of the problem food, in respect of intolerance this is not generally the case. Food chemicals, such as salicylate and solanine, build up in the body and it is only when the individual's tolerance is breached that problems appear. Challenge testing with a concentrated form of the chemical can be misleading as most are cumulative in the body and the amount varies from day to day. A positive reaction is of no help in ascertaining the level you can in fact tolerate.

We all want a quick and easy answer but the reality is that this is not always possible. If you do use one of these tests and are presented with a list of foods to avoid, do not accept the list as definitive proof of your problems. By far the wisest course of action would be then to test each of these foods using an elimination diet. If you don't do this you could be restricting your diet far too severally and unnecessarily.

Why bother with an elimination diet when you know someone who has had massive improvements by following the advice given as a result of one of these tests? Because your health matters and what works for one person will not necessarily work for someone else. Two of the most common foods that people are asked to eliminate are milk and wheat and I think you will be a rare individual not to experience some positive health changes if you eliminate these but this is not always indicative of a food intolerance problem. Wheat and milk are two foods that are consumed daily, often at each meal, and removing them from the diet often leads to some improvement. It is possible that your body is simply enjoying a rest, that you are intolerant of gluten or are lactose deficient or that you have a problem with amines and so on.

In 1998 a survey by 'Health Which?' (163) examined four different services costing between £20 and £105. They found that the tests could not "reliably diagnose true food allergies or intolerances". Soutter et al (389) in their study of food allergy and food intolerance in children state that food chemical intolerance can only be assessed by means of an appropriate elimination diet and challenge protocol. Blood and skin tests are not helpful or appropriate. Sadly few doctors, allergists or other health practitioners are aware of the problems these chemicals can cause. Elimination diets are the only accurate way of determining most forms of food intolerance and a simple easy to use system is outlined later in this book.

3

EVIDENCE

More than 2000 years ago Hipocrates said "Let your food be your medicine and your medicine be your food". He, like many doctors down the centuries, accepted the link between food and illness. In the twelfth century, Maimonides stated that no illness that could be treated by diet should be treated in any other way. They understood that simple changes to the diet were sometimes all that was needed.

Despite overwhelming amounts of evidence accumulated by modern day doctors and researchers, this is not a view that has been embraced by Western medicine. The search remains focused on finding 'cures' that have nothing to do with diet and doctors prescribe treatments that relieve symptoms rather than cure them. Yet, it seems that the basic truth that food can make you ill and a change in diet can make you well is continuously being rediscovered by doctors.

It is a sad fact that many people discover that they are food intolerant without the help of a doctor and when they present this information to the doctor they are not believed. As much as I find this highly annoying, I also find it understandable. Vickers and Zollman (430), in their 1999 study, found that, although nutrition as a science has always been part of conventional medicine, doctors are not taught, and therefore do not practise, much in the way of nutritional therapeutics.

Dieticians in conventional settings tend to work mainly with particular patient groups such as those with diabetes, obesity, digestive, or cardiovascular risk factors. Apart from the treatment of severe nutritional deficiencies and rare metabolic disorders, other nutritional interventions generally fall outside the mainstream and have therefore come to be seen as complementary medicine.

Also, if you have never witnessed for yourself a food reaction then you will be sceptical. Doctors who begin to use elimination diets, a method of testing for food intolerance, are also at first taken aback at the range of symptoms and the number of foods that their patients claim they have a reaction too. But in the words of Dr Mansfield (251): "Patients do not want to react adversely particularly to their favourite foods, and are more likely to ignore a minor reaction to a favourite food than to invent reactions that do not exist." Obvious really.

In 1998 the British Allergy Research Foundation stated that there is now abundant evidence that conditions such as irritable bowel syndrome and asthma are linked to food allergies but that the connection is still not recognised by many GPs with the result that many people suffer years of misery before they are properly diagnosed (if they ever are). They estimated that one in four people suffers from some form of allergic disease and found evidence that food intolerance causes or exacerbates conditions such as asthma, migraine, nasal congestion, eczema, hyperactivity, irritable bowel syndrome and Crohn's disease. In respect of Crohn's disease, 50% feel better when a particular food is eliminated from the diet.

In 1999 the BBC ran a mini series called "Allergy Alert". Their review of studies in different western populations showed at least 15% of the population to be allergic which in Britain means around eight million people. Yet, the British Nutrition foundation estimates that only 1.4% of the United Kingdom population has allergies but that 20% believe they have an allergy.

French Allergy researchers recently reported that multiple food intolerance in infants and young children is increasing. Moneret-Vautrin et al (274) estimate that more than 40% of infants less than one year old could be effected. The most common food allergens are milk, egg, soya and wheat but other foods are also implicated.

I could continue quoting figures but at best they are estimates and do not give a true picture of the ways in which food affects health. Part of the problem is with definitions. The focus of these statistics is usually allergies that can be observed objectively using scientific methods of testing. Yet, food intolerance which causes problems for countless people cannot be measured in this way.

Some doctors when quoting statistics will estimate far greater numbers because they are aware of food intolerance but others don't. So what is the truth? At the moment we don't know. I suspect that the number of people with food intolerance problems is far greater than ever suspected but until methods of identifying and classifying these cases is carried out we will not know for definite.

Before continuing, I would like to extend a very big thank you to the doctors, scientists, researchers and the individuals who have participated in the studies outlined below. Without this type of research there would be no hope at all of the medical profession exploring the role of food in illness and health. Maybe, just maybe, we are at stage three in the development of a new medical idea as put forward as a 'joke' in Dr Mumby's book 'The Complete Guide to Food Allergies and Environmental Illness' (281):

1. You are mad.
2. There might be something in it.
3. There might be something in it but where is the proof?
4. Of course, we knew all along.

The purpose of this chapter is to highlight some of the research that has been carried out that has identified food as the cause of ill health. It is by no means comprehensive, there are thousands of articles out there, but is presented here to give you an idea of the work being done and also to show you that many doctors do recognise this problem. Before we start a special mention needs to be given to weight problems.

Weight Problems
The slimming industry is worth millions of pounds and many people seem to be permanently on one type of slimming diet or another. Bray and Macdiarmid (50) quote figures that suggest by 2025 there will be 300 million people in the world who are obese. They state that obesity "is a chronic disease that is caused by eating more calories than are expended". Is it really that simple? Although concern about increasing weight problems is very evident, rarely is the question asked 'why and why now?'. It surely is not simply that more food is available than in the past. Nor, given the torment that individuals go through in attempts to lose weight, can the answer always be over eating.

Friedman (133) has estimated that most people will lose weight if they reduce their calorie intake to below 1,500 a day although some will require less than 1000 to continue to lose weight. He also found that most obese people are unable to achieve their ideal weight and of those that do the overwhelming majority will regain the weight within two years. A depressing scenario for anyone intent on losing weight but excellent news for the slimming industry. If reducing calories and increasing exercise don't work what will work?

One of the first things anyone concerned with their weight should do is to ascertain if they have any food sensitivities as these can and do lead to weight gain. The main ways in which food sensitivities effect your weight is by:

1. Effecting blood sugar levels which leads to artificial feelings of hunger that need to be satisfied - a problem that never ends if the 'hunger' is satisfied with a problem food.

2. The body attempting to avoid withdrawal from a problem food. Many food sensitivities appear to lead to a form of addictive eating - you quite simply must have the coffee, cake, drink, chips or whatever to keep on going. What is taking place here is that the level of the 'poison' drops in your body and signals you to top up the level, you reach for the problem food and immediately feel better. Unfortunately the feeling doesn't last and you reach out for more food.

Both of these reasons can lead people to consuming far more food than they need to but they will not be able to stop for any length of time until they eliminate the problem foods from their diet. No slimming diet will be successful unless it accidentally removes the offending food from your diet. One of the most positive aspects of finding the foods that truly work for you is that you will never again need to try to lose weight. Once the body is receiving food that is healthy for you the need to over eat quite simply disappears and excess weight gradually fades away. Sounds fantastic but it is true. Now let's turn our attention to some more specific conditions

Acute Pancreatitis

Matteo and Sarles (259) report on two cases of acute recurrent pancreatitis, lasting for 8 and 10 years, characterised by acute abdominal pain. Pain attacks were associated with headache or typical migraine, myalgia, pruritis, and diarrhoea. In one case, the IgE serum level was increased but for both individuals the symptoms were reproduced in the 2 hours following the consumption of some particular food. Symptoms abated when the food was avoided. They concluded that both cases were due to food allergy and that food allergy could, for some people, be the cause of acute recurrent pancreatitis. The problem foods, for these people, were beef, milk, potato, fish, and eggs.

Another study (89) gives details of a 23 year old with recurring episodes of acute pancreatitis. Other symptoms, that occurred at the same time, included red patches on the face, generalised itching and diarrhoea. They were all found to be induced by the consumption of milk. Gastaminza et al (140) report on a case of acute pancreatitis being caused by an allergy to kiwi fruit.

Although these studies describe these as rare occurrences it does make you wonder how many other people are suffering from this condition and have never had food allergy and intolerance explored as a possible cause.

Arthritis

Links between food and arthritis have been recorded in the medical literature as far back as 1917. Dr John Mansfield (251), a British doctor specialising in allergy and nutrition, states that "Most forms of arthritis are environmentally and nutritionally induced."

In a study of alternative treatments, including dietary changes, for rheumatoid arthritis, Gaby (137) states that although the response of patients is variable and, at times, unpredictable, some patients have shown dramatic improvement and long-lasting remission. A few of the numerous studies are summarised below, these are presented in chronological order.

1953: Kaufman (202) found food allergy to be a causative factor in some cases of arthritis.

1979: Skoldstam et al (382), placed 16 individuals, selected at random, with classical rheumatoid arthritis on a 7-10 day fast followed by a 9-week period on a lactovegetarian diet. Pain, stiffness, medication, and clinical and biochemical findings were recorded before fasting, on the first day after the conclusion of the fasting period, and at the end of the lactovegetarian period. One third showed objective signs of improvement including reduced pain and stiffness after the fast, only one person had any improvement on the lactovegetarian diet.

1980: Hicklin et al (168) administered an elimination diet to 22 patients with rheumatoid arthritis. Twenty of the patients (91%) noticed an improvement in their symptoms, and 19 found that certain foods repeatedly caused a return or aggravation of symptoms.

1982: O'Banion (295) reported on the cases of three patients with rheumatoid arthritis whose arthritic pain was totally removed by the avoidance of foods they were found to be allergic to.

1983: Panush et al (305) tried a 10-week, double-blind trial with 26 patients with chronic, progressive rheumatoid arthritis. They were asked to consume an experimental diet which excluded additives, preservatives, fruit, red meat, herbs, egg yolks and dairy products, or a 'placebo diet' which excluded selected foods from the major food groups. Two of the 11 patients consuming the experimental diet improved significantly; however, there were no significant differences between the two groups in terms of clinical improvement or changes in laboratory parameters. The lack of significant benefit in this study may have been due to the fact that the experimental diet did not exclude a number of common allergens, such as wheat, corn, egg whites, sugar, and coffee.

1985: Ratner et al (332) presented the case of a 14-year-old girl with a six-year history of juvenile rheumatoid arthritis who recovered after elimination of all cow's milk protein from her diet. In the same year, Ratner et al (331) studied 15 women and 8 men with rheumatoid or psoriatic arthritis. The patients were instructed to remove dairy products and beef from their diet. Seven patients improved. The authors concluded that a diet free of dairy products and beef is of value in lactase-deficient women with seronegative rheumatoid arthritis or psoriatic arthritis.

1986: Panush et al (306) outlined a detailed case study of a 52 year old woman whose inflammatory arthritis was severely exacerbated by milk. Placebo and other foods had no effect.

1988: Beri et al (33) prescribed an 'elimination and rechallenge' diet to 27 patients with rheumatoid arthritis. Of the 14 patients who completed the diet program, 10 (71%) showed significant clinical improvement.

1990: Panush's (304) study of allergy and arthritis found that, for a small number of patients, food was a key factor in their rheumatic arthritis. Problems were caused by, amongst others, milk, shrimp and nitrates. The conclusion was that probably not more than 5% of rheumatic disease patients have immunologic sensitivity to foods but that the observations made do suggest a role for food allergy in the treatment of at least some patients with rheumatic disease.

1991: Kjeldsen-Kragh et al (210) had 27 patients with rheumatoid arthritis undergo a partial fast, followed by individual food challenges. Foods which provoked symptoms were avoided, as were animal foods, refined sugar, citrus fruits, preservatives, coffee, tea, alcohol, salt, and strong spices. A control group of 26 patients ate an ordinary diet. After four weeks, the diet group showed a significant improvement in the number of tender joints, Ritchie's articular index, number of swollen joints, pain score, duration of morning stiffness, grip strength, sedimentation rate, and C-reactive protein. In the control group, only pain score improved significantly. The benefits in the diet group were still present after one year.

1991: Darlington (84) treated 70 patients with rheumatoid arthritis by identifying and eliminating symptom-provoking foods. Of these 70 patients, 19 per cent remained well and did not require any medications during follow-up periods (ranging from 1.5 to 5 years). The foods that most commonly caused symptoms were: corn (56%), wheat (54%), bacon/pork (39%), oranges (39%), milk, oats (37% each), rye (34%), egg, beef, coffee (32% each), malt (27%), cheese, grapefruit (24%

each), tomato (22%), peanuts, cane sugar (20% each), and butter, lamb, lemon, and soy (17% each).

1991: Skoldstam and Magnusson (383) reported that otherwise healthy and well-nourished patients with rheumatoid arthritis showed significant clinical improvement from fasting for 7 to 10 days. The improvement was reversible and lost when eating was taken up again. This is one of many studies with similar findings and I am a little puzzled as to why the studies do not then go on to investigate specific intolerance problems.

1992: After a study of 94 patients, van de Laar and van de Korst (419) concluded that there is a group of patients with rheumatoid arthritis in which food intolerance places a part and that food intolerance, therefore, merits serious consideration in the management and treatment of the disease.

1994: Borg et al (46) reported that arthritis is a recognised complication of untreated coeliac disease and that symptoms and signs usually improve on introduction of a gluten-free diet.

1998: Nenonen et al (286) tested the effects of an uncooked vegan diet, rich in lactobacilli, in rheumatoid patients. They experienced subjective relief of rheumatic symptoms during the diet and a return to an omnivorous diet aggravated symptoms. Half of the patients experienced adverse effects, including nausea and diarrhoea, during the diet and stopped the experiment prematurely.

2000: Slot and Locht (386) reported on two adults with silent coeliac disease presenting with arthritis of a knee and a sacro-iliac joint, respectively. In both patients the arthritis was relieved on a gluten free diet.

It seems deeply sad that so many of the above studies identified food as a factor but did not then go on to ascertain in exactly what way the problem was being caused. I remain convinced of the view that *you are unique* and if food is implicated in an arthritic condition then the individual needs to find out what it is within their own diet that is not right for them.

Most of the above studies have dealt with rheumatoid arthritis but there is also a large amount of anecdotal evidence that links gouty arthritis with a diet too high in purines, and arthritic and joint pain, more generally, has been linked with a diet too high in solanine. It is also the case that many people with arthritis type conditions, whether diagnosed as such or not, have gained tremendous relief from eliminating problem foods from their diet.

Asthma
Asthma is a condition that has been studied extensively and individual foods, food additives and food chemicals have all been found to be responsible for some individuals' asthma. Businco et al (62) state that, currently, wheezing is considered unusual in food intolerant people but that cases of food-induced asthma have been observed particularly in children. Food allergy may trigger allergic respiratory symptoms through two main routes: ingestion or inhalation.

Back in 1959, Rowe and Young (348) presented findings on 95 patients whose asthma was successfully treated by eliminating allergenic foods from their diet. In 40 per cent of those over the age of 55, food allergy alone appeared to be the cause of their asthma. Stevenson and Simon (402), Stenius and Lemola (401), and Freedman (131) all found that sensitivity to food additives such as metabisulfites, tartrazine, sodium benzoate, and sulphur dioxide acted as trigger factors for asthma in some individuals.

Ogle and Bullock (297) reported on a study of 188 children under one year of age with allergic rhinitis and/or bronchial asthma. The children were placed on an elimination diet for six weeks. Sixty-two per cent had total symptom relief, and a further 28 per cent had partial relief. Pelikan and Pelikan-Filipek (312) found that out of 107 patients with perennial asthma, 60 (56%) had an asthmatic response to ingestion of one or more foods.

If you do your own research you will also find studies that can find no significant relationship between allergy and asthma. One example is the study conducted by Onorato et al (301) which found that only 9 per cent of 300 asthmatic patients had a clinically proven allergy. The key phrase here is 'clinically proven'. As I explained earlier the current tests for allergy are unable to detect food intolerance so although the subjects of these tests may not have had 'allergies', it is still quite possible they had sensitivities to food, food chemicals or additives. These were not looked for in the studies.

Allen et al (5) investigated the asthma provoking potential of monosodium glutamate (MSG). Thirty two people with asthma, some with a history of severe asthma after Chinese restaurant meals or similarly spiced meals, were placed on an additive-free diet for 5 days then challenge tested with MSG. Thirteen had an adverse reaction. Seven developed asthma and symptoms of the Chinese restaurant syndrome 1 to 2 hours after ingestion of MSG. Six did not develop symptoms of Chinese restaurant syndrome and their asthma developed 6 to 12 hours after ingestion of MSG. They concluded that their challenge studies confirm that MSG can provoke asthma and note that the reaction to MSG is dose dependent and may be delayed up to 12 hours making recognition difficult.

Eriksson (112) found that 24% of adults with bronchial asthma and/or allergic hay fever had some kind of food sensitivity - hazelnut, apple and shellfish being the most often named. A correlation was found between birch pollen allergy and food sensitivity with nuts, apple, peach, cherry, pear, plum, carrot and new potato. A correlation was also found between acetylsalicylic acid (aspirin) intolerance and food sensitivity with some foods including nuts, strawberry, almond, green pepper, chocolate, egg, cabbage, milk and wine.

Eriksson suggests that the connection between birch pollen allergy and food sensitivity is probably explained by the structural relationship between birch pollen allergen and some allergens of the foodstuffs, whereas the high incidence of food sensitivity in acetylsalicylic acid-intolerant patients is probably explained by additives in foods as well as salicylates or benzoates naturally occurring in some food.

Rousquet et al (345) reported that between 7 and 29% of asthma sufferers have a milk sensitivity. Petrus et al (318) reported on the case of a young girl with asthma who was found to be sensitive to sodium benzoate. Avoidance of this additive was followed by complete and prolonged disappearance of episodes of coughing and wheezing. To be successful certain drugs that contained benzoates, which had been used in the treatment of the asthma, also had to be avoided.

Genton et al (142) challenge tested individuals with asthma with a number of compounds including acetylsalicylic acid, sodium benzoate, sulfur dioxide, sodium glutamate and tartrazine. Over half of those in the study were found to be intolerant of at least one compound. For some of the group, a diet free of additives resulted in a marked improvement within 5 days.

Attention Deficit Hyperactivity Disorder
Kidd explains that the exact aetiology of ADHD, which often persists into adulthood, is unknown but that adverse responses to food additives and food sensitivities do play a role in the condition for some individuals. The pioneer in this field was Dr Feingold (121) who in the 1970s identified sensitivity to food additives, and often salicylates, as the cause of hyperactivity in up to 50% of children so diagnosed.

Although Feingold has been much criticised, it is the case that links between food and behaviour had been previously noted. As early as 1922, Shannon (375) had published information on the successful treatment of children with hyperactivity and learning disorders using an elimination diet; 30-50 percent of children improved.

More recently, Schardt (364) reviewed more than 20 double-blind studies that examined whether food dyes or ordinary foods worsened behaviour in children with ADHD or other behavioural problems. In the majority of the studies, the behaviour of some children worsened after consumption of food dyes or improved on an additive-free diet. Individual foods also caused problems for some children.

Kidd (205) tells us that Feingold's original case histories covered 1,200 cases in which food additives were linked to behavioural and learning disorders, and implicated a vast number of additives yet subsequent research attempting to verify his work has focused on less than a dozen additives. "It is interesting to note that studies conducted in non-U.S. countries produced results markedly more favourable to the Feingold interpretation, and that most of the U.S. investigations were sponsored by a corporate food lobby group, the Nutrition Foundation."

As Boris (47) demonstrates, studies that eliminate a single additive tend to show little improvement whilst those eliminating a wider range are a great deal more successful (47, 48). Up to 88 percent of ADHD children react to these substances in sublingual challenge testing, (282) but in blinded studies no child reacted to these alone.

Carter et al (64) found that on an elimination diet, 59 out of 78 children with hyperactive behaviour problems improved. They concluded that doctors should give weight to the accounts of parents and consider dietary treatment if it is indicated from the medical history. Data from two double-blind studies indicated that 73-76 percent of ADHD children respond favourably to food elimination diets (79, 64). Maintenance on even more-restricted, low-antigen (oligoantigenic) diets raised the success rate as high as 82 percent. Invariably in these studies, reintroduction of the offending foods led to reappearance of symptoms (105, 107, 408).

A study by Boris and Mandel (48) found that dietary factors may play a significant role in the condition of the majority of children with ADHD. Of the children tested, 73% responded favourably to an elimination diet. The children reacted to various foods, dyes and preservatives.

Breakey (51), in a 1997 review of key research, mainly from 1985-1995, on the relationship between food and behaviour concluded that the research has shown that diet definitely affects some children. But rather than becoming simpler the issue has become noticeably more complex. The range of suspect food items has broadened, and some non-food items are also implicated. Symptoms which may change include those seen in attention deficit disorder (ADD) and attention deficit hyperactivity disorder (ADHD), sleep problems and physical symptoms, with later research particularly emphasising changes in mood. The reports reviewed also show the range of individual differences both in the food substances producing reactions and in the areas of change.

Rowe and Rowe (350) set out to establish if there is an association between the ingestion of synthetic food colourings and behavioural change in children who had been referred for assessment of 'hyperactivity' to the Royal Children's Hospital (Melbourne). Two hundred were included in a 6-week open trial of a diet free of synthetic food colourings. The parents of 150 children reported behavioural improvement with the diet, and deterioration on the introduction of foods containing synthetic colouring. After further tests they concluded that behavioural changes in irritability, restlessness, and sleep disturbance are associated with the ingestion of tartrazine in some children. A dose response effect was also observed perhaps indicating that, like some food chemicals, colours build up in the body.

Rowe (349) placed 55 children suspected of 'hyperactivity' on a 6 week trial of the Feingold diet. Forty (72.7%)

demonstrated improved behaviour and 26 (47.3%) remained improved following liberalisation of the diet over a period of 3-6 months. The parents of 14 children claimed that a particular cluster of behaviours was associated with the ingestion of foods containing synthetic colourings so further studies were conducted with some of the children and behavioural changes were noted. The findings raise the issue of whether the strict criteria for inclusion in studies concerned with 'hyperactivity' based on 'attention deficit disorder' may miss children who indicate behavioural changes associated with the ingestion of food colourings.

Weiss et al (437) tested 22 young children for reactions to 7 artificial colours in a double-blind trial. Two children were recorded as having negative reactions: one of them, a 34-month-old female, showed a significant increase in aversive behaviours. Kaplan et al (201) in 1989, conducted a 10-week study in which all food was provided for the families of 24 hyperactive preschool-aged boys whose parents reported the existence of sleep problems or physical signs and symptoms. The diet used was far broader in scope than most that had been used in previous studies. It eliminated not only artificial colours and flavours but also chocolate, monosodium glutamate, preservatives, caffeine, and any substance that families reported might affect their child. The diet was also low in simple sugars, and it was dairy free if the family reported a history of possible problems with cow's milk. More than half of the boys showed a reliable improvement in behaviour and negligible placebo effects. In addition, several non behavioural variables tended to improve including waking during the night and halitosis.

Sugar intake makes a marked contribution to hyperactive, aggressive, and destructive behaviour (79, 282, 323). A large study by Langseth and Dowd (221) found 74 percent of 261 hyperactive children manifested abnormal glucose tolerance in response to a sucrose meal. Other studies have been conducted, but industry interests may have influenced their outcomes in a manner inconsistent with good scientific research.

Wolraich and collaborators (445) conducted a trial on sugar and hyperactivity that was published in the New England Journal of Medicine in 1994. The findings were portrayed by the study investigators and the media as proving that sugar did not significantly contribute to hyperactivity. Yet the control 'low-sugar' diet averaged 5.3 teaspoons of refined sugar per day, fed to children aged 6-10 years. This 'baseline' level of sugar intake is arguably so high that the investigators should not have been surprised that the test group on a higher sugar diet did not show significantly more symptoms than the controls. No attempt was made to eliminate dietary allergens such as milk, wheat, and egg, which trigger behavioural problems in some hyperactive children, and all the children were allowed to consume soda drinks during the study. At the end of their report, the authors acknowledged their gratitude to General Mills, Coca-Cola, PepsiCo, and Royal Crown.

Autism
A number of studies have reported a worsening of neurological symptoms in autistic individuals after the consumption of milk and wheat. Lucarelli et al (238) tested the effectiveness of a cow's milk free diet, as well as some other foods, in 36 autistic patients. They noticed a marked improvement in the behavioural symptoms after 8 weeks on an elimination diet and found high levels of IgA antigen specific antibodies for casein, lactalbumin and beta-lactoglobulin and IgG and IgM for casein. They concluded that there is a link between food allergy and infantile autism.

O'Banion et al (294) studied the effect of particular foods on levels of hyperactivity, uncontrolled laughter, and disruptive behaviour in an 8-year-old autistic boy. They found that, for this child, foods including wheat, corn, tomatoes, sugar, mushrooms, and dairy products produced behavioural disorders.

Waring and Klovrza (435) on examining the low plasma sulphate levels found in many autistic children state that "the most useful advice that can be given to parents of autistic children is to try a gluten-free, casein-free diet for at least 6 months, also removing chocolate, bananas and citrus fruit". Reichelt (340) found that for some autistic children diets that were either gluten-free and milk-reduced or milk-free and gluten-reduced resulted in an improvement in some behaviour problems and also a decrease in epileptic seizures.

A study by Tettenborn (30) found improvement in 28 out of 57 autistic children, aged between 2 and 15, when they were given anti-fungal therapy and/or fed a diet low in yeast and milk products. The children who responded to treatment shared several characteristics in common: most had developed autism after 16 months, many had poor socialisation skills, a history of altered bowel habits that developed at the same time as the autistic symptoms, many had been ill when symptoms developed and had been given antibiotics. They also had a tendency to feel excessive thirst, cravings for milk or wheat products, nasal congestion, and presented a very pale face with dark shadows under the eyes and abdominal distension.

Behaviour

A survey of allergists in N. America in 1950 found that more than half had noticed changes in personality when patients known to have allergies were exposed to food triggers (72). Schauss (365) reported that when several Michigan detention centres reduced their inmates' milk consumption, the incidence of antisocial behaviour also decreased.

Crook (78), in 1980, reported on cases where dietary changes have had startling results in children. The examples he cites include aggressive behaviour being triggered by red dye, peanuts, wheat, sugar, and milk; hostile behaviour induced by milk; hyperactivity and irritability by red colours, citrus fruits, and potatoes.

Swain et al (408) found that 81 out of a group of 140 children with behavioural disorders experienced significant improvement following the elimination of certain foods and food additives. Novembre et al (291) report on cases in which reactions to the food additives tartrazine and benzoate group led to a range of symptoms effecting the central nervous system including headaches, concentration and learning problems, depression and over activity.

In a review paper, Hall (155) notes that allergies of the nervous system have been found to cause diverse behavioural disturbances including headaches, convulsions, learning disabilities, schizophrenia and depression. Treatment includes using elimination and rotation diets. The observation is made that whilst some of the biological mechanisms have been established by research, others remain to be explored.

Mills (270) describes a case of a woman with chronic depression who exhibited classic signs of food intolerance but had remained untreated for ten years. Using elimination diets and testing, her food problems were identified and long-term follow-up revealed a continuing marked improvement in psychological and physical functioning.

In 1986, Vlissides et al (432) carried out a double blind study on the effect of a gluten-free versus a gluten-containing diet in a ward of a maximum security hospital. Most of the 24 patients suffered from psychotic disorders, particularly schizophrenia. Out of the 12 who had a gluten-free diet, 2 improved and relapsed when the gluten diet was reintroduced. A controlled test by King (207) demonstrated that allergens can induce cognitive and emotional symptoms in some individuals.

A not uncommon view is that it is psychological problems that lead to individuals believing they have food problems. Joneja and Ehmann (189) set out to assess whether client referrals to a clinic specialising in the assessment and treatment of food intolerance might benefit from psychological intervention for management of stress in addition to changes in diets. The answer was *no*. Some of those studied even scored significantly below normal on personality factors related to psychological disturbances (e.g. driven behaviour and low relaxation potential). None of them showed elevations on indices of anxiety, depression or hostility. A small sub group of individuals with IBS were found to engage in fewer relaxing activities compared to individuals without gastrointestinal symptoms and scored higher on the stress test than others but that was the only group.

Further examples of the way food can influence behaviour can be found in the preceding chapter. But, despite the evidence, there does seem to be a reluctance to accept that food can influence behaviour. Odd really when we use drugs to affect behaviour and some of the most potent poisons exist in nature. Just because the food we eat is classed as 'safe' does not mean it will have no effect on the mind. If you eat food that your body cannot tolerate then emotions, feelings and behaviour will be effected.

One area that has received more attention than others is the condition known as Attention Deficit Hyperactivity Disorder (ADHD) in children and that is explored more fully in the section above.

Breast Pain
A study in 1989 by Russell (356) demonstrated a link between breast pain in patients diagnosed with fibrocystic breast disease and caffeine intake. After the first year, 81.9% of the patients involved had reduced their caffeine intake substantially and 61% of these reported a decrease or absence of breast pain. Other studies have disputed this connection.

Heyden and Muhlbaier (166) found that it seemed as if there was improvement on a low caffeine diet but that given the variability in the disease and the subjective assessment of pain it was difficult to accurately measure any link between caffeine consumption and breast pain.

Chronic Fatigue Syndrome

In a paper 'Allergy and the chronic fatigue syndrome' Straus (405) concludes that allergies coexist with the chronic fatigue syndrome in more than 50% of patients. Manu et al (253) found that intolerance to various foods is reported often by patients seeking evaluation for chronic fatigue. On investigation they found that intolerance to multiple foods is probably not a cause or the effect of chronic fatigue, but rather one of the symptoms often presented by CFS sufferers.

In his book 'Chronic Fatigue Syndrome' Dr Stoff (404) outlines how food allergies and sensitivities are often a secondary problem that arises with CFS.

There is also a great deal of anecdotal evidence of cases where individuals with debilitating CFS have had their symptoms reduced substantially, even eliminated, by a change in diet. Whether a cause or not, food sensitivities can not be ignored by anyone suffering from CFS. Following general advice on a 'healthy' diet will not be enough, sensitivities will need to be identified and accommodated in the diet.

Coeliac disease

It is accepted that coeliac disease is caused by food intolerance. Feighery (119) writes in the British Medical Journal that coeliac disease is an inflammatory disease of the upper small intestine and results from gluten ingestion in genetically susceptible individuals. Treatment consists of permanent withdrawal of gluten from the diet which results in complete remission. This has been the view since 1952 when Anderson et al (114) published a paper identifying gluten as the cause of coeliac disease.

However, as Gottschall (150) describes in her paper 'Whatever happened to the cure for coeliac disease?' coeliac disease was already being treated as a carbohydrate intolerance problem by a specific carbohydrate avoidance diet. She argues that the gluten free diet now used does not work for all sufferers because of the continued use of carbohydrates.

An Australian study by Faulkner-Hogg et al (118) set out to explore why some people with coeliac disease continue to have symptoms even when following a gluten free diet. Thirty nine adults who had persistent gastrointestinal symptoms despite adhering to a gluten free diet were evaluated. They discovered that 22 (56%) were consuming a gluten free diet as defined by the WHO/FAO Codex Alimentarius (Codex-GFD), in which foods containing up to 0.3% of protein from gluten-containing grains can be labelled as 'gluten free'. The remaining 17 were following a 'no detectable gluten diet' as defined by Food Standards, Australia.

All 39 followed the 'no detectable gluten diet' during the study. For 5 of the 22 who made the change in diet symptoms disappeared and were reduced for a further ten. Food elimination diets were then tried with 31 of the participants leading to further improvement for 24 (77%). Three common problem foods/food chemicals were soya, amines and salicylates. They argue that if symptoms persist after following a 'no detectable gluten diet' then other food sensitivities should be explored.

Colic and Colitis

Food allergy has been identified as one major cause of colitis in children which may become a life long problem leading to more serious conditions or resolve spontaneously (170, 188). Hill et al (170) studied the role of food allergies and problems with additives in babies suffering from colic and found a link between food problems and colic in 39 per cent of the babies studied. They suggest that treatment of healthy babies with colic would usefully include a low allergen diet and appropriate nutritional support.

A study by Lust et al (240) suggests that maternal intake of cruciferous vegetables, cow's milk, onion, or chocolate during exclusive breast-feeding can be associated with colic symptoms in young infants. Jenkins et al (188) presented information on 8 children under the age of two who had food allergic colitis which resolved completely after exclusion of certain foods. For most of them, the onset was soon after starting foods other than breast milk. The most common offending food was cows' milk protein but soya and beef were also implicated.

Colic related to cow's milk sensitivity can be an early indication of a deeper problem. Bishop et al (40) found that children who are sensitive to cow's milk frequently have similar reactions to other foods such as eggs, nuts, soya, and wheat. Iancono et al (180) placed 70 cow's milk formula fed infants with severe colic on a soy milk formula. After one week, 50 had improved and reintroduction of cow's milk resulted in a relapse within 24 hours. Unfortunately the soy milk formula was not without problems as, within three weeks, 8 of the infants had developed soya allergy. They also found that, at 9 months, 18 of the 50 developed symptoms other than colic to cow's milk.

Lothe et al (235) had similar findings. Eighteen per cent of 43 infants with colic who responded to a cow's milk exclusion diet developed other features of cow's milk allergy by the time they were 6 months old and 13% retained these features to at least 12 months of age.

Crohn's Disease

Rudman et al (354) maintained four patients with Crohn's disease on a gluten-free and lactose-free diet for 12 days, after which they were challenge tested. Within 4-9 days of beginning the gluten challenge they all developed reactions including fever, abdominal pain, diarrhoea, and nausea. The reactions subsided within 2-4 weeks after discontinuation of gluten.

Riordan et al (342) placed 136 patients with active Crohn's disease on an elemental diet. Of the 93 patients who continued the diet for 14 days, 78 (84%) achieved clinical remission and were then randomly assigned to receive corticosteroids or dietary treatment. The diet group was instructed to introduce one new food daily and to exclude any food that precipitated symptoms. The remission time in the diet group was nearly fifty per cent higher than in the group receiving corticosteroids. Forty five per cent of those who followed the diet remained disease-free for at least two years.

Jones et al (191) induced remission in twenty patients with active Crohn's disease by dietary changes. After the patients had achieved remission, they were randomly assigned to receive a control diet (high in fibre and unrefined carbohydrates) or to a diet that, after food challenges, excluded foods which provoked symptoms. Seven of the ten patients on the exclusion diet remained in remission for 6 months, compared with none of 10 patients on the control diet. In a further trial, 51 of 77 patients on an exclusion diet remained well for periods of up to 51 months.

After 2 years, 65 per cent of those patients were still in remission. The most frequent symptom-provoking foods were wheat, dairy products, brassicas (cabbage, broccoli, cauliflower, etc...), corn, yeast, tomatoes, citrus fruits, and eggs. They also reported that, in an uncontrolled study, an exclusion diet allowed 51 out of 77 patients to remain well on the diet alone for periods of up to 4 years 3 months, and with an average annual relapse rate of less than 10%.

Dermatitis
Dermatitis is an inflammation of the skin that produces flaking, thickening, scaling, colour changes and, quite often, itching. Many cases are the result of contact allergies caused by items such as perfumes, cosmetics, rubber and nickel. Others are linked with food intolerance and allergy problems. The most notable being dermatitis herpetiformis which has frequently been linked with the consumption of foods containing gluten and, sometimes, dairy products.

Reunala (336) writes that dermatitis herpetiformis is a lifelong, gluten-sensitive, blistering skin disease yet less than 10% of those with the condition also have gastrointestinal symptoms suggestive of coeliac disease yet they all have gluten-sensitive enteropathy with the rash responding to gluten withdrawal. Atherton (20) states that there can be no real doubt that dietary gluten is responsible for most, if not all, dermatitis herpetiformis.

The Department of Dermatology, St Mary's Hospital in London, has been using gluten-free diets to treat individuals with dermatitis herpetiformis since 1967. Garioch et al (139) report that of the 212 people with dermatitis herpetiformis attending between 1967 and 1992, 133 managed to maintain a gluten-free diet to some extent. Seventy eight of these achieved complete control of their rash by diet alone. Of the remaining 55, all but three were on a partially gluten-free diet, and over half of these managed to substantially reduce the dose of medication required. Of the 77 people eating a normal diet, eight entered spontaneous remission, giving a remission rate of 10%. A further two who had been on gluten-free diets were found to have remitted when they resumed normal diets.

They list the advantages of a gluten-free diet in the management of dermatitis herpetiformis as being a reduced need or no need at all for medication, a resolution of the enteropathy (disease of the intestine), and individuals experiencing a feeling of well-being after commencing the diet. They, therefore, propose a gluten-free diet as the most appropriate treatment for patients with dermatitis herpetiformis.

Fry (134) reports that the eruptions experienced by sufferers tend to be persistent with only 10-15% having spontaneous remission over a 25-year study period. The initial treatment of the rash is usually with one of the following drugs, dapsone, sulphapyridine or sulphamethoxypyridazine but the rash also clears with gluten withdrawal. To achieve significant reduction in symptoms using drugs takes on average 6 months and can take over two years before the drugs are no longer required. Individuals following the gluten-free diet find that the eruption recurs when gluten is reintroduced.

Gawkrodger et al (141) describe a long term study of 76 patients with dermatitis herpetiformis and conclude that a gluten free diet is of therapeutic benefit and that spontaneous remission is uncommon in those not on a diet. Gluten, however, is only part of the story.

Kadunce et al (196) found that dietary factors other than gluten are also important in the pathogenesis of the skin lesions in dermatitis herpetiformis. See also the section on eczema below.

Eczema (and Dermatitis)
There are numerous studies linking the conditions known as eczema and dermatitis with food sensitivities. Atherton (20) writes that foods appear to play an important provocative role in many instances of atopic eczema. The reaction often appears to be slow and insidious, is almost always unrecognised by the patient, and is not detected by skin testing or tests for IgE antibodies.

Van Bever et al (418) in a study of 25 children with severe atopic dermatitis found the condition linked to reactions to eggs, wheat, milk, soya, and various additives including tartrazine, sodium benzoate, sodium glutamate and sodium metabisulphite. They concluded that some foods, food additives, tyramine and acetylsalicylic acid, can cause positive double-blind placebo-controlled challenges in children with severe atopic dermatitis.

Soutter et al (389) found that in 68 children with eczema, 79% had food allergies before the age of 10 months and 23% at 7 years of age. In a separate study of people with eczema, food chemical intolerance reactions were shown to irritate the rash in 47% of cases.

In an evaluation of 46 patients with atopic dermatitis for food hypersensitivity, Burks et al (58) found that 61% had a reaction to one of the foods tested; egg, milk and peanut were the most common culprits. As in previous studies, patients developed skin, respiratory or gastrointestinal symptoms during the testing. They concluded that children with atopic dermatitis that is unresponsive to routine therapy or who continue to need daily treatment after several months would benefit from evaluation for food hypersensitivity.

A further study by Burks et al (59) of 165 patients found that 60 per cent had at least one positive prick skin test. Milk, eggs, peanut, soya, wheat, cod/catfish and cashew accounted for 89 per cent of the positive challenges. Sampson and McCaskill (359) studied 113 children with severe atopic dermatitis. Fifty six per cent responded positively and, once again, egg, milk and peanut were the most common culprits. They concluded that, for some children with this condition, appropriate diagnosis of a food problem followed by an exclusion diet can lead to significant improvement in their symptoms.

Hanifin (158) in his study of the links between diet and atopic dermatitis suggests that between 10 and 20% of children and 10% of adults have eczema that is aggravated by food. The most common culprits being eggs, milk, peanuts, seafood, wheat and soya.

Sloper et al (385) examined the role of foods in the exacerbation of atopic eczema in children. The children's eczema improved in 49 of 66 cases after eliminating cow's milk, eggs and various other foods. Fiocchi et al (125) estimated an incidence of beef allergy of between 3.28% and 6.52% among children with atopic dermatitis. Hoffman et al (173) found that 48% of those studied with eczema tested positive for allergy to the milk protein a-lactalbumin.

Veien et al (426) carried out a randomised, placebo-controlled oral challenge with preservatives and food colourings on 101 individuals with eczema of undetermined origin but who suspected that the intake of certain foods aggravated their dermatitis. Thirty seven reacted to one or more of the food additives but not to a placebo. They did not find it possible to correlate the reactions to food additives to specific foodstuffs containing the same additives. They concluded that if intolerance to food additives is suspected, an elimination diet was warranted, regardless of whether there was a measurably reaction to an oral challenge with food additives.

A further study (427) found improvement in the dermatitis of 262 of 675 patients who followed a restrictive diet for approximately 1 month. Sensitivities included metal salts, balsams, classic food allergens and food additives. A follow-up study was carried out 1-3 years later in which each of the 262 patients was asked to complete a questionnaire to describe the long-term course of the dermatitis. Two hundred and six responded to the questionnaire and 144 of them had experienced long-term improvement. They also found that symptoms of contact urticaria were more common among those with hand eczema than those with other types of eczema.

Epilepsy
There have been studies that have shown improvement or recovery from epileptic seizures as a result of ruling out food sensitivities. These were usually most marked in individuals who had additional symptoms such as migraines and digestive problems.

A study of children by Egger et al (106) identified forty two different foods that caused seizures and symptoms in forty five children who had epilepsy with recurrent headaches, abdominal symptoms, or hyperkinetic behaviour. Thirty six of these recovered or improved when their problem foods were removed from their diets.

Pelliccia et al (313) explored the link between cow's milk allergy and epilepsy. Three children with cryptogenetic partial epilepsy and behavioural disorders such as hyperactivity and sleeping difficulties were placed on a milk-free diet. An improvement was observed in the children's behaviour and the electroencephalographic anomalies disappeared. Double blind oral provocation tests did not present an immediate reaction. Reactions occurred a few days after the test but, once placed on the diet again, they disappeared. They concluded that it was feasible that food intolerance could lead to the onset of convulsive crisis.

Kinsman et al (208) tried the ketogenic diet (high fat/low carb) with 58 epileptic children who required multiple medications. They found that seizure control improved in 67%, medication could be reduced in 64%, also greater dexterity and improved behaviour was noted in 36% and 23% respectively. And, back in 1964, Millichap et al (269) found that a high fat diet was helpful when drugs alone were unable to control seizures.

Fatigue
Fatigue is a very common symptom of food intolerance but has rarely been studied in isolation as it is usually one of a number of symptoms. Randolph and Moss (327) present the case of a male college student with unexplained fatigue and other symptoms such as irritability and nervousness. After a food testing protocol was carried out, it was found that his fatigue was always brought on by dairy products and eggs. In another case the incriminating foods were pork, milk, egg, potatoes, beets and beet sugar.

In an experimental study (396), seven women were tested with high carbohydrate/low protein and high protein/low carbohydrate diets. It was found that the high carbohydrate diet significantly increased fatigue which could not be attributed to hypoglycaemia as plasma glucose remained elevated.

A Japanese study by Kondo et al (213) showed how traditional methods of testing were not successful in identifying sensitivities to cow's milk and buckwheat in individuals with allergy tension fatigue yet these substances were the cause of their fatigue.

As Dr Stewart (403) says: "An exclusion diet may be an invaluable approach when chronic fatigue has persisted and no underlying physical cause has been found, or chronic fatigue is accompanied by several complaints that may be related to food allergy or intolerance such as migraine headaches, irritable bowel syndrome, asthma, nettle rash (urticaria) and eczema".

Gallbladder disease

Breneman (53) conducted a study of 69 patients with gallstones or post-cholecystectomy syndrome. They were all placed on elimination diets with foods being gradually reintroduced. All the patients were relieved of their symptoms usually within 3-5 days. Egg was the most frequent offender (93%), followed by pork (64%) and onion (52%).

Gastrointestinal Problems

Gastrointestinal symptoms including diarrhoea, nausea, abdominal cramping, and gastrointestinal bleeding are frequently associated with food sensitivity (185). In a study of 71 children with chronic abdominal pain, Ignys et al (183) found that food allergies were implicated and that many improved after being placed on an elimination diet. Pfaffenbach et al (319) present the case of a 23 year old woman who suffered from chronic abdominal pain, nausea and diarrhoea. After an elimination diet was used as treatment she became, and stayed, symptom free.

Kokkonen et al (212) studied 12 children with lymphonodular hyperplasia of the duodenum for recurrent abdominal pain, and 4 children with lymphonodular hyperplasia of the colon. All were evaluated for food allergy and the condition was found to be associated with food allergy in 9 of the 12, and, amongst the group of 4 with lymphonodular hyperplasia of the colon, three reacted to milk and two to cereals. They concluded that preliminary observations indicate that lymphonodular hyperplasia of the duodenum or the colon is related to the gastrointestinal type of food allergy to basic foodstuffs.

Pelto et al (314) hypothesised that milk hypersensitivity in adults may be the cause of gastrointestinal disorders. From the people they tested they did find a link that was not always associated with lactose intolerance and did not always show up as an actual allergy. They concluded that milk hypersensitivity in adults, occurring as gastrointestinal reactions, may be more common than previously thought.

Read et al (334) studied 27 patients with severe chronic diarrhoea for which no diagnosis had previously been found. For one of the patients the cause turned out to be an allergy to beef. In a study of 50 patients with ulcerative colitis, food allergy was found to be the cause in 67 per cent of the patients (11).

In 1960, Rowe and Rowe (347) reported that nearly 50 per cent of 170 people with ulcerative colitis needed no medication as their condition could be managed successfully with anti-allergy therapy alone. In 1962, Rider and Moeller (339) tested 20 patients with ulcerative colitis for wheat, egg and milk intolerance; 14 of them experienced complete remission or significant improvement.

In 1965 Wright and Truelove (448) placed 50 patients with ulcerative colitis on a milk-free diet or a control diet for one year. During the follow-up period, 38 per cent of the patients on the milk-free diet remained free of relapses, compared with 21 per cent of those on the control diet.

Farah et al (117) reported on a study in which 13 out of 49 individuals, suspected of having specific food intolerance after withdrawal and reintroduction of specific foods, were further subjected to double blind placebo controlled food challenges. Only 3 of these were shown to have proven specific food intolerance. Of the remaining 10, nine were strong 'placebo reactors'. (I do wonder what was in the placebo.) They go on to say that the study suggests that a small number of individuals with gastrointestinal symptoms have verifiable specific food intolerance but that a greater number have symptoms attributable to psychogenic causes. But just because it was not 'verifiable' by the techniques used by these researchers does not mean that it does not exist. Placing symptoms down to psychological causes is surely not acceptable when not all foods, food additives, and food chemicals were tested.

See also: Coeliac Disease, Colic and Colitis, Crohns Disease, Irritable Bowel Syndrome.

Glaucoma

In a review of the research, Mindell (271) found that glaucoma can be caused by long term use of steroid drugs or by "over consumption of optic nerve toxins like aspartame and MSG (monosodium glutamate)".

Gulf War Syndrome

A paper by Holland (178) in 1995 outlined the theory that the Persian Gulf Syndrome was caused by beef allergy. It is supposed that during the first symptomless phase, as a result of the US Army immunising program, the soldiers developed immunity to the targeted substances and also became sensitised to other substances in the immunising sera, specifically to beef protein. Whilst in the war zone their diet was restricted and essentially free from beef so they remained healthy. On return to the US symptoms began to develop as a result of the change in diet.

Head and Neck Pain

Seltzer (370) reviewed the existing literature to uncover the existence of head and neck pain syndromes caused by foods, and food and drug combinations. they found at least 25 such syndromes including those induced by colourings, flavours, chocolate, coffee and tea, and foods containing tyramine.

Hemiplegia
Staffieri et al (398) reported on a case of right sided hemiplegia that took place immediately after a meal. It was associated with angioedema, urticaria, purpura, and eosinophilia. A wheat elimination diet resulted in a clearance of the symptoms within a few days. Cooke (74) reported on a case of transient 3rd cranial nerve palsy associated with hemiparesis, followed by an episode of contralateral blindness and paresthesia in a food allergic patient. Symptoms were resolved with avoidance of beef and pork.

Hypoglycaemia
Blood sugar problems are usually linked with diets that are high in refined carbohydrates such as white bread and sugar. The advice is to avoid refined carbohydrates and to switch to a high carbohydrate/high fibre diet or a high protein/low carbohydrate diet. However, for many people neither of these will work as their blood sugar problems are caused by a food sensitivity.

Breneman (54) identified food sensitivities as the cause of blood sugar problems in 75% of those with the condition.

Irritable Bowel Syndrome (IBS)
Petitpierre, Gumowski, and Girard (317) investigated food hypersensitivity as a cause of irritable bowel syndrome using exclusion diets and blind provocation. They found that one or several foods or food additives could induce the typical symptoms of IBS and that adequate exclusion diets could result in dramatic clinical improvements.

In 1989, Nanda et al (285) reported their findings after some 189 patients with irritable bowel syndrome were placed on an elimination diet for three weeks. The diet excluded dairy products, cereals, citrus fruits, potatoes, tea, coffee, alcohol, additives, and preservatives. Ninety-one patients (48.2%) improved. Subsequent challenges with individual foods provoked symptoms in 73; of these, 72 remained well on a modified diet. Some were intolerant of only one food and others had multiple food intolerances, the maximum being 19. The most common problem foods were: dairy products (40.7%), onions (35.2%), wheat (29.7%), chocolate (27.5%), coffee (24.2%), eggs (23.3%), nuts (18.0%), citrus fruits (17.8%), tea (17.6%), rye (17.6%), potatoes (15.4%), barley (13.3%), oats (12.1%), and corn (11.1%).

In a study by Jones et al (192) 21 patients with irritable bowel syndrome limited their diet for one week to a single meat, a single fruit, and distilled or spring water. Fourteen of the patients found that their symptoms disappeared on the elimination diet. Individual food challenges identified the following foods as problems: wheat, corn, dairy products, coffee, tea, and citrus fruits. Six of the patients underwent food challenges. In each case, double-blind testing confirmed the food intolerance. Changes in plasma histamine, immune complexes and eosinophil counts were similar after challenge with symptom-provoking foods and control foods, indicating that these food reactions were probably not immunologically mediated - i.e. they were not allergies.

In 1989, Antico et al (16) concluded that food additives may be a major factor in the development of irritable bowel syndrome.

Joint Pain

In the cases studied by Novembre et al (291), tartrazine and benzoates were linked with joint pain. Golding (148) reported on 9 patients who had attacks of joint pain and sometimes swelling that were precipitated by certain foods or associated with allergic manifestations. It was not always the case that an actual 'allergy' could be determined so indicating an intolerance that does not result in a measurable immune system change. The conclusion was that allergy was an occasional cause of rheumatic pain or synovitis in some patients whether or not they had an underlying condition of arthritis.

Alexander (3), a Naturopath and Orthomolecular Nutritionist, writes that he has found "70 per cent of the people he treats for joint pain and stiffness and/or muscle pain have a sensitivity to the nightshade group of plants". He also found that this sensitivity rarely showed up as an allergy to one of these plants. His experience leads him to write: "An important part of the treatment of arthritis is the removal of this food group from the diet". Solanine is a naturally occurring chemical that is found in these plants and full details can be found in a later section.

Mekersson-Rosenthal Syndrome
Food allergy and intolerance to food additives have been implicated in Mekersson-Rosenthal syndrome, a rare disorder with chronic orofocal granulomatosis (especially of the lips), peripheral facial paralysis, and fissuring of the tongue. Mckenna et al (260) report on the case of a 34 year old man whose symptoms were triggered by sodium benzoate and tartrazine. Elimination of these from his diet led to progressive improvement and complete remission lasting at least one year.

Memory Loss
Impaired memory is a not uncommon symptom of food intolerance but it is rarely one that is studied in isolation as it invariably comes in tangent with other symptoms. Randolph and Moss (327) present the case of a woman who had an excellent memory and then began to experience memory loss. Initially her problem was thought to be psychological in origin but was found to be caused by a susceptibility to wheat, corn and, especially, oats.

Dr Mandell (250) refers to a condition known as 'allergic amnesia' in which the allergy sufferer often lashes out verbally, has irrational outbursts, and may be aggressive but later has no memory of the incident. He also cites cases of memory loss caused by food intolerance: one of a woman with periodic memory lapses, the other of a boy who after eating chocolate suffered from an impaired memory.

Meniere's Disease

Derebery and Berliner (94) examined the prevalence of allergy in a population of individuals with Meniere's disease. Out of 734 sufferers, 40.3% had or suspected they had food allergies. Their conclusion was that allergy was more prevalent in people with Meniere's disease than in the general population or the population of patients visiting an otologic clinic for other symptoms.

In a different study, Derebery (93) evaluated the effect of allergy immunotherapy and elimination of suspected food allergens in individuals with Meniere's disease. A group of 137 people with Meniere's disease for whom allergy treatment had been recommended were identified. Out of these, 113 had received allergy treatment, the remaining 24 served as a control group. The 113 had shown a significant improvement in both allergy and Meniere's symptoms. Their ratings of frequency, severity, and interference with everyday activities of their Meniere's symptoms were also better than ratings from the control group. In particular, hearing was stable or improved in 61.4%. Derebery concludes that people with Meniere's disease can show improvement in their symptoms of tinnitus and vertigo when receiving specific allergy therapy.

Derebery et al (95) identified various factors that can contribute to the development and severity of the symptoms associated with Meniere's disease. These included food reactions to very common 'hidden' foods that are frequently ingested in the diet. They suggest that by proper recognition and treatment of the underlying allergic factors affecting

Meniere's disease, significant improvement can be obtained even in long standing cases.

Endicott and Stucker (110) reported on an going study using double-blind techniques that included several people whose Meniere's symptoms were related to specific food ingestion. Haid et al (154) in a study of 574 individuals suffering from Meniere's disease concluded that, amongst other factors, allergy may trigger the disease.

Migraine

Migraines have over the years been linked with a wide range of foods. Some studies also link them with naturally occurring food chemicals such as histamine and tyramine. Vasoactive amines found in food are known to affect blood vessels in the brain causing the vasodilation associated with migraine pain.

Food allergy as a cause of migraine is mentioned in the scientific literature as early as 1930 when Blayeat and Brittain (25) published the results of their study of fifty five migraine patients. In that study, twenty nine patients (52.7%) achieved complete or near-complete freedom from symptoms by avoiding allergenic foods, combined with general supportive care; a further twenty one (38.2%) had some degree of partial improvement.

In 1935, Sheldon and Randolph (376), tell us of a study in which 66.3 per cent of 127 migraine patients experienced partial or complete relief of symptoms after following an elimination diet. In 1952 Heymann (167) found that food reactions were the cause of migraine in 15 of 20 patients studied. In 1971, Speer (391) also found that foods, mainly milk, chocolate, cola and corn, were common triggers for migraine.

A 1979 study by Grant (151) of 60 patients with a history, some as long as twenty two years, of frequent and recurring migraines had 85% of them become headache-free after following an elimination diet. The number of headaches in the group fell from 402 to 6 per month. The commonest foods causing reactions were wheat (78%), orange (65%), eggs (45%), tea and coffee (40% each), chocolate and milk (37% each), beef (35%), corn, cane sugar, and yeast (33% each).

Scheife and Hills (366) found that amongst the most common precipitating factors for migraine were foods including coffee, tea, and cola beverages, chocolate, cheese, and alcohol. Egger et al (108) placed 88 children suffering severe and frequent migraines on an oligoantigenic diet for 3-4 weeks. Those who didn't improve were offered a second oligoantigenic diet, with no foods in common with the first diet. Seventy-eight children recovered completely and four improved markedly. They found that most of the children reacted to several foods. In total, they identified fifty-five different foods that provoked symptoms, the most common of which were cow's milk, egg, chocolate, orange, and wheat.

Merret et al (263) tested to see if food allergy was a major cause of migraine. Their findings were that allergies could not often be detected and concluded that the food intolerance associated with migraine headaches was not related to the conventionally defined allergic mechanism. Peatfield et al (310) found that 19% of about 490 patients with classical or common migraine reported that headaches could be precipitated by chocolate, 18% by cheese and 11% by citrus fruit; some were sensitive to all three foods. Twenty-nine percent also reported sensitivity to alcohol which was significantly associated with sensitivity to the three food stuffs. They concluded that the correlations found suggest that food induced headaches are 'caused' by chemical constituents common to these foods.

Peatfield (311) reports on a study of 577 people attending the Princess Margaret Migraine Clinic from 1989 to 1991 who were questioned about dietary triggers of their headaches. Of those who had migraines (429), 16.5% reported that headaches could be precipitated by cheese or chocolate and nearly always both. A sensitivity to alcohol, especially red wine and beer, was also found. They discovered that there was a definite statistical association between sensitivity to cheese/chocolate and to red wine and also to beer and concluded that cheese/chocolate and red wine sensitivity, in particular, have closely related mechanisms in some way related more to migraine than to more chronic tension-type headache (no food sensitivities were reported in this category).

Mansfield (292) noted that clinical observations and studies support the role of food in causing migraine and sinus headache and clearly makes the point that the benefits of an avoidance diet include the need for fewer medications.

Lucarelli et al (238) studied 92 children affected by migraine. Forty nine had positive skin tests to one or more foods and 40 of these improved after following an elimination diet for 4-6 weeks. Elimination diets worked for migraine sufferers in a 1992 study by Mylek (284). The food most usually implicated was cow's milk but other problem foods included cabbage, eggs, preservatives and colours, some cheeses, and chocolate.

A study by Wantke (434) of 100 patients on a histamine free diet found considerable improvement in 57 patients, 15 of whom had total remission. Sixty four per cent of those with headaches obtained relief. In the same year Guariso (153) found that food testing for 12 young (7 to 18 years old) migraine sufferers brought freedom from headaches for half, a significant improvement for 5 and no change for one of them. The foods responsible included cocoa, banana, egg and hazelnuts.

Trotsky (417) found that treatment with elimination and rotation diets or provocation neutralisation may successfully control headaches without the need for continuous medications in some patients. Leira and Rodriguez (228) reported that some foods in our diet can spark off migraine attacks in susceptible individuals. They identified a number of food based triggers for migraine including individual foods such as cheese, citrus fruits, nuts, tea, coffee, pork, chocolate, milk, vegetables, and substances within food such as tyramine, phenylalanine, phenolic flavonoids, alcohol, caffeine, food additives including sodium nitrate, monosodium glutamate and aspartame.

Mouth Ulcers (Aphthous Ulcers)

Wray (446) reports on a study in which 20 individuals who had suffered from recurrent aphthous ulcers, some for more than 11 years, were given a gluten-free diet to follow. Five of these (25%) became ulcer free and when challenge tested with gluten the ulcers returned.

A study by Hay and Reade (162) placed 17 individuals with recurrent aphthous ulcers that had not responded to conventional therapy on an elimination diet. Of the 12 patients who followed the diet for six to eight weeks, four became symptom-free and one had marked improvement. In four of these cases a particular food was identified which, when eliminated from the diet, led to marked improvement or complete resolution of the ulcers. Similar results were found by Wright et al (447) in their 1986 study.

In 1991, Nolan et al (290) reported on a study involving 21 individuals with recurrent mouth ulcers. Each of them was tested for allergies to foods, food additives, flavouring agents and essential oils. Twenty of the 21 showed positive patch-test reactions to one or more of the following substances: benzoic acid, cinnamaldehyde, nickel, dichromate, fragrance mix, methyl methacrylate, parabens, sorbic acid, phosphorus, mercury, colophony, and balsam of Peru. Avoidance of the allergens which had tested positive, during a follow-up period of six months to six years, resulted in improvement in 18 patients,. For me, this study raises the question as to whether some of the unsuccessful subjects of other studies had simply not been tested for the correct 'allergen'.

Movement Disorders

Gerrard et al (144) present three cases where the individuals had episodic movement disorders triggered by foods or components of the diet. In one person, the movement consisted of shaking the head from side to side and was triggered by milk and a number of other foods. Repeated shrugging of the shoulders, in another, was triggered by egg and coffee. Rhythmic contractions of the arms and legs, in the third individual, were triggered by aspartame. Their observations led them to conclude that foods can trigger movement disorder by acting on dopamine and other neurotransmitter pathways in the brain.

Multiple Sclerosis

Dr Mandell (250) describes the case of a woman who had been diagnosed with multiple sclerosis. After extensive allergy testing it was found that most of her symptoms were in fact caused by food sensitivities. As the cause of multiple sclerosis is still not known recent attention has turned to possible links with food and environmental allergies. Little research has so far been done in this area but it does seem clear that many individuals with multiple sclerosis also have food allergies. Although the cause/effect relationship is not established it seems likely to be of value for a multiple sclerosis sufferer to check whether they have food sensitivities.

Murray and Pizzorno (282) state that "the consumption of two common allergens - gluten and milk - has been implicated in MS. Small intestinal biopsy in a small group of MS patients indicated an increased frequency of significant damage to the intestinal lining. The damage was similar to that which occurs in celiac disease and food allergies."

Kruger and Nyland (214) have proposed that "multiple sclerosis arises due to the effect of various mediators (histamine and protease) released from the perivascular mast cells after stimulation by some diet factor."

Nephrotic Syndrome

Nephrotic syndrome is a condition marked by very high levels of protein in the urine, low levels of protein in the blood, swelling especially around the eyes, feet, and hands, and high cholesterol. It can occur with many diseases but some causes are unknown. The following studies all demonstrate how in some of these cases the problem can be food sensitivities.

Sandberg et al (361) studied 6 children, aged between 10 and 13, who all had nephrotic syndrome of unknown origin. Drug treatment was stopped and a diet that avoided milk was prescribed. Once the protein in the urine had dropped to a certain level, within 3 to 10 days, the children were challenge tested with milk. The milk challenge resulted in a return of significant amounts of protein in the urine and oedema in four of the children.

Gaboardi et al (135) report on the case of a six year old girl with dermatitis herpetiformis, coeliac disease, and nephrotic syndrome. All three conditions disappeared when she was placed on a gluten-free diet.

Lagrue et al (217) tested 34 individuals with idiopathic nephrotic syndrome and 19 blood donors. Five foods were tested - wheat flour, cow's milk, whole egg, beef and pork. The tests were positive in 22 out of the 34 with nephrotic syndrome (64%) and in 1 out of the 19 blood donors (less than 1%). The test was 9 times positive for wheat flour, 9 times for pork, 6 times for cow's milk, 6 times for beef and 5 times for whole egg.

Laurent et al (223) placed 13 individuals with idiopathic nephrotic syndrome on an oligoantigenic diet for 10 days. At the end of the oligoantigenic diet, proteinuria was significantly reduced in the 13 patients; it decreased by more than 50% in 9 patients and disappeared completely in 5. They argue that it seems likely that an oligoantigenic diet is helpful in cases of idiopathic nephrotic syndrome that do not respond to corticosteroids and that diet should be tried before the initiation of immunosuppressive therapy. Various other studies have confirmed that for some individuals there is a link between food sensitivities and idiopathic nephrotic syndrome (180, 218, 222, 224).

Oral Allergy Syndrome
Oral allergy syndrome refers to symptoms that arise as a result of direct contact of the oral mucosa with the offending food. Symptoms are usually in the form of oral itching and lip swelling. It has been frequently associated with sensitisation to fresh fruits and vegetables in those with a pollen allergy. Bircher et al (39) found that about 35% of patients allergic to pollens showed allergic symptoms to fresh fruit and vegetables.

Oral allergy syndrome has also been described in cases of egg and shrimp allergy (10). Adults seem to be more likely to develop oral allergy syndrome to fresh fruit and vegetables than children.

Phlebitis
Rea et al (333) divided 20 individuals with recurrent intractable non-traumatic phlebitis into two groups, matching them for age and severity. The control group continued on their usual anticoagulant treatment, bed rest and support hose. The other group were placed in an 'Environmental Control Unit' where all the air, water and food could be controlled. All medication, for this group, was stopped. In 8 out of 10, of this group, the phlebitis was found to be triggered by food sensitivities and inhaled chemicals such as formaldehyde.

In a five year follow up study this group showed two 48 hour episodes of phlebitis cleared by home bed rest and food abstinence. In contrast, the control group had more than 60 episodes of phlebitis at home and 41 episodes in hospital. Medical costs in these comparable groups showed a differential of $20 per person in the Environmental Control

Unit treatment versus more than $20,000 per person in the control group over the 5 year follow up.

Pre Menstrual Syndrome
Although it is unlikely that PMS is as such 'caused' by food intolerance, reactions to problem foods can be exacerbated in the pre-menstrual phase and may mimic PMS symptoms. Abraham (1, 2) found that symptoms of the pre-menstrual syndrome could be reduced or eliminated by changes in the diet - either by eliminating/reducing certain foods or increasing supplementation of certain vitamins.

Wurtman et al (449) found an association between changes in mood and eating carbohydrates. They found that women who reported having pre-menstrual symptoms increased their intake of carbohydrates when feeling depressed. They speculate that this is an attempt to increase serotonin production and hence improve mood. It seems possible that certain foods will 'agree' or 'aggravate' more at certain times in the menstrual cycle.

Psoriasis
Skin conditions are frequently linked with contact or food sensitivities. Psoriasis is no exception. Douglas (98) reported on patients with psoriasis improving after eliminating certain foods. The foods varied from individual to individual but included citrus fruits, nuts, corn and milk. Others noticed improvement when eating a diet low in acidic foods such as coffee, tomatoes, soda and pineapple.

Michaelsson et al (266) found that a gluten free diet was helpful to some people with psoriasis. The people who improved all had measurable antibodies to gliadin and this would indicate that testing for allergy/intolerance is worthwhile for someone with psoriasis.

Recurrent Otitis Media

Inflammation of the middle ear is a common childhood complaint. In 1994, Nsouli et al (292) evaluated 104 children, with recurrent serious otitis media, for food allergy by means of skin testing, specific IgE tests, and food challenges. Children who had evidence of allergy eliminated the suspected offending foods for 16 weeks, after which individual food challenges were done. Eighty-one (78%) of the children had evidence of food allergy. Elimination of the allergens resulted in significant improvement in 86 percent of the children. The problem foods were cow's milk, wheat, egg white, peanut, soya, corn, orange, chicken and apple. They concluded that considering food allergies in children with these problems "might prevent surgery and might prevent permanent damage".

Viscomi (431) presents an approach to allergic management for use in cases of children with otitis media arguing that there is often a history of allergy. Fifty allergic children with recurrent secretory otitis media, despite conventional surgical therapy, were treated for inhalant and food allergy for one year. There was a significant reduction in the recurrence of the condition.

A study by Bernstein et al (36) of 100 children with recurrent otitis media with effusion tested for six inhalant and two food allergens. They concluded that allergic reactions may play a role in otitis media with effusion in about 23% of young allergic patients. One wonders if the percentage would have been significantly higher if a greater range of foods had been tested.

The significance of elimination diets in the treatment of secretory otitis media was investigated by Lehti using the cytotoxic leucocyte test. The findings showed that using the test and then the appropriate elimination diet leads to total clearance of the symptoms or a significant improvement in a large number of individuals.

Rousquet et al (345) reported that between 7 and 29% of asthma sufferers have a milk sensitivity. They also found it was often a cause of rhinoconjuctivitis in young children and may be implicated in serious otitis media.

Restless legs syndrome
In a study of patients with restless legs syndrome, Lutz (241) found patients improved on a caffeine free diet.

Rhinitis
Rhinitis is a symptom usually associated with hay fever but studies, including those carried out by Pelikan (312), Pastorello (308), and Freedman (131), have shown that when food, including additives, are tested there is a surprisingly high number of patients who have some degree of intolerance, sensitivity or allergy.

Sampson and Eigenmann (358) estimate that the prevalence of food-induced allergic rhinitis, even among patients referred to allergy clinics, appears to be less than 1 percent, although 25 to 80 percent of patients with documented IgE-mediated food allergy have nasal symptoms during oral food challenges. Raphael et al (329) explores 'gustatory rhinitis', a form of rhinorrhea caused by spicy foods in which the reactions are not immunological ones, being influenced rather by neurologic mechanisms.

Sexual Dysfunction
Armani et al (18) had 7 young men eat 7 grams of liquorice each day for a week, They found that after 4 days their testosterone levels had dropped by an average of 44%. These findings led them to suggest that doctors should consider liquorice as a potential culprit when treating men with sexual dysfunction.

Sinusitis

Although Host (179) believes that food allergy is an extremely rare cause of chronic sinusitis, allergy can both produce sinusitis and effect the severity of an episode. Derebery (92) suggests that the treatment of chronic sinusitis and nasal polyposis requires consideration of allergy as well as looking for more traditional disease factors. In cases where allergy is implicated treatment would be both medication and avoidance of the allergen.

Allergy was demonstrated to be an underlying factor in 40% to 67% of patients with chronic sinusitis and is present in as many as 80% of patients with bilateral sinusitis according to Spector (390) in 1992.

Mansfield (292) noted that clinical observations and studies support the role of food in causing migraine and sinus headache and clearly makes the point that the benefits of an avoidance diet include the need for fewer medications.

Sleep Disorders

Okudaira et al (298) gave 12 healthy men 250mg of theophylline in order to test the effects on their 24 hour rhythms. They found that the rhythms of sleep/wake and subjective sleepiness were delayed. Ingestion of xanthines such as theophylline and caffeine in coffee, tea, colas, and chocolate could therefore contribute to some sleep disorders.

Kahn et al (198) in a study of 146 children referred for sleep disturbance identified 15 whose sleep problems were resolved within 5 weeks of starting a diet free from cow's milk. In a subsequent challenge, the sleep disturbances returned within 4 days of reintroducing the cow's milk. Food chemicals, such as salicylate, have also been implicated in sleep disturbances.

Tinnitus

Tinnitus is an accepted symptom of salicylate toxicity as has been frequently shown in various studies. For example, Brien's (55) review of toxicity associated with salicylates cites tinnitus and hearing loss, usually reversible, with acute intoxication and long term administration of salicylates such as aspirin.

And, Cazals (66) notes that tinnitus may be the first subjectively recognised symptom of salicylate toxicity and presents evidence going back to 1877 which shows links between salicylates and tinnitus. The dose of salicylate medications, for the treatment of rheumatoid arthritis, was often set below the point at which the individual started to experience tinnitus.

Although these studies have focused on manufactured forms of salicylate there is also evidence that dietary salicylate, in a sensitive individual, may also lead to tinnitus. In 1989 DeBartolo (88) reported that over a twelve year period they had identified individuals who are sensitive to salicylates and have improved or relieved their tinnitus with a salicylate free diet. Shulman (377) in his book on the diagnosis and treatment of tinnitus includes one of the potential triggers as being foods high in salicylate.

In a study of people with Meniere's disease, Derebery (95) found that 61.4% had significant improvement of their hearing symptoms, mainly tinnitus, when they received treatment for various allergies. Salicylates are the biggest food group to have been implicated in tinnitus but other foods can also cause problems. Various anecdotal evidence has implicated foods including cheese and avocados. Aspartame and MSG have also been identified as causes.

Urticaria
Atherton (20) writes that food has been demonstrated to play a major role in urticaria. In some patients whealing occurs within minutes of ingestion of the problem food, in others the reaction can be much slower and less easy to identify. It is not only foods that cause these reactions but food additives, especially azo dyes, have been implicated.

Swain et al (407) found that 86 out of 140 children with recurrent urticaria improved significantly on a salicylate free diet. They also observed reactions to preservatives, azo dyes and brewers yeast. Juhlin (194) also found that many sufferers of urticaria improved on a diet free from additives.

Henz and Zuberbier (165) reported that in the majority of cases of urticaria the symptoms are provoked, and sustained, by food ingredients. On a diet largely avoiding preservatives, dyes and natural pseudo allergens, 73% of patients experienced remission of more than 6 months duration, starting within the first 3 weeks after starting the diet (the spontaneous remission rate is 14%). Eighteen per cent reacted to food preservatives and dyes, and 71% to pureed tomatoes.

Zuberbier et al (453, 454) had success in identifying food additives as the cause of urticaria in some patients and improvement in the symptoms of others. Verschave et al (429) used an elimination diet for additives and tyramine with 67 individuals with chronic urticaria; 55% per cent reacted favourably. Rudzki et al (353) placed 158 people with chronic urticaria on a diet free of salicylates, benzoates and azo dyes. Fifty were found to be sensitive to food additives.

Thirty per cent of individuals with chronic urticaria and angioneurotic oedema, in a study by Montano et al (275), were found to be sensitive to sodium benzoate, tartrazine or sodium metabisulfite.

Lindemayr and Schmidt (232) found that of the individuals with recurrent urticaria who were placed on a diet avoiding salicylates, benzoates and colours, 20% recovered spontaneously and became symptom-free and a further 55% of cases showed marked improvement. Genton et al (142) challenge tested individuals with urticaria with a number of compounds including sodium benzoate, tartrazine, and sulfur dioxide. Virtually all those tested were found to react to at least one compound. Most went on to experience a marked improvement in symptoms after 5 days on an additive free diet.

Vasculitis

Veien and Krogdahl (428) in 1991 reported on the case of a 24 year old woman with leukocytoclastic vasculitis. She experienced a severe eruption of vasculitis after a placebo controlled oral challenge with 50mg of ponceau (E214, a red colour dye). She followed an additive free diet and, after two months, the vasculitis was found to have faded.

Vertigo

Dunn and Snyder (101) presented information on 3 children who were found to be milk sensitive. Their vertigo attacks were eliminated by removing milk from their diets and reappeared with milk challenges. Chocolate was suspected in another child but could not be confirmed. Duke (100) reported on a case of adult vertigo in Meniere's syndrome that improved on an elimination diet.

*****

Not all illness is food related but, as the studies above demonstrate, it can be the sole cause or a major factor for many individuals and in a wide range of conditions. Without food we would die and given this crucial role that food plays in our lives it does seem strange that its role in illness (and health) is not more fully acknowledged and used in treatments. The cost to the individual is enormous - loss of health and a deterioration in the quality of life. The financial cost to society of continuously treating recurring conditions is enormous yet treatments relying on food avoidance cost virtually nothing in comparison. This is highlighted in the study by Rea on phlebitis cited above. The cost to society is not just financial, it is also a massive loss of work time, creativity and energy. Changing your diet can change your life and so effects everyone you come into contact with and everything that you do.

In October 2000, the British government apologised for the mistakes and delays that took place during the BSE crisis.

Wrong advice was given to the public about the dangers of eating beef and people died, and continue to do so, from the human variant CJD. It took 15 years for this apology to materialise and the report cast serious doubts on our ability to believe government reassurances and advice on food safety. What struck me at the time of this report was that it had taken deaths and very specific scientific proof that these were linked with mad cow disease before any real action was taken. The long term debilitating effects of food substances such as additives and artificial sweeteners are not visible in the same way but this does not mean they do not exist. Will sufferers ever receive an apology? Will we ever be totally able to rely on government advice? On the doctors that advice governments? Can we truly trust others with our health?

If you think that food, in some form, might be effecting your health do not let yourself be dismissed by health care professionals. Persist - it is your life, your health. You might be wrong but you also might be right. There comes a time when you have to set the advice aside, find out more for yourself and listen to your body. There is only one person who is going to take your health totally seriously and that is *you*. We have now reached the end of the first part of this book. The next part is the 'Seven Step Plan' which will be your guide to finding your way to better health.

4

SEVEN STEP PLAN

The Seven Step Plan is a simple and easy to use system for identifying food intolerance problems. It is designed to help you take things at your own pace and to place as little stress on your body as possible.

Step 1: Decide to take some action

In many ways this step is the hardest. Change is something that is constantly happening within and around us yet our naturally tendency is to resist change. This is a normal human response but one we need to be aware of when reviewing our diet and health.

In respect of health, we are more used to being told what to do rather than choosing a course of action for ourselves. If a doctor says there is nothing wrong with us, then, despite our symptoms, we accept the diagnosis often interpreting it as meaning that there is nothing that can be done. As you are reading this book and have reached this stage within it, you are probably fed up with being ill, over weight or depressed and you will probably have already tried many other avenues of help. Please don't despair - I managed to find a route to better health after more than thirty six years of being ill and miserable. If I can do it then I have every faith that others can also do it.

I am not offering a quick fix - I wish I could - rather a slow evaluation of your situation and a move towards finding the diet that works for you which, when found, will change your life.

CHANGE YOUR DIET AND CHANGE YOUR LIFE

What you most need to know and remember is that the only true expert on you is yourself. Your instincts may have become a little clouded but they are still there and will re-emerge to help you. I used to laugh when I read advice like 'listen to your stomach' or liver or some other organ. I couldn't differentiate one from another. Neither could I trust my inner voice about whether a food was good for me or not - it was all simply food, in the shops and therefore safe.

The self-preservation instinct does re-emerge when you start to remove the layers of toxins and you do come to be able to listen to what your body is saying, whether it is because it needs something different or needs you to stop eating something. This will happen for you but for now trust more in observation and logic than feelings.

However, we are not going to completely ignore feelings. Before you decide to take some action you need to be clear about what it is you are trying to change. Your overall goal will be to find the ideal healthy diet for you but the other details will be very specific to you. Start by writing out how you feel about your health and how you feel about what you have read so far in this book.

This will be useful for you to later look back on - as you get better you will begin to forget how awful things were and having something in writing will boost your confidence and help you keep going. If you don't know where to start then take a pen and some paper, sit somewhere quiet, let yourself go still and simply begin to write. Don't worry if you start writing gibberish. Just let the words flow - this is for your eyes only.

Why bother? Not feeling well, whether physically or mentally, takes a massive toll on us especially if we simply have to get on with all the usual demands of life - work, family, housework, seeing friends etc... You will have strong feelings about your health and it is better to get these out than to keep them locked inside. You may be surprised at what you discover.

Later... Take some more paper and list all your symptoms. For each symptom note any diagnosis and treatment and how effective it's been. Identify the symptoms that just do not seem to change no matter what you do (and this can include changes you have made in your diet). Now decide that you want to take some action. Write a note to yourself promising yourself that you are going to do the best you can to make yourself better by changing your diet.

Step 2: Simplify Your diet

Food, even in its simplest form, is a complex substance. Combine a whole range of foods and additives together and you increase the complexity. If you are sensitive to any foods or food chemicals you need to find out which ones. To find out you will have to test foods. In order to test foods you will need to eat them in their simplest, most natural form possible. The more complex your diet the harder it will be to unravel a food intolerance problem. It is essential that you simplify your diet.

Reactions to products such as chocolate, ice cream or white bread tell us nothing. We need to know which ingredient in these products brought about the reaction. If we don't then it is likely that our problems will recur. To clarify let us look at a couple of examples. A reaction to chocolate could be a reaction to milk, cocoa, vanilla, caffeine or any other ingredient. So, if your problem was milk and you did not reduce this more generally in your diet then you may get a brief respite from your symptoms but your tolerance would soon drop and the problems would begin again. If white bread causes you a problem is it because the flour has been bleached, that you need to eat wholewheat, is it a gluten problem or are you sensitive to yeast or a preservative?

If you don't simplify your diet you will not be able to answer these questions and will find yourself getting very confused and eliminating foods that are okay for you whilst eating others that are not. This is a very common problem.

CHANGE YOUR DIET AND CHANGE YOUR LIFE

Save yourself time and misery by truly simplifying your diet before testing for food intolerance problems.

By far the easiest way to simplify your diet is to reduce the amount of processed food you eat and to eliminate, as much as you can, food additives. Your goal should be to eat your usual diet in as natural form as possible. Ideally you would remove all processed food and all additives but we live in a busy world and even with the best of intentions you will find this difficult but aim to get as near to it as you can - don't sell yourself short.

We have become very dependant on processed food and at first it is daunting to consider breaking this dependency. Make the change gradually. Do not make any drastic change to your diet - simply try replace the more complex foods with similar ones with fewer added ingredients. There are lots of ways in which you can do this. Let's look at snack foods and drinks.

- Plain crisps often contain only potatoes, vegetable oil and salt. Flavoured crisps are far more complex as they include a variety of flavourings and colours.
- Breakfast cereals can contain colours and preservatives. Choose a similar one that contains fewer ingredients or make your own from ingredients purchased at a health food shop.
- Chocolate bars can be packed with added flavourings, colours, emulsifiers, raising agents and other ingredients. Choose one that has the fewest number of ingredients. A simple chocolate bar will have far fewer ingredients than one that has been flavoured or had other things added.
- Sweets can be extremely complex products but there are now some on the market that contain very few, or no, artificial colours and flavours. The brighter, more unnatural the colour the greater the number of additives.
- Fizzy drinks can often be a cocktail of chemicals - check the labels and choose the one with the least or, if you feel ready, change to drinking mineral water.

♦ Nuts can be bought in their original form without added oils and flavourings.

A few tips:

♦ Go as natural as you can.
♦ Cook your own meat and do not buy processed meats like salamis and sausages. If you absolutely have to eat these products search out the ones with the fewest ingredients.
♦ If you eat yoghurt then buy the natural variety and add your own fruit.
♦ Avoid tinned vegetables and fruit - stick with fresh or use frozen.
♦ Never buy ready made meals as these are incredibly complex. Buy the ingredients instead and make your own (if you're not a cook then buy a cook book and you'll soon be on a journey of discovery to the true taste of food).
♦ Dishes requiring sauces are easy enough to make if you take the time to find out. A tomato based sauce using tomatoes, onion, garlic and a sprinkling of herbs takes only minutes longer to prepare than a shop bought one.
♦ If you eat sandwiches for lunch then make your own rather than taking your chance at the sandwich bar or eating too much in a cafe or restaurant. If you are interested in losing weight this will also help you reduce your calories without trying - most of us do not use the amounts of margarine and dressings that a commercial outlet does.
♦ Margarines can be highly coloured - choose the one with the smallest number of ingredients and preferably one that tells you which type of oils are actually used. The term 'vegetable oil' can mean one or a combination of many different types.
♦ If you have a freezer then cook meals ahead and freeze them.

- If you have to eat away from home choose the simplest menu option and avoid sauces.
- Always have a low additive snack food or fruit with you.
- Avoid buying on impulse.

If it still seems impossible then do it for at least one or two meals in the week. For the others think simple - there is nothing wrong with the traditional meal of meat and two veg. You *can* reduce the complexity of your food. The easiest way of helping yourself is to plan ahead. Sit down and work out the meals you will eat for the week and buy accordingly. If you leave the decision till half an hour before you need to make a meal your options will be limited and you are more likely to succumb to heavily processed food.

Takes too much time? No way. Believe me it is far quicker than going through thinking process and frantic supermarket shopping or queuing at fast food outlets each day. Still seems difficult? Don't worry and don't panic. I am not expecting you to make a total change overnight. Gradually decrease the amount of processed food in your diet. Do not, however, change the basic structure of your diet . Eat the same type of foods you were eating only in a more natural and simpler form. So if you are vegetarian do not suddenly start eating meat. If you have never eaten nuts then do not start. If you have always avoided lettuce do not start eating it. And so on.

I am frequently asked why I am so keen that you reduce the number of additives as surely these are safe. I shall try address this issue. The UK government releases information on food and additives via the Ministry of Agriculture, Fisheries and Food (MAFF). Their booklet "about food additives" (245) states that additives allowed in the UK are "considered safe for almost everyone". They go on to state that: "There are a few additives to which a few people may react badly. But this is not good enough reason to ban such additives: substances in everyday food like milk, wheat, oranges or strawberries upset far more people. The value of the additive to everyone is weighed against upset it may cause to a small number of people."

So safe for some but not safe for all. The truth is that you can be intolerant of any additive, or group of similar additives. As it is rarely possible to test these in isolation from food it is far better to begin your food intolerance testing with real food. As Hannuksela and Haahtela (159) point out, food additives seldom provoke true allergic (i.e. measurable) reactions. Intolerance is more likely to take place and this type of individual intolerance may change and fluctuate from time to time.

Additives have been implicated in a wide range of health problems including behaviour problems, bloating, headaches, gastrointestinal problems, respiratory difficulties, and skin problems. Antico and Di Berardino (16) found additives to be a frequent cause of skin complaints. Leira and Rodriguez (228) found them implicated in migraines. Novembre et al (291) saw them induce symptoms in other organs including the joints and central nervous system, symptoms included over activity, concentration and learning difficulties, and depression. Rowe and Rowe (350) found they caused hyperactivity in some children. Kanny et al (200) demonstrated a link between additives and dermatitis. The list goes on and on.

Food additives can cause serious problems for some people. They also make your diet incredibly complex and that is why I want you to reduce them. Basically if it was not something you would place in food when cooking at home then avoid it. Not only will you simplify your diet but you will also discover how food is supposed to taste. You need to be aware that many additives are present in food but are not listed amongst the ingredients (this may vary from country to country).

The law, in the UK, does not require the listing of any additive that has been incorporated into one of the ingredients used for preparing the food or beverage. It would be interesting to see how long ingredients lists would actually be if all of these had to be disclosed. There are also foods that are exempt from having to list their ingredients. Some of the ways in which additives are hidden in food as well as other labelling problems are listed below:

♦ A product made up of a number of ingredients only needs to list the ingredients and not what is in each of them. For example: If a vegetable oil has been treated with an antioxidant only the term 'vegetable oil' needs to be stated - you will not know if an antioxidant has been used and if one has been used you will not know which one it is.

♦ If a preservative was added to a colour to give it a longer shelf life the preservative would not have to be declared.

♦ If the product contained 'dried apples' you do not need to be told if these contain sugar, preservatives or colours.

♦ Flavourings do not have to be individually listed only the term 'flavouring' need appear. There are more than 3000 flavourings in use. You will have no idea which one has been used or how it was produced.

♦ Terms such as 'vegetable oil' and 'sugar' can be potentially misleading. If your tomato sauce bottle says 'sugar' it could be cane, beet or corn sugar. Even if you are able to identify which sort it is, say it is cane sugar, there is no guarantee that the next bottle will include cane sugar. The manufacturer could make his choice depending on which is the most readily available and cheapest at the time of manufacture.

♦ The same principle applies to vegetable oil. Some manufacturers are now beginning to tell us at least which types of oil it might be but many don't. This could be a serious problem for anyone sensitive to corn, sunflower seeds, sesame seeds, peanuts or soya.

♦ Modified starch frequently appears on labels but we have no knowledge of the source and this could again vary from batch to batch depending on economic factors at the time of manufacture.

♦ Additives are manufactured substances but their identifying name and number provides us with no indication as to the origin of the substance. This can cause problems for some individuals. For example: Anyone sensitive to aspirin is best avoiding azo dyes which are often used in the production of food colourings. Someone with a lactose intolerance may need to avoid, among others, E325 which is the sodium salt of lactic acid.

♦ Some food and drinks are exempt from listing their ingredients including: Alcoholic drinks - beer, lager, cider and wine are all likely to contain a number of additives; unwrapped foods such as bread, cakes and sweets; take-aways and fast foods. Consume any of these foods and you will not know what you are eating.

♦ Additives used as processing aids do not have to be declared. These include powders and greases to stop foods sticking, anti-caking agents to stop powders forming lumps, acids that produce raising agents, and bleaches. In theory only a residue will remain in the food you bought but you will not know what has been used or how much of it has been left behind in the product you're eating.

The complexity of any processed food is further increased by these hidden additives - the sausages with fifteen listed ingredients could in reality contain more than thirty different substances.

The comfort of added vitamins could also, rather than helping, be hurting. BHT and BHA are frequently found in margarines and other vitamin fortified foods. Feingold (122) identified vitamins A, D and E as frequently containing BHT, one of the substances he identified as being linked with hyperactivity. It is also the case that for many additives there is a safe daily intake level. Even if you knew the amounts you would not be able to gauge the amount you were ingesting as the amount per serving is not declared on labels and many substances do not have to declare the amounts available. For example, sulphites (E numbers 220 to 227) are frequently used in wines, beers and ciders but this information does not have to be declared. Drink too much and you could exceed the safe daily intake (161, 381).

Sadly the argument that labelling will enable us to avoid additives if we wish to do so is not an accurate representation of the picture. There are far too many hidden ingredients in processed food for us to be ever fully sure we are not consuming one of the additives that 'upsets' us. Lists of additives implicated in certain conditions are outlined in the appendix for your information but I would advise you to invest in a book on additives and check your next lot of shopping. Do you really want to be eating cocktails of chemicals whose effects we know so little about? If your answer is "No, but it is easier, convenient and probably okay", I know exactly how you feel. All I can say, is that in time it does get easier.

As you make the changes you may begin to experience some improvements. If you do please make a note of them as the information could prove valuable later. And remember, even if you start to feel much better, this is only the beginning, better things are yet to come. If, however, you find yourself becoming more irritable, tired and feeling stressed stop and think before you revert to your normal diet. It takes time for your body to adapt. It also takes longer amounts of time for your body to detoxify itself.

Additives are thought to accumulate in the body (350) so it can take some time for the body to eliminate them. If you have had a problem with some food additives then your body could be experiencing withdrawal and this, not the change in your diet, is probably making you feel ill. Persevere but please remember to eat the more natural versions of what you were eating rather than introducing foods unfamiliar to your body.

You need to stay at this stage for a least two weeks but you can stay here for as long as you like or need. If the improvements have been startling you may decided not to continue with the following stages, you can always do so later. If you have felt ill then you need to give yourself time to build your strength and allow your body to continue with its elimination of built up toxins and heal before continuing with specific food tests. If there has been little or no change then press on to the next stage.

Step 3: Know what you are eating

Food intolerance is difficult to diagnose and, at the moment, the only accurate way is to eliminate foods from your diet and then reintroduce them. If you are doing this for more than one food or for any food chemical you will get confused. Don't assume you will be able to remember what you've eaten or how you felt - you won't. Keep a food diary and keep it diligently. Not only will it help you keep track of the food you've eaten and how you felt but it will also help you monitor changes. I recently found one of my very early food diaries and was quite shocked at how ill I had been and also how complex my diet used to be. I had forgotten and it was a very helpful reminder especially as I was going through a bad reaction at the time.

Many people discover that they are food intolerant without the help of a doctor and when they present this information to the doctor they are not believed. This is understandable. If you have never witnessed for yourself a food reaction then you will be sceptical. One way of helping present the evidence to your doctor is by use of a food diary - he may still be sceptical but at least you have it down in black and white and are not just waxing lyrical about the changes that have taken place. If you are going to use your food diary as evidence for your doctor do endeavour to keep it as clear and concise as possible. The more professional it looks the more he is going to be inclined to read it and, hopefully, accept your findings.

Buy a notebook or paper and binder and create a diary. You will need one page for each day. Divide the day into four segments: midnight to 6am, 6am to 12 noon, 12 noon to 6pm, 6pm to midnight. Draw a line down the centre of the page, dividing it in two. List the food you eat on the left side and your symptoms on the right hand side. You can download example pages from the Food Can Make You Ill Web site: http://www.foodcanmakeyouill.co.uk.

As you need to list all the ingredients in every meal, you will find it easier if, at the back of your notebook, you keep a list of any complex foods that you eat and their ingredients. For example, if you eat muesli then in your complex foods list add 'muesli and list the ingredients fully - oats, wheat flakes, coconut, sunflower seeds, almonds, sultanas, hazelnuts and so on. Then when you eat muesli you only need to write 'muesli'. Why so detailed? It can be extremely difficult to identify some food intolerance problems and a very detailed food diary can provide you with the clues that you need. By the way, a complex food is one that contains more than one ingredient such as muesli, soup, biscuits, sauces, pastries.

Use your diary fully. List all ingredients of every meal and their scores (when applicable). Make a note of any medication you may be taking. Write down any changes whether positive or negative - include all physical and mental changes. If you get a cold, flu or tummy upset write it down so that you can try separate it from any other changes. Write down anything you feel is significant. For example, if you had a headache after being stuck in traffic for two hours note down that the journey was the probable cause.

Write up your diary every day. If you forget or find yourself too ill to do it then don't punish yourself or give up on the idea. Simply write down what you can remember and also why you didn't write it at the time - this could be vital information as many mental symptoms can be produced by food intolerance, most classically brain fogging and confusion.

DAY and DATE: *Monday 8/5/00*   **EXAMPLE**

Midnight to 6 a.m.

| | *Restless night* |
| | *Woke with headache - suspect too much coffee* |

---

6 a.m. to 12 noon

MUESLI	
Milk	*OK but totally ran out of - steam by 11 - very hungry*
Black coffee x 4	*Headache cleared*
CRISPS - plain	

Noon till 6 p.m.

Jacket potato with butter and cottage cheese	
Salad - lettuce, tomato,. cress, chives	*Felt better after lunch but energy dropped by 4 p.m.*
Mineral water	*Return of headache -*
Coffee black x 4	*definitely not stress as*
Apple	*today has been a lovely day*
FLAPJACK	*out*

---

6 p.m. till midnight

Lamb chops - grilled	
Brown rice - boiled	
Stir fry veg - greens,	
mushrooms bamboo	*Very restless and tired but*
shoots fried in	*not sleepy. Aching legs.*
cold pressed sunflower oil	
Banana	*Trying tea rather than*
Tea - black x 3	*coffee on an evening*
HEADACHE PILLS	

Step 4: Develop a strategy

At this stage you need to decide on which you foods or food chemicals you are going to test. To help you decide read through the sections on food chemicals and food problems. It is likely that at least one of these will leap out at you. If it doesn't think about the foods that you eat and have eaten in the past. Are there any you feel you just cannot live without? Unfortunately, this probably indicates a food addiction whose underlying cause is usually an intolerance problem. Remember any food can cause problems.

You may have refused certain types of food as a child but been made to eat them because they were 'good for you' (children who are 'picky' eaters could be signalling a food intolerance problem) and you may know that some foods give you stomach problems or a hangover effect but because you enjoy them or they are 'good for you' you keep on eating them.

Make a list of the foods or food chemicals you want to test and prioritise them - put the one you think is the most likely culprit at the top of your list and the reason why. Do not be tempted to try to eliminate more than one food or food chemical at a time. Rather than speeding up the process this will lead to confusion and cause additional stress to the body. Please, also, do not be tempted to fast and then introduce one food at a time. This places enormous stress on the body, leads to confusing results and the slow process of reintroducing foods can lead to a diet that does not sustain health. There is a time and place for fasting and this isn't it.

I receive many requests from people asking me where they should start and it is impossible for me to direct them, or you, to the specific food, foods or food chemicals that may be causing them or you a problem. You are a unique individual and what causes you a problem may be totally okay for someone else. As I've said before although a food may cause a certain type of reaction in some people it will not always cause this symptom.

However, I do understand how difficult starting out on this journey can be and I accept that you may need some further guidelines so, if you are truly uncertain as to where to begin, use the check list below to guide you. Find your main symptom and then read the corresponding sections in the book and see if any 'speak' to you.

Acid reflux: Caffeine, capsaicin.
Anxiety: Caffeine, MSG, salicylate.
Asthma and breathing difficulties: Benzoates, histamine, lectins, milk, MSG, sulphur and sulphites.
Catarrh and sinus problems: Milk.
Depression: Caffeine, grains, salicylate, sugar, wheat.
Fatigue: Caffeine, MSG.
Gastrointestinal problems: Capsaicin, gluten, grains, lectins, legumes, milk, oxalic acid, purines, sulphur and sulphites, wheat.
Gout: Purines.
High blood pressure: Tyramine.
Hyperactivity: Caffeine, salicylate.
Joint pain: Purines, serotonin, solanine, wheat.
Kidney/bladder stones: Oxalic acid, purines.
Migraines: Amines, caffeine, histamine, phenylethylamine, serotonin, tannins, tyramine.
Mouth problems: Capsaicin, fruit, histamine.
Mood swings: Gluten, MSG, salicylate, solanine, sugar, tyramine, wheat.
Panic attacks: Caffeine.
Restless legs: Caffeine.
Skin problems: Benzoates, fish, fruit, grains, histamine, milk, peanuts, salicylate, wheat.
Sleeping problems: Caffeine, milk, salicylate.
Tics: Caffeine, salicylate.
Tinnitus: Salicylate.

If you still remain uncertain as to where to start then consider testing wheat and/or milk. I only suggest these as they are two foods that are often consumed many times a day. A 'holiday' from either of them will not do you any harm. If there is any other food that you have eaten each and every day of your life then that food could also go on your suspect list.

Be gentle, take it slowly.

At this stage you need to consult your doctor. Dr Michael Tettenborn (412), a consultant paediatrician at the Frimley Children's Centre in Surrey, suggests that many doctors have been turned against dietary management because some people have made excessive claims about its potential impact and that their scepticism is fuelled by the range of tests in use by non-medical practitioners. Bearing this in mind I have outlined a strategy that you can use in preparing for your appointment:

1. Make a list of the symptoms that concern you with details of how long these have been a problem.
2. List any treatments you have tried and their outcomes.
3. Make a few notes for yourself as to why you want to test for food intolerance - this will help give you confidence when talking to your doctor (we all get nervous and if you are unwell your self confidence will be low).
4. Take the food diary you will be using - this will show your doctor how he can follow your progress. The food diary is going to be your way of presenting evidence.
5. If you want to take additional information along with you make sure it is information that is acceptable to your doctor. Many doctors are suspicious of information obtained on the Internet so ensure that you know the source of what you are presenting. Details of articles in medical journals are going to carry more weight than somebody's home page.
6. Remember that your doctor is an individual who has been trained in medicine - he is there to help not hinder you. If you are not happy with your doctor you always have the option of changing to another one.
7. Remember it is okay to ask questions, make suggestions and take notes.
8. If your doctor is obviously pushed for time then suggest you make an appointment for a longer session later.

9. Remember your doctor is a human being like you. He, like you and I, is not perfect. Your doctor does not know everything but then neither do you or I. Respect and co-operation are better than hostility and antagonism.

As unravelling illness can be a complex process I advocate the path of co-operation with the medical profession but I am also very aware that you may meet resistance. If at all possible seek help from another doctor or an alternative practitioner. If you do decide to go ahead with testing on your own please take extreme care when testing foods - it is always best to have someone else, who understands what you are doing, present just in case you have a severe problem. NEVER stop medication without your doctor's consent.

Once you have decided on your strategy then decide when you are going to begin the next step - eliminating the suspect foods. You can repeat the next three steps as many times as you need and at your own pace, returning to step two whenever you need.

Step 5: Eliminate suspect foods
The key to successfully eliminating a suspect food lies in planning. Know when you are going to start and know, in detail, what you are going to eat. It is essential that you plan your meals carefully so that you do not unwittingly eat any of the test food.

You may have read about other elimination diets that involve periods of fasting or insist that you stop drinking tea and coffee and stop smoking. The approach outlined in this book asks that all you do is eat your newly simplified diet and eliminate only the food, in all its forms, that you are testing. If you try to eliminate other foods or drinks or try stop smoking at the same time you will make it virtually impossible for yourself to identify what substance is causing what problem - one food or food chemical at a time.

Elimination diets that ask you to remove a range of foods at one time may, at first, seem like the easiest and most straightforward option. Although avoiding a host of foods at one time may in fact be just as easy as avoiding one, the difficulties arise at the time of testing. Reactions can be delayed and confusing and tests may need to be repeated.

It is also possible to misread results as a study by Bethune et al (37) showed. They reported on how three individuals had self-diagnosed a carbohydrate intolerance and had gone on to develop increasingly restrictive diets as their symptoms kept on appearing. They found that carbohydrate restriction can disturb glucose metabolism and that this may be interpreted falsely as food allergy. Mumby (281) confirms this and advises against remaining on a very low carbohydrate diet for too long. Although these type of diets can help correct low blood sugar problems they can then go on to reproduce the symptoms if the body is not able to convert sufficient protein into carbohydrate.

These type of blood sugar problems can cause a variety of symptoms many of which mimic allergy problems as well as sometimes being caused by them. These include cravings for sweet foods, feeling tired, anxiety, shaking and inner trembling, depression, irritability, difficulty concentrating, light-headedness, and joint pain. If eating relives the symptoms at least temporarily then you are likely to have a low blood sugar problem. It is not just eating too little carbohydrate that can cause this it can be that you are simply not eating enough - a risk for anyone changing diets especially if you are keen to lose weight. Make sure that you are eating enough and regularly. Don't worry about the calories as, once your diet settles into one which works for you, the excess weight will gradually fade away without you trying.

Make sure you check all the labels of any food or drink you are going to consume to ensure it is free of the test food. Eating out could cause problems so phone ahead to the restaurant to see if they can cater for you. How you approach elimination is effected by which food or food chemical you are testing. Detailed advice is given in the appropriate sections later in this book. The length of time that any food or chemical needs to be eliminated from the diet varies so check carefully. If your test food is not listed then you can assume that four days totally clear is a reasonable guide but if you know you have a sluggish system extend this to six.

If you have been reacting to the food you have eliminated you can expect a sudden weight loss. This is linked with fluid retention. Breneman (54) found that it is possible to retain as much as 4% of your body weight as fluid as a result of a food sensitivity. This weight is gained within 6-8 hours after ingestion and lost within 18-24 hours after the food has been removed from the diet. You could also find yourself with a headache and feel tired. This is the body detoxifying itself and nothing to worry about. Drink lots of water and rest as much as you can. You may find you suddenly feel amazing and then just as suddenly feel wretched - again this is just detoxification.

And of course, you could just start feeling much better. Be meticulous about keeping your food diary and you will be able to track your progress over time.

Step 6: Test suspect foods

You have now gone the required number of days without eating the test food and the time has come to find out if you have a problem. One very clear indicator is that you have had a noticeable improvement in your symptoms. If this is the case you may want to delay testing for a few more days to ascertain the extent of the 'recovery'. If you are testing a food chemical then consult the appropriate chapter for fuller details on how to go about this.

If you are testing a single food then choose the time at which you test with care. If you have a busy day planned you do not want to be dealing with unpleasant symptoms at the start of the day.

Eat a reasonable amount of the test food in it's simplest, most natural, form and wait. Some reactions occur immediately or within the first thirty minutes. Common responses are mild swelling in the mouth, headache, feeling disorientated, stomach irritation, a feeling of heaviness and/or lethargy. If you have any of these responses do not continue with the test. You have an intolerance problem to that food.

If nothing happens then continue with your day and note any changes as they occur. Leave at least a few hours before eating any more of the test food. Delayed responses are not uncommon and include a return of your previous symptoms, skin rashes, blood sugar problems, and bloating (hands, feet, abdomen, face, as well as more generally). Reactions can be delayed for as much as 36 hours.

Do not attempt to eliminate/test any other food for at least five days. You need to give yourself this amount of time to be sure there is no problem. If after this time you have not experienced any unwanted symptoms then you can assume that the test food is safe. If the test has been inconclusive then you may need to repeat it. Other factors such as illness do have an effect and should be taken into account. You should also know that it is quite possible to tolerate a food in one form but not another.

For example: Boiled eggs may be okay but not fried, raw cabbage may make you feel ill but when cooked there is no problem, steak may be okay but mince could leave you feeling uncomfortable, milk in yoghurt may lead to no symptoms whilst milk on its own causes problems. Test the food in its various forms to be sure you are not unnecessarily eliminating foods from your diet.

Step 7: Review
Was the test food a problem or not? If it was a problem then eliminate it from your diet - you can always retest late. If it

wasn't a problem then you can include it in your diet but remember to keep it simple if you are planning further tests. If you have found yourself getting confused then eliminate the test food again and eat your simplified diet for a few days before testing again.

Decide on whether to continue with another test and plan accordingly. Repeat steps 5 to 7 as often as you need and over as long a time period as is appropriate to you.

If your problems continue to remain after food testing then you may like to consider checking your environment for other possible causes - it is not uncommon to react to fragrances and chemicals commonly found in the home, school or work place. Again this is a very hidden problem and only comes to light after you have removed the offending chemical from your environment. It is also worth exploring whether you have a nutritional deficiency of some sort as these have also been linked with a wide range of conditions and symptoms.

5

FOOD CHEMICALS

No matter how 'natural' you attempt to make your diet, you cannot avoid chemicals in food as many, potentially hazardous, chemicals occur naturally in food especially in plant based foods. Plants produce toxins to protect themselves from spoilage and from being eaten by predators.

The complexity of each individual plant is immense and any one of its constituent chemicals can, potentially, cause problems for someone sensitive to it. Emsley and Fell (109) estimate that there are about half a million natural chemicals in the food we eat. Only a few of these have been identified and even fewer have been tested, analysed and their implications for health understood.

A food chemical, natural, or man made, becomes a problem for some people when it is eaten in large amounts, is eaten on a regular basis, or the body cannot detoxify it due to illness or a deficiency in the metabolic pathways.

This section of the book looks at some of the natural chemicals, as well as some of the man made versions which have often been produced to mimic those produced by nature.

The information presented is based on the research done to date and will provide you with information on the main chemicals that have been identified as causing problems for some.

5.1

AMINES

Amines are naturally occurring chemicals in certain foods which, like salicylates, are cumulative in the body. Over a period of time these can build up in your system causing reactions that mimic allergies. Amines are produced in food as a result of protein breakdown and/or fermentation which means they are often highly concentrated in processed foods. If you noticed a substantial decrease in your symptoms when you simplified your diet you may want to consider testing to see if you have an amine problem. If you also regularly suffer from constipation then the amine problem could be more pronounced.

Naturally occurring amines are generally thought to act in the body as neurotransmitters and the term 'biogenic amines' is now frequently applied to these. These 'biogenic' amines include amongst their number - histamine, phenylethylamine, serotonin and tyramine. Each of these is dealt with separately as each has been found to have clearly defined symptoms in certain individuals. Some people, however, seem to have a more general sensitivity to amines. Diets low in food chemicals usually include amines in this more general way.

Cooking certain foods, in particular meats, at high temperatures produces a set of amines that were not present before. One group of these is heterocyclic amines (HCAs). More than 17 different types of HCAs have been found in meat cooked at high temperatures. Stewing, barbecuing and frying appear to produce the most HCAs. Gravies made from meat juices, therefore, also have a high amine content. Apparently, cooking in a microwave does not produce HCAs to anywhere near the same extent.

The other form of amine produced by cooking is polycyclic aromatic hydrocarbons (PAH). These are formed by the browning of carbohydrate based foods such as bread and are found in foods such as smoked and grilled meats and coffee. A sensitivity to these amines can often be misinterpreted as an intolerance specific to one type of food. For example, if toast doesn't agree with you it is easy to think that wheat is the problem; if a grilled steak upsets you then you might think you have a problem with beef.

What everybody should know is that various studies have linked these types of amines with cancer. The rule of thumb here is do not overcook food and always eat your food as fresh as possible. Pickling, smoking and other forms of preserving all increase the number of amines.

There is no specific list of symptoms indicated for amines but migraines that don't respond to other treatments may be relieved by a diet low in amines (see also: histamine, phenylethylamine, serotonin, tyramine). The key to testing amine intolerance is to reduce the amount of amines in your diet, and hence your body, over a period of two weeks. Stick to your simplified diet as much as possible but eliminate all the high and very high amine foods. Read the food lists carefully - if you are a regularly consumer of the foods in the moderate list reduce these also.

A way of keeping track of the amount of amines you are eating is to allocate each portion the number 1 and add these up each day. If then find you have some improvement but not a lot you could reduce the amount of amines more easily in this way.

Re-think your cooking style. Avoid over cooking anything and avoid meat cooked in sauces as these will have a high amine content. Never eat anything that has been burnt and avoid toasted breakfast cereals. After two weeks, eat some of the high and very high foods and monitor your response. Remember that amines are cumulative in the body.

Some people may immediately get a reaction such as a headache and others will only get similar symptoms after their level has increased - this can take up two weeks. Keep your food diary up to date and continue with scoring the number of amine portions you have had in any one day.

At the end of the testing time, if you have felt no better at all then you are unlikely to have an amine problem. If there has been a little improvement you may want to consider reducing your level even further and seeing if that increases the improvement. You should, however, also note that individuals who are intolerant of one chemical in food often are intolerant of another so you may need to test some of the other food chemicals.

If you have had a substantial improvement then you are amine sensitive and need to now work on establishing the level of amines you can generally tolerate. At this stage you may find your tolerance is very low but that over time this may change.

Testing for amine content in food has been slow in taking place. The lists that follow are based on the available research but must not seen as the end of the story. Amine content will vary within the same foods especially as it is so effected by the ageing and cooking process. You are welcome to try foods not on the lists but so as not to confuse the results it would be advisable to treat them as suspect and only introduce them at a later stage when you can clearly determine what is happening. The categories of food are very low, low, moderate, high and very high

Amines in food: **VERY LOW**

Fruit: Apple, apricot, blueberry, gooseberry, lime, peach, pear, rhubarb, strawberry.

Vegetables: Asparagus, cabbage, carrot, celery, corn, courgette, cucumber, french beans, green pea, lettuce, lima beans, onion, peppers, potato, radish, soya bean, turnip.

Nuts: Chestnut, horse chestnut, sunflower, pine nut, pistachio.

Condiments: Herbs and spices.

Dairy: Butter, cottage cheese, milk, ricotta cheese, plain yoghurt but as fresh as possible.

Sweets and sweeteners: Carob, golden syrup, maple syrup, sugar.

Beverages: Cow and goat milk, lemonade, soya milk, decaffeinated coffee.

Misc: Tofu, tofu ice cream.

Amines in food: **LOW**

Fruit: Black currant, cherry, grapefruit, honeydew melon, mandarin, red currant.

Nuts: Almond, cashew, coconut, macadamia.

Meat, fish, and poultry: Chicken eggs, beef, chicken (no skin), fish (white), lamb, rabbit, turkey (no skin), veal.

Misc: Plain corn chips, plain potato crisps, tacos.

Amines in food: **MODERATE**

Fruit: Dates, kiwi fruit, orange, passion fruit, paw paw, tangerine.

Vegetables: Broccoli, cauliflower, olives.

Nuts: Brazil, hazelnut.

Meat, fish, and poultry: Any meat, fish and poultry older than two days. Any frozen meat. Chicken liver and skin, salmon (tinned), tuna (fresh).

Condiments: Malt vinegar.

Beverages: Coffee, coffee substitutes, tea, decaffeinated tea, most herbal teas.

Amines in food: **HIGH**

Fruit: Avocado, banana, fig, grapes, lemon, pineapple, plum, raspberry.

Vegetables: Aubergine, gherkin, mushroom, tomato.

Nuts: Pecan, walnut.

Meat, fish, and poultry: Bacon, hot dogs, frozen fish, gravy, ham, mackerel (tinned), meat juices, meat loaf, offal, pork, sardines (tinned).

Dairy: Mild cheeses.

Condiments: Meat extracts, soy sauce, vinegar, Worcestershire sauce.

Sweets and sweeteners: Cocoa, milk chocolate, white chocolate.

Beverages: All fruit juices.

Amines in food: **VERY HIGH**

Vegetables: Sauerkraut, spinach.

Nuts: Butternut.

Meat and fish and poultry: Any form of dried, pickled, salted, or smoked fish and meat. Anchovies, beef liver, fish roe, pies and pasties, processed fish products (such as fish fingers, cakes, and pastes), salami, sausages, tuna (tinned).

Dairy: Virtually all cheeses including brie, camembert, cheddar, cheshire, Danish blue, edam, emmental, gloucester, gouda, gruyere, jarlsberg, leicester, mozarella, parmesan, processed cheese, provolone, roquefort, stilton, swiss, wensleydale.

Sweets and sweeteners: Dark chocolate.

Condiments: Hydrolysed protein, miso, tempeh, yeast extracts.

Beverages: Chocolate flavoured drinks, cocoa, cola type drinks, orange juice, tomato juice, vegetable juices.

5.2

BENZOATES

Benzoic acid occurs naturally in many berries, fruits, herbs and spices (such as cinnamon and cloves), vegetables and tea. The existence of benzoic acid in its natural form has been known since at least the sixteenth century. The body generally excretes benzoic acid as hippuric acid in the urine within 9-15 hours of eating it but it's presence in the body can temporarily inhibit function of digestive enzymes and may deplete amino acid glycine levels. In around 1860 it was produced synthetically from compounds derived from coal tar.

Today it is commercially manufactured by the chemical reaction of toluene, a hydrocarbon obtained from petroleum with oxygen in the presence of cobalt and manganese salts as catalysts.

The commercial form is used in the food manufacturing process as a preservative and also has widespread non-food uses. The use of derivatives such as benzoyl peroxide for bleaching flour is an example of how this can become a hidden sensitivity as bleaching agents rarely have to be declared on products they have been used in. The intakes from natural sources are low in comparison with potential intakes from food additive uses.

Symptoms of benzoate sensitivity have included asthma aggravation, gastrointestinal problems, hyperactivity, itching, numbing effect in the mouth, recurrent urticaria, rhinitis, skin sensitivity.

Jacobsen (184) writes that people with asthma, chronic urticaria-angioedema, rhinitis, and purpura may be predisposed towards benzoate and paraben sensitivity. Wuthrich and Fabro (450) found benzoate sensitivity in some individuals suffering from asthma, rhinitis, and urticaria. Juhlin et al (195) examined the sensitivity of aspirin-intolerant patients to p-hydroxybenzoate and sodium benzoate by oral provocation testing; urticaria was induced in 5 of 7 patients.

Michaelsson and Juhlin's (267) study of 57 patients with recurrent urticaria or angioedema found that 52% reacted to sodium benzoate and/or p-hydroxybenzoic acid. August (21) reported that 33 of 86 patients with chronic urticaria gave positive reactions to tartrazine and sodium benzoate. Gibson and Chancy (146) found that 52% of patients studied with chronic idiopathic urticaria had a benzoate sensitivity.

Ortolani et al (303) found 21% of a patient group with chronic urticaria-angioedema were intolerant to benzoic acid. They also noted a high incidence of cross reactivity to aspirin. Chafee and Settipane (67) found that sodium benzoate might have been responsible for the provocation of asthma in a patient who had taken a dye-free vitamin supplement preserved with benzoate. Investigations showed a sensitivity to tartrazine; the reaction to the supplement could have been due to the fact that tartrazine and benzoates have the same aromatic ring structure and carbohydrate group and hence are viewed as virtually the same by the body.

Reactions to this group of additives have been observed in people with an aspirin or salicylate sensitivity and should be avoided by anyone with this condition. Benzoic acid has also been found to react with the preservative sodium bisulphite (E222). If you suspect a problem, the food additives you need to avoid are:

> E210 Benzoic Acid
> E211 Sodium benzoate
> E212 Potassium Benzoate
> E213 Calcium Benzoate
> E214 Ethyl 4-hydroxybenzoate
> E215 Ethyl 4-hydroxybenzoate, sodium salt
> E216/21 Propyl 4-hydroxybenzoate/sodium salt of

You may also need to limit your intake of foods in which benzoates occur naturally, such as anise, cinnamon, cloves, prunes, tea, and many berries most notably raspberries and cranberries.

If you suspect benzoates are causing you a problem then eliminate them in all their forms from your diet for at least two weeks. If there are signs of improvement then continue to avoid them for a further two weeks before testing. Partial improvement with a reaction after testing could indicate that you need to check non-food substances for benzoates and also avoid these but if this does not work then testing for a salicylate sensitivity is probably indicated as both salicylates and benzoates have similar chemical structures.

Esters of para-hydroxybenzoic acid, more commonly known as parabens, are used widely in medications and cosmetics. In fact, benzoates can be found in a variety of non-food products including medicines, perfumes, cosmetics, toothpaste, lice treatments, resin preparations, in the production of plasticisers, in dyestuffs, synthetic fibres, as a chemical intermediate, as a corrosion inhibitor in paints, a curing agent in tobacco, as a mordant in calico printing and in insecticides. Some exposure may also result from inhalation of auto exhaust, tobacco smoke and other combustion sources.

An example of non food use is the use of benzyl benzoate as a treatment for lice and scabies infestations. It is believed to be absorbed by the lice and mites and to destroy them by acting on their nervous system. Benzyl benzoate has been classed as a potential neurotoxicant. Symptoms of neurotoxicity can include muscle weakness, loss of sensation and motor control, tremors, alterations in cognition, and impaired functioning of the autonomic nervous system.

5.3

CAFFEINE

Caffeine is one of three dietary methylxanthines, the other two being theobromine and theophylline. All three are readily absorbed from the gastrointestinal tract and distributed throughout the body, metabolised in the liver and excreted in the urine. Theobromine is weak in comparison to caffeine, and theophylline is only found in small concentrations in food so the only methylxanthine dealt with in this book is caffeine.

Caffeine naturally occurs in the leaves, seeds or fruits of at least sixty three plant species world-wide. The most familiar sources of caffeine in our diet are through drinks such as coffee, tea and cola. The amount of caffeine in any product varies depending on the plant variety used and also how it was prepared.

Caffeine is so readily available in coffee, tea and chocolate that we have come to accept it as harmless but the truth is that caffeine is a powerful drug which effects both your body and your mind. It has the strange quality of at first decreasing the heart rate and then increasing it about an hour after intake. It, also, has a powerful effect on the nervous system and can in small doses help improve concentration but the reverse takes place with a higher dose.

Even a relatively moderate amount, two to three cups of tea a day, leads to observable effects and caffeine abuse can result in symptoms that mimic mental illness. Children, because they have smaller bodies, are at greater risk from caffeine toxicity, and insomnia in children could be linked to the amount of cola drinks they consume (44, 45). How much caffeine you can tolerate will depend on a number of factors including the amount you consume, how often you consume it, and your individual metabolism.

Some people seem to experience no noticeable effects whilst others have uncomfortable symptoms after just a small amount. Products containing caffeine are often used to boost energy which takes place as a result of caffeine's ability to stimulate adrenal gland activity. This constant abuse of the adrenal glands can, however, lead to a state of burn out where the adrenal glands quite simply become exhausted. Fatigue, although it can have many causes, can often be the result of diminished adrenal function. If this is the case, no amount of additional coffee or chocolate will help.

The speed at which your body is able to eliminate caffeine depends on factors such as age, state of health and your own unique biochemical make-up. The rate at which it is cleared is decreased by liver disease, pregnancy and oral contraceptives. Women taking oral contraceptives have been found to have significantly lower rates for breaking down caffeine than women not using these contraceptives and men (395).

Fluoroquinolines, drugs used to treat bacterial infections, impair caffeine and theophylline metabolism leading to a greater concentration in the body (254). Other medications, including theophylline, can also cause a problem as these can add to the stimulant effects of caffeine- containing foods and drinks.

Sadly, caffeine is habit forming and tolerance develops so that more and more is required to obtain the desired effect. Silverman et al (380) found that even consuming smaller regular doses of caffeine can lead to addiction. A variety of conditions have been linked with a caffeine sensitivity. Charney et al (69), in a placebo controlled study of patients with panic disorder or agoraphobia with panic attacks found that caffeine significantly increases anxiety, nervousness, fear, nausea, palpitations, restlessness and tremors. These effects all correlated with plasma caffeine levels.

Observations made by Davis and Osorio (87) suggest that caffeine may precipitate tics in susceptible children. Greden (152) found that caffeine in large quantities of tea and coffee could produce symptoms that mimic anxiety and panic disorders. Even caffeine induced urticaria has been noted (138, 322).

The symptoms that have been linked to a caffeine sensitivity or to a high intake of caffeine include:

Agitation, anxiety, blood sugar problems, depression, disorientation, dry mouth, headache, heart burn, increased need to urinate, insomnia, irritability, nausea, palpitations, panic attacks, restless legs syndrome, rhinitis, stomach problems, sweating, tinnitus, tremors, urticaria.

It is quite possible that regular headaches or migraines are linked with caffeine withdrawal. If you have regular headaches and migraines and consume caffeine rich products then do consider taking this test.

If you have any of the above symptoms and you know you consume large amounts of caffeine then you may want to consider testing for caffeine sensitivity. The only way of assessing sensitivity is to eliminate all caffeine from the diet for ten days, reassess the situation and then reintroduce it if you choose too. If you consume large amounts of caffeine and are concerned about the effect of withdrawal symptoms then reduce the amount that you use over a period of ten days until you are as caffeine free as you can manage. Make a list of how much you eat and drink and draw up a reducing strategy. Choose the best option for you. The foods you need to eliminate/reduce are all forms of:

Coffee, tea, chocolate and cocoa, cola drinks, guarana, mate and any other soft drinks that contain caffeine.

Substitute with decaffeinated versions where possible and if you want too. To be on the safe side also check any medications, supplements and tonics. Any prescribed forms of medication containing caffeine should be continued until you have discussed them with your doctor and been given permission to reduce or stop taking them.

You will either find that you very quickly begin to feel calmer and less stressed or you may experience withdrawal symptoms. Do not be alarmed if you find yourself feeling ill. All of the following have been linked with caffeine withdrawal: low attention span, depression, nervousness, problems sleeping, mood swings, and irritability. Drink lots of water and be gentle with yourself and let your body do the job of detoxification.

The positive changes you are looking for are an increase in energy but less manic, fewer sleeping problems, increased ability to concentrate, more relaxed, less irritable and nervous, and a peaceful sense of well being. If you experience any of the above then you really should question the sense of returning to using any products containing caffeine.

Replacements in the form of decaffeinated coffee and tea, caffeine free drinks and carob bars are all now readily available and make acceptable substitutes. If you do return to using caffeine products ensure you keep them to a minimum in your diet - if you don't then before you know it all the symptoms will have returned. For example, some people may get away with 2 cups of coffee and a bar of chocolate, or 3 cups of tea, or two cans of cola and some may not be able to tolerate any at all.

If you have gone through withdrawal then the safest course of action is to quite simply say NO to caffeine. This also applies to anyone that has or is suffering from anxiety or depression as the intensity of both of these states can be exacerbated by caffeine.

The amount of caffeine in various products is a matter of some dispute. For example, some studies show no caffeine in chocolate, others have shown a large amount. As caffeine has definitely been found in chocolate and cocoa it is safest to eliminate it at this time. Also please note that even decaffeinated drinks still contain some caffeine albeit in small amounts.

One example of amounts of caffeine in products comes from the MAFF UK survey (246):

Non decaffeinated cola drinks	33 to 213 mg/l
Low caffeine colas	less than 0.2 mg/l
Energy drinks	0.5 to 349 mg/l
Standard tea products	95 to 430 mg/l
Instant and ground coffee	105 to 340 mg/l
Decaffeinated instant coffee	10 to 11 mg/l
Chocolate products	5.5 to 710 mg/kg
	(highest in chocolate bars)

Rozin et al (352) found that a chocolate bar contains 20mg of caffeine compared to 80-100mg in a cup of coffee. This relatively low dose in comparison with other sources of caffeine, such as coffee and cola drinks, which are not craved to the same extent, suggests that caffeine is not the major reason that chocolate is craved. However, if you are extremely sensitive to caffeine it could be a problem.

5.4

CAPSAICIN

The genus 'capsicum' encompasses several species including chilli peppers, red peppers, and paprika. Capsaicin is the most important biologically active compound within these and it is known for providing pain relief in conditions such as arthritis and neuralgia. It can also have an adverse effect if you are sensitive to it.

The most common adverse reaction is a burning sensation in the mouth but others have also been noted. Serio et al (372) outline a case of plasma cell gingivitis linked with exposure to capsaicin. Myers et al (253) found it led to a significant increase in gastric acid secretion as well as mucosal bleeding.

Evidence of nausea, vomiting and abdominal pain after ingestion have also been noted, and exposure in the workplace has led to cases of coughs being linked with its inhalation and to contact dermatitis.

To test for a sensitivity eliminate all of the following from your diet for at least 5 days:

Bell pepper	Hot pepper
Cayenne	Paprika
Cherry pepper	Red chilli
Chilli	Spur pepper
Cone pepper	Sweet pepper
Green pepper	Tabasco

Be very careful with any pre-prepared meals and sauces or restaurant food as some of these may contain capsaicin under the term 'spices'. After the elimination period test by eating whichever one you used to eat most often in as simple a form as possible. If you get a reaction then wait another five days before trying a different food from the list.

The reason for testing more than one is to ensure that the problems you are experiencing stem from capsaicin and not the individual food. If you experience no reaction then capsaicin is unlikely to be a problem for you.

5.5

HISTAMINE

Histamine is a biogenic amine that occurs in many different foods. At extremely high concentrations, usually as a result of food spoilage, it can lead to poisoning. In some individuals smaller concentrations can lead to food intolerance which is often misinterpreted and can lead to the wrong food being eliminated.

The problems associated with an overload of histamine were first recorded in 1830 when crew members of a vessel became ill with severe headaches, flushing, bloating, diarrhoea and shivering after eating bonito, a member of the Scomberesociade fish family. The illness was called 'scombroid poisoning'. As other types of fish were also found to cause similar symptoms, research was conducted to find the common link. That 'link' turned out to be histamine.

Histamine poisoning differs from histamine sensitivity. In cases of histamine poisoning the person is likely to have eaten a contaminated form of fish and experienced a reaction almost immediately. The symptoms, usually a combination of sweating/shivering, rashes, flushing, burning sensation in the mouth, stomach pains, diarrhoea and headache, last for about twelve hours and then abate.

Histamine sensitivity is unlikely to result in such severe symptoms and may not abate as quickly. The body already has a supply of histamine which it stores in a safe form for use when needed. Food too high in histamine swamps the body's defences. If the body becomes flooded with histamine in a 'non-safe' form problems can arise. The body has to act to clear it and fast and in some people this clearance mechanism is slow and, whenever their tolerance level is breached, unwanted symptoms arise.

The suspected cause is a deficiency of diamine oxidase in the small intestine resulting in diminished histamine degradation in the gastrointestinal tract, and thus absorption. Tyramine is also metabolised by this enzyme. Alcohol and up to 94 drugs, including dihydralazine, isoniazid, clavulanic acid, promethazine, verapamil and metoclopramide, can inhibit the action of diamine oxidase.

The only treatment is to avoid foods containing histamine (and tyramine if indicated).

A sensitivity to histamine can produce allergy type symptoms which no allergy test will recognise. Histamine is heat stable - cooking does not remove it. Wantke's study (434) in 1993 found that sensitivity to histamine in food and drink could result in bronchial asthma, headache, and urticaria. He also found the ingestion of food rich in histamine brought about a recurrence of atopic eczema in those affected. Doeglas et al (97) identified histamine intoxication after eating cheese in some individuals; the symptoms included nausea, vomiting, urticaria, headache, difficulty swallowing and thirst.

Ingestion of 25 to 50mg of histamine can trigger headaches, and 100-150mg can lead to flushing (278). However, figures such as these can only ever be estimates. Scombroid toxicity has been identified after ingestion of only 2.5mg of histamine (276).

Histamine sensitivity can lead to:

Abdominal cramps, asthma like symptoms, bronchial asthma, burning sensation in the mouth and throat, diarrhoea, difficulty swallowing, dizziness, flushing, headaches, low blood pressure, migraines, nausea and vomiting, palpitations, peppery taste in the mouth, rhinitis, shortness of breath, skin itching, sneezing.

Conditions like eczema can be made worse. Testing for a histamine sensitivity is advisable in cases of chronic headaches, migraines and skin complaints that don't respond to other solutions. A common indicator of a histamine problem is if you know that red wine always gives you a headache. The key to testing for histamine sensitivity is to ensure you eat your food as fresh as possible. Then totally avoid all the foods on the list below. As so many cheeses are implicated I would suggest that you avoid all cheese for the duration of the test which should be at least seven days.

After seven clear days eat a meal containing one of the foods on the list that you would ordinarily eat (not cheese) and monitor your reaction. If you have unpleasant symptoms within a few hours you would be advised to avoid foods high in histamine. If you have no problems then you can gradually reintroduce the foods but keep a food diary and monitor your progress - it could be that you can tolerate a reasonable amount but not too much. When you are secure in establishing your tolerance then reintroduce cheese (not one of those listed).

The reason for postponing the testing of cheese is that it is possible to have a hidden milk sensitivity and this would cloud the results of the histamine test. Should you find that you have a problem with cheese not on this list I recommend that you test for milk intolerance.

More detailed information on histamine content of food is difficult to come by as measurement is not a straightforward process due to variations in food effected by factors such as storage and fermentation. The list below is, therefore, not a definitive list and the amounts of histamine in foods included will vary considerably.

Fish: Anchovy, herring, mackerel, sardine, salmon, tuna.
Cheese: Blue, camembert, cheddar, emmenthal, gouda, harzer, mozzarella, parmesan, provolone, roquefort, swiss, tilsiter.

Meat: All dried or cured meats such as hams and salamis.
Vegetables: Aubergine, pickled cabbage, spinach, tomatoes.
Alcohol: Beer, champagne, red wine, sparkling wine, white wine.
Other: Tamari, soy sauce.

More generally avoid food that has been smoked, pickled or fermented.

You will need to use a food diary to monitor your responses. Some foods without a significant histamine content have been thought to trigger a histamine release (9). Foods with this capacity include egg white, crustaceans, chocolate, strawberries, tomatoes and citrus fruit

How long the effects of histamine will last depends upon its metabolism in the body. Under 'normal' circumstances, histamine is rapidly converted to its inactive metabolites by either histamine methyltransferase or diamine oxidase (DAO) (24). It has also been found that eating a histamine containing meal and taking drugs that inhibit DAO can produce symptoms so check with your doctor about any medication that you are taking.

Once you have established your level of histamine tolerance, adjust your diet to accommodate it. You will need to ensure that you never eat too many foods high in histamine in succession but if you are able to tolerate some you will be to included these in your weekly meal plan.

5.6

LECTINS

Lectins are a class of proteins, chiefly of plant origin, which bind specifically to certain sugars and cause agglutination of particular cell types. It has now been found that lectins are toxic and/or inflammatory, resistant to cooking and digestive enzymes, and present in much of our food. Initially it was thought that lectins only caused digestive problems that often mimicked the symptoms of food poisoning but it is now believed that some of these leave the gut and effect other organs in the body leading to more widespread symptoms. Many lectins are powerful allergens in their own right, such as prohevin, the principle allergen of rubber latex, but it is also possible to be more generally sensitive. One of the most commonly known lectins is phytohaemagglutinin which is found in beans.

Gilbert (147) reports on a case of a hospital holding a "healthy eating day" which resulted in illness. The canteen served a dish containing red kidney beans which was chosen by 31 customers. Over the next few hours cases of severe vomiting and diarrhoea were reported. All had recovered by next day. Investigations showed no signs of traditional food poisoning but the beans were found to contain an abnormally high concentration of the lectin phytohaemagglutinin.

Ordinarily, phytohaemagglutinin is only a danger after consumption of raw or undercooked kidney beans. The reactions experienced after eating beans in this state are not, as such, classed as an intolerance problem rather as a form of poisoning. In these situations the symptoms usually appear within 1 to 3 hours and are marked by extreme nausea, followed by vomiting, abdominal pain and diarrhoea. Some people have been hospitalised but recovery is usually rapid.

Phytohaemagglutinin is found in many species of bean but it is found in highest concentrations in the red kidney bean. The unit of measurement is the hemagglutinatins unit (hau). Raw kidney beans contain between 20,000 to 70,000 hau, cooked beans from 200 to 400 hau. White kidney beans contain one third the amount of toxin as the red beans and broad beans only one tenth. Some people find that, even when cooked correctly, red kidney beans cause problems most notably abdominal discomfort. The only solution is to avoid the beans. Information on testing for a sensitivity to beans can be found in the section on Legumes.

The different ways in which we deal with lectins has also been linked with blood groups types (82). And, reviewing the available research, Freed (129) suggested that it was possible that insulin dependent diabetes, rheumatoid arthritis, and peptic ulcers could all be triggered by problems with lectins. The avoidance of large numbers of lectins in diets such as the 'stoneage' diet could be the reason why some people notice an improvement in their symptoms especially in reducing respiratory symptoms as without lectins in the throat the lining provides a more effective barrier to viruses. Freed goes on to offer an explanation as to how disease such as rheumatoid arthritis and diabetes can often develop after illnesses such as flu. Basically, the protective coating of our cells can be stripped away during illness leaving us open to the damaging effect of lectins.

5.7

MSG

MSG, monosodium glutamate, is the sodium salt of a naturally occurring amino acid - glutamic acid. Glutamate is essential to life and is found in cells throughout our body. It occurs in two forms, naturally in food and as an added flavour enhancer. Most of the glutamate our bodies receives is in a 'bound' form and is gradually released as enzymes digest the protein food that it is part of. MSG, on the other hand, is a form of 'free' glutamate that is instantly available to us and it is too much of this type that can lead to problems.

The degree of sensitivity experienced depends on the individual. Some people can tolerate vast amounts, others find themselves shaking and in an anxiety state after very little. The 'toxic' reactions experienced by some people are generally because of an overload of MSG in it's form as a flavour enhancer.

MSG intensifies some flavours and lessens others. It is an ideal additive for food manufacturers to 'adjust' the taste of highly processed food and you can, without realising it, be ingesting quite large amounts of MSG. Generally made from the fermentation of corn, sugar beets, or sugar cane, MSG is a potential problem for anyone with an intolerance of these foods.

MSG has been linked with a number of conditions. It has been found to bring on asthma in some individuals, with the asthma developing anywhere from 1 to 2 hours to as long as 12 hours after ingestion (4,5).

Squire (397) reported on a case of a 50 year old man whose recurrent angioedema of the face, hands and feet was related to MSG intake. The angioedema occurred 16-24 hours after ingestion of MSG. Botey et al reported on 3 children whose urticaria was caused by MSG. Symptoms developed between 1 and 12 hours after the MSG challenge was given.

In summary, the various symptoms and conditions that have been linked with MSG sensitivity are listed below.

Fatigue has been noted as a side effect of too much MSG. As this often occurs up to 12 hours after ingesting MSG it is sometimes difficult to link the symptoms to the cause (a food diary will help). Note that, because MSG effects the neurological system, the symptoms include ones which effect behaviour and feelings. If you frequently eat food containing large amounts of MSG, such as Chinese takeouts, then you may have a hidden MSG problem.

MSG does seem to set of an addictive response and hence cause food cravings. One of the difficulties with diagnosing if you have an MSG sensitivity is that it is often an ingredient that is hidden. You will need to follow the avoidance process very carefully.

MSG sensitivity - possible symptoms

Anxiety	Asthma
Balance problems	Behavioural problems
Bloating	Blood pressure changes
Blurred vision	Breathing difficulties
Burning sensation in the back of the neck/forearms	
Changes in heart rate	Chest pain
Depression	Diarrhoea
Difficulty focusing	Disorientation
Dizziness	Dry mouth (extreme)
Facial tightness	Flu-like achiness
Flushing	Headache
Hyperactivity	Insomnia
Irritable bowel	Joint pain
Lethargy	Light-headedness
Loss of balance	Mental confusion
Migraine	Mood Swings

Nausea
Panic attacks
Runny nose
Seizures
Skin rashes
Slurred speech
Stomach cramps
Urinary and prostate problems
Wheezing

Numbness or paralysis
Rapid heartbeat
Sciatica
Shortness of breath
Sleepiness
Stiffness

To test for MSG sensitivity avoid all foods containing MSG both naturally and as an added flavour enhancer for at least five days. Test in two stages. During the first stage, eat some of the foods in which MSG occurs naturally and monitor your response. If there is no adverse reaction then continue to the second stage of testing. If you do have a reaction then return to a no MSG diet for five days and then continue to the second stage. During the second stage, eat one of the food you would have eaten before that contains added MSG.

Some people react immediately on eating any MSG whilst for others it is dose related - whereas one meal containing MSG may cause no problems, a second meal followed by a snack food with high levels can produce the symptoms. It is a cumulative process - you may be able to eat it once a week but not over a number of days in succession. If a large, for you, amount of MSG is ingested it is possible that the initial reaction will be severe but of short duration. You should not be fooled into thinking this is the only reaction you will get.

Monitor yourself carefully over the next few days and notice any additional changes such as bloating, rashes, mental confusion, false energy and headaches. If you had no reaction to added MSG but reacted to some of the foods in which it occurs naturally then you may have a problem with another food chemical such as salicylate rather than MSG.

Foods in which MSG naturally occurs:

Apricot, broccoli, grape, green pea, meat extracts, mushroom, plum, prune, raisin, sultana, soy sauce, spinach, sweet corn, tomato, yeast extracts. Cheese (especially blue vein, brie, camembert, gouda, gruyere, parmesan, roquefort).

Drinks in which MSG occurs:
Brandy, liqueur, port, rum, sherry, tomato juice, vegetable juice, wine.

Processed Foods:
Avoid those containing any of the above foods or drinks.
Snack foods such as cheese and spicy flavoured crisps, chips, tacos.
Soya products, mainly soy sauce, miso, tamari, tempeh.
Most sauces, gravy mixes, and stock cubes.
Meat and yeast extracts, pastes and pates made from fish and meat.
Watch out for the additive MSG - it can be listed as MSG, Monosodium Glutamate or Flavour Enhancer 621.
Check labels very carefully - MSG now creeps into foods as diverse as crisps and soup.

Hidden MSG: It is possible that each of the following may contain MSG.
Autolyzed yeasts, bouillon, barley malt, broth, calcium caseinate, flavourings (including those listed as natural), HVP (hydrolysed vegetable protein), HPP (hydrolysed plant protein), kombu extract, malt extract, seasonings, sodium caseinate, textured protein.

Restaurants and take outs:
Beware! Many restaurants and fast food outlets sprinkle MSG onto fresh foods such as fruit salads to prevent browning. Chinese food often uses MSG as an ingredient. MSG is also often one of the hidden or "secret" ingredients in fast food.

5.8

OXALIC ACID

Oxalic acid and oxalates are naturally occurring toxins in many foods. They are generally dealt with in the gastrointestinal tract and removed from the body in the faeces as calcium oxalate. In some people oxalates have been detected in the urine indicating that absorption from the gastrointestinal tract has taken place. It appears that this absorption takes place when calcium in food is tied up with other dietary components.

A build up oxalic acid can lead to kidney and bladder stones. Other symptoms that have been linked with high oxalic acid levels include abdominal pain, diarrhoea and sore throats.

Plant leaves, especially rhubarb, beet tops and spinach, have the highest concentrations: the concentration is so high in rhubarb leaves that they have been classed as poisonous.

It is not possible to provide a full list of foods containing oxalic acid but the ones listed below have all been found to contain it.

Beer	Peanuts
Beetroot	Pears
Blackberries	Potatoes
Broad beans	Red currants
Celery	Runner beans
Cocoa powder	Sorrel
Gooseberries	Spinach
Green peppers	Strawberries
Leeks	Tea
Parsley	

An average serving of each of these provides about 15mg of oxalate. Rhubarb has the highest amount, followed by spinach, beetroot, and cocoa powder. No oxalates have been identified in cereals, cheese, eggs, and most other fruit and vegetables (109).

If you suspect an oxalic acid problem the general advice is to avoid the foods high in oxalate, limit your fat intake and increase your calcium intake. Do discuss these changes with your doctor first.

5.9

PHENYLETHYLAMINE

Phenylethylamine, derived from the amino acid phenylalnine, has been associated with changes in mood, behaviour and co-ordination. Emsley and Fell (109) state that "there is no evidence that the body treats phenylethylamine as anything other than a chemical to be removed". Cases of chocolate 'allergy' have in fact turned out to be a problem with phenylethylamine. It appears that some people simply do not have sufficient quantities of the enzyme that breaks this amino acid down and prepares it for removal from the body.

Reactions to phenylethylamine have included

Abdominal cramps, diarrhoea, dizziness, flushing, headache, low blood pressure, nausea, respiratory problems, urticaria.

The symptoms often appear to mimic an allergic reaction but when tested no allergy is identifiable. The phenylethylamine in chocolate could be one of the causes of chocolate related migraines.

Sandler et al (363) identified a headache occurrence rate of 50% in those suffering from migraines when exposed to phenylethylamine as opposed to 6% of those receiving a placebo. It could be that some people are unable to fully metabolise phenylethylamine so leaving it in their systems longer and strengthening its effect on the vascular system. Some migraine sufferers and children diagnosed with hyperactivity have been found to have elevated plasma phenylanine (49).

Phenylethylamine is highly concentrated in high-protein foods such as meat and dairy products especially cheese. To reduce the level of the free form that is most likely to cause problems you would need to avoid all processed meat and fish products, meat extracts, cheese, chocolate, wines and beer. You also need to avoid products sweetened with aspartame.

To test for a problem with phenylethylamine avoid all the above foods, including aspartame, for at least two weeks and then reintroduce them gradually. Keep a food diary and remember that problems with phenylethylamine are probably dose related so a single test of, say, some processed meat is unlikely to provide a reaction unless you are extremely sensitive (do also remember that processed meats often contain other ingredients that can cause problems).

By carefully recording what you eat over a period of time, as well as any symptoms you experience, you should be able to see a pattern emerge that shows you how much food high in phenylethylamine you can tolerate before symptoms arise. If you use products containing aspartame please also read the section in the chapter 'Sugars and Sweeteners'.

If there has been some improvement but symptoms, especially migraines, continue to persist then consider testing for a tyramine sensitivity - the foods that need to be avoided are very similar.

5.10

PURINES

The production of uric acid is a normal bodily function. It is a waste product of digestion and is excreted via the kidneys as urine. In some individuals the removal of uric acid is impaired and it accumulates in the body eventually leading to unwanted symptoms. Foods that contain the compound purine can raise the uric acid levels in the body leading, if you are susceptible, to conditions such as gouty arthritis or joint pain. These conditions are generally recognisable by their accompanying sudden and severe attacks of pain, redness and swelling of joints. The condition has been found to be helped by eating a low purine diet.

Gout generally comes on very suddenly with pain, swelling, warmth and redness usually in one joint. It has been commonly been associated with the big toe but can in fact afflict any joint. Some types of kidney stones can also be caused by uric acid build up and autism in some children has also been linked with an inability to correctly metabolise purines.

Other problems have also been linked with purines. Moss reported on a study of the relationship between the consumption of alcohol, purines and boron, and the incidence of irritable bowel syndrome or frequent diarrhoea. The findings showed that individuals on diets high in alcohol, purines and boron had a higher prevalence of irritable bowel syndrome or frequent diarrhoea. The relationship was found to be significant.

You will find it useful to test for purine sensitivity if you have recurring gout like symptoms, only recently had a gout like episode but are also overweight and drink alcohol, or if you have irritable bowel syndrome that has not fully responded to other forms of dietary intervention. It should be noted that not everyone with gout will have a purine sensitivity.

To test for a purine sensitivity, read the food lists carefully and avoid all the very high purine foods for at least two weeks. Reduce your intake of high and moderate purine foods as far as you can remembering that you need to find sources of protein that you can tolerate. Increase your intake of fruit and vegetables (choosing from those not on the lists) that you can eat as these increase the alkalinity of the blood and can help in the removal of excess uric acid. Avoid alcohol.

Foods that are **very high** in purines include:
Anchovies, brains, gravies, kidneys, liver, sardines, sweetbreads.

Foods that are **high** in purines include:

Bacon	Lentils
Beef	Perch
Calf tongue	Pork
Carp	Rabbit
Chicken soup	Shellfish
Cod	Trout
Duck	Turkey
Goose	Veal
Halibut	Venison

Foods that have a **moderate** purine content include:

Asparagus	Mushroom
Bluefish	Mutton
Bouillon	Navy beans
Cauliflower	Oatmeal
Chicken	Oysters

CHANGE YOUR DIET AND CHANGE YOUR LIFE

Crab	Peas
Ham	Salmon
Herring	Spinach
Kidney beans	Tripe
Lima beans	Tuna
Lobster	

For some the relief will be quite sudden but for others it can take time for the body to deal with removing the excess uric acid. If after a fortnight you are noticing some improvement you should maintain the diet. To actually test for a purine sensitivity is difficult as it is effected by the build of uric acid to a level that is a problem for the individual - in some the response can be sudden, in others it can take weeks.

Persevere and monitor your success. As always with food testing, keep a food diary.

5.11

SALICYLATE

The word 'salicylate' is derived from the botanical name for the willow family 'salicaceae' In 1838 salicylic acid was isolated from willow bark and, by 1899, acetylsalicylic acid was synthesised and marketed as aspirin. We come into contact with salicylate in two forms: In man made substances such as medicines, solvents and perfume fixatives, and in its natural form in vegetables, fruit, herbs and plants.

In nature, salicylates appear to exist as a natural preservative or insecticide protecting the plant and elongating its life span. The work of Anne Swain (407) and others in Australia in the mid 1980s demonstrated the extent to which salicylate is present in food. Virtually every meal we ever eat contains some salicylate and for most people this causes no problem but for an individual who is salicylate sensitive the consequences for their long term health can be disastrous. The brain is often seriously effected as an overdose of salicylate first stimulates and then depresses the central nervous system leading to emotional and behavioural problems.

It has been particularly linked with hyperactivity as a result of the work Dr Feingold in the 1970s. The results of research carried out in 1989 by Williams et al (444) support the theory that some food additives and industrial chemicals induce intolerance because of their aspirin-like properties. And a study of aspirin allergy by Speer et al (393) in 1981 found that 90% of those with aspirin sensitivity are also sensitive to inhalants, food or other drugs. Others, including Thune and Granholt (414), have also found a cross reactivity with aspirin. So if you have an aspirin sensitivity consider testing salicylates more generally.

Many of the symptoms that arise as a result of salicylate intolerance mimic those of allergy but a reaction to salicylate is not an allergy. No current method of food intolerance or allergy testing will accurately establish salicylate sensitivity. Salicylate is cumulative in the body and symptoms will only arise when the tolerance level of the individual has been exceeded. A large number of symptoms and conditions have been linked with salicylate and these are outlined in the lists below.

Identified Salicylate Symptoms - mainly physical

Abdominal pain	Aching legs
Asthma	Bed wetting
Dermatitis	Ear Infections
Eye muscle disorders	Fatigue
Hives	Nasal polyps
Persistent cough	Physical sluggishness
Rhinitis	Sinusitis
Sleep disorders	Skin problems
Stomach irritation	
Swelling of face/hands/feet	Tics
Tinnitus	Urticaria

Identified Salicylate symptoms - emotions, behaviour and feeling

Accident proneness
Anxiety or agitation for no reason
Bouts of excessive energy followed by fatigue

Confused thinking	Depression
Distraction	Dyslexia

Erratic sleep pattern
Excessive or constant talking

Hyperactivity	Impatience

Lack or loss of concentration

Memory problems	Mental sluggishness

Mood swings	Needing to be left alone
Nervousness	Poor self image
Sudden bouts of paranoia	Sudden highs
Temper flare ups	Unpredictability
Visual disturbance	Workaholism

How do you know if you are salicylate sensitive?

Check the symptom list. How many of the symptoms do you currently have or have frequently had before? The greater the number the more likely you are to be sensitive. Have you had periods of times when you have experienced clusters of the symptoms? Salicylate sensitivity is generally a life-long condition and a pattern of symptoms and behaviour will be noticeable. Do spices, herbs or vegetables make you feel ill or do you have an aversion to them? This is not necessarily an indicator as we have often been conditioned about our responses but think back to childhood and how you responded to these at that time.

Salicylate sensitivity is most likely an inherited condition. If, from the above, questions, you feel that you are probably salicylate sensitive you should be able to identify similar traits in another family member. Some caution is needed here - the extent of the sensitivity will vary and salicylate sensitive people often find ways of coping that mask their problem so it may not be immediately obvious.

The only way to determine if you are salicylate sensitive is to reduce the level of salicylate in your system and the only way of doing this is to eat food containing no salicylate or very low levels. Once the body has eliminated the stored salicylate it is then possible to reintroduce foods containing a higher level and to assess the extent of any reaction.

If you suspect that salicylates may be a problem for you and you are taking any medication containing aspirin or another form of salicylate DO NOT undertake this test. Check ALL your medicines first. If in doubt ask your pharmacist. Ideally, all medications should also be additive (especially colour) free. If you are taking a salicylate medication then consult your doctor before even considering this test. Please do take the above advise seriously. Aspirin, and other salicylate based drugs, contain a very concentrated form of salicylate. If you stop taking them, reduce the overall salicylate level in your system, and then take one you could be putting your life at risk. Death can result from anaphylactic shock.

As salicylate is cumulative in the body you need to lower your level over a period of at least two weeks. During this time you must be absolutely certain that you do not expose yourself to any high levels. Choose your fortnight with care as meals away from home will be very difficult to deal with. You can eat any amount of the foods listed as safe. If you are currently a vegetarian do not suddenly start eating meat, if you know that lettuce or one of the other foods makes you ill or you have an aversion to it then don't eat it - stick to foods you are used to eating, you can (if you want to) try the other ones later.

To make it easier for you the foods have been allocated a number so that you can keep score of how much salicylate you are eating - the score relates to an average portion. Your maximum allowance during this fortnight is FIVE a day and it is essential that you do not exceed this amount on any day. Keep a food diary and write down the total score for each day. Your food diary is going to become an incredibly important ally in unravelling your food sensitivities. Use it fully.

None of us are perfect and if you slip up don't beat yourself up about it. Correct it. If you find that on one day you unwittingly had a score of ten then make sure the next day's score is zero. Do not do the reverse - this means that if, for example, on the Friday, you scored three you must not increase Saturday's score to seven. KEEP TO FIVE. If you have slipped up on more than two consecutive days you will probably need to start your fortnight again.

At the end of the fortnight you will need to decide on the next stage. The degree of your sensitivity, your age, your overall health and the speed at which your body can detoxify will all have influenced what took place. You will probably find yourself in one of the following categories:

1. There was no noticeable change.
2. There was a gradual improvement in symptoms.
3. There was no change at first then you had two or three days of feeling wonderful followed by days of being generally unwell and very tired - not too dissimilar to flu symptoms. Unless you have contracted a virus this is probably detoxification and nothing to be unduly concerned about.
4. There was a substantial improvement in symptoms.

If you had no improvement in your symptoms then it is unlikely that you are salicylate sensitive. You can test this by eating as many foods from the high lists as you like. If after a fortnight these cause you no problem you can safely assume that you do not have a problem with salicylates. If there was a gradual improvement then you are probably salicylate sensitive. You can try to increase your salicylate level gradually. Increase your score allowance to ten a day over a two week period. If your symptoms begin to get worse again drop your level to five for a few days and then increase slowly until you find the level you can tolerate.

If you can tolerate a score of ten a day then increase to 15 a day, once again for two weeks, and keep on doing this until you reach the level at which your symptoms reappear. The easiest way of dealing with a return of symptoms is drop your level to five for a few days and then take it back up when you feel better.

If you had a few days of feeling great and then feeling generally ill and tired it is likely that you have some degree of salicylate sensitivity. To give your body a chance to detoxify it is safest if you stay at this level for at least a further two weeks.

Testing for salicylate content in food has been slow in taking place. The lists that follow are based on the available research (407) but must not seen as the end of the story. Salicylate content may vary from different crops and harvests, not all foods have been examined, results have not been retested and, in the future, newer methods of analysis may be discovered. It is however, the clearest list you will find available and, if you follow the guidelines above, you should soon have an idea of whether you are salicylate sensitive and be able to establish your level of tolerance.

You are welcome to try foods not on the lists but so as not to confuse the results it would be advisable to treat them as suspect and only introduce them at a later stage when you can clearly determine what is happening. The categories of food are safe, very low, low, moderate, high, very high and extremely high.

Safe Salicylate Foods   **Score = 0**

Fruit: Banana, pear (peeled).

Vegetables: Bamboo shoot, cabbage (green/white), celery, dried green split peas, lentils, lettuce (iceberg), swede.

Potatoes are fine but they must be of the old white variety and you must peel them.

Beans - dried (not borlotti). You may use canned beans but avoid any that have added ingredients such as sugar and salt. It is possible to buy beans in filtered water only and there are some organic varieties available. Check in your local health food shop.

Grains: Barley, buckwheat, millet, oats, rice, rye, wheat. To avoid additives and hidden preservatives, all bread, biscuits, cakes etc.. should be home-made.

Seeds and nuts: Poppy seeds.

Sweeteners: Maple syrup, white sugar.

Meat, fish, poultry: Meat, fish, poultry and eggs are generally salicylate free but avoid liver and prawns and do not eat any processed meat.

Herbs, spices and condiments: Malt vinegar, saffron, sea salt, soy sauce.

Oils and fats: Cold pressed oils such as soy or sunflower. Butter. Margarine and processed rapeseed (canola), safflower, soya bean, sunflower oils although probably low in salicylate are likely to contain preservatives that may mimic salicylate reactions and are best avoided.

Dairy: Butter, cheese (not blue vein), milk, yoghurt - natural only but you can add your own fruit.

Misc: Carob powder, cocoa, tofu.

Beverages: Decaffeinated coffee, milk, ovaltine, home made pear juice, soya milk, rice milk, water. Water should be the drink of your choice.

Very Low Salicylate Foods   Score = 1

Fruit: Golden delicious apple without the peel (green variety only), paw paw, pomegranate, tamarillo.

Vegetables: Brussel sprouts, borlotti beans, chives, choko, garlic, green peas, leek, mung bean sprouts, red cabbage, shallot, yellow split peas.

Nuts and seeds: Cashew nuts.

Herbs, spices and condiments: Fennel - dried, fresh parsley.

Sweeteners: Golden syrup.

Meat and fish: Liver, prawns.

Low Salicylate Foods   Score = 2

Fruit: Fresh figs, lemon, mango, passion fruit, persimmon, red delicious apple (peeled), rhubarb.

Vegetables: Fresh asparagus, beetroot, cauliflower, green beans, onion, marrow, potato - with peel, pumpkin, tomato, turnip. Frozen spinach.

Seeds and nuts: Hazelnuts, pecan, sunflower seeds.

Herbs, spices and condiments: Fresh coriander leaves.

Oils and fat: Ghee.
Beverages: Dandelion coffee, shop bought pear juice.

Moderate Salicylate Foods   Score = 3

Fruit: Custard apple, kiwi fruit, loquat, lychee, pear with peel.
Vegetables: Aubergine - peeled, carrot, lettuces other than iceberg, tomato juice, mushrooms. Tinned asparagus, beetroot, black olives, sweetcorn.
Seeds and nuts: Desiccated coconut, peanut butter, walnuts.
Sweeteners: Molasses.
Beverages: Coco cola, rose hip tea.

High Salicylate Foods   Score = 4

Fruit: Avocado, most other varieties of apples, cantaloupe melon, cherries, grapefruit, mandarin, mulberry, nectarine, peach, tangelo, watermelon.
Vegetables: Alfalfa sprouts, aubergine with peel, broad bean, broccoli, cucumber, tinned okra, parsnips, fresh spinach, sweet potato, tinned tomatoes and tomato puree, watercress.
Grains: Maize.
Seeds and nuts: Brazil nuts, macadamia nuts, pine nuts, pistachio, sesame seeds.
Herbs, spices and condiments: Yeast extracts.
Oils and fats: Almond oil, corn oil, peanut oil, sesame oil, walnut oil.
Beverages: Coffee.

Very High Salicylate Foods   Score = 5

Fruit: Fresh apricots, blackberry, blackcurrant, blueberry, boysenberry, cranberry, fresh dates, grapes, guava, orange, pineapple, plum, strawberry, sultana.
Vegetables: Chicory, chilli peppers, courgette, endive, tinned green olives, peppers, radish, water chestnut.
Seeds and nuts: Almonds, peanuts with skins on.
Sweeteners: Honey.

Herbs, spices and condiments: Basil, bay leaf, caraway, chilli powder, nutmeg, vanilla essence, white pepper.
Oils and fats: Coconut oil, olive oil.
Beverages: Peppermint tea.

Extremely High Salicylate Foods   Score = 6

Fruit: Dried apricots and dates. Currant, loganberry, prunes, raisin, raspberry, red currant.
Vegetables: Gherkins.
Herbs, spices and condiments: Allspice, aniseed, black pepper, cardamom, cayenne, celery powder, cinnamon, cloves, cumin, curry powder, dill, fenugreek, garam masala, ginger, liquorice, mace, mint, mustard, oregano, paprika, rosemary, sage, tarragon, turmeric, thyme, wine and cider vinegars.
Beverages: Cordials and fruit flavoured drinks, fruit and vegetable juices, tea.

Alcohol varies in amount. Given the difficulty in fully ascertaining the ingredients of alcoholic beverages, it is best to avoid drinking alcohol during the first two weeks. The following list can be only be treated as a very basic guide to levels. The safest course of action would be to introduce your favourite drink as a test.

Gin, whisky and vodka are probably safe.
Beer, brandy, cider, and sherry have a high salicylate content.
Liqueurs, port, rum, and wine are extremely high in salicylate.

If you get a reaction, be gentle with yourself. If salicylates effect your mind you may find it useful, when well, to write yourself a note you can read when a reaction takes hold - it should explain what is happening and reassure you that it will pass. If you have someone who understands what is happening talk to them - sometimes this helps minimise the effects of the anxiety.

Increase the number of safe fruit and vegetables you can eat as this increases the alkalinity of your blood. Taking extra Vitamin C can also help. If your blood sugar has been effected, don't worry. Eat lots of small meals for as long as you need - include 'safe' treats. If you need to rest then take the time do so. It will pass. The length and severity of reactions will vary from individual to individual but, as it takes time for the body to eliminate salicylate, you can expect to experience symptoms for at least a few days.

Living with salicylate sensitivity is not easy. To maintain a level of salicylate that you can tolerate in your diet then you really are going to have to take responsibility for your diet - you can never allow anyone else to make a meal for you without first ensuring that they have a full list of the foods you can eat (it is easier to give a list of foods you can eat than those that need to be avoided).

Some food additives can also be a problem not necessarily because they contain any salicylate but because some of them mimic salicylate in the body. A list of these is given in the appendix. Adverse reactions to tartrazine are common in people who also react badly to salicylate (374), probably because both are similar in structure and are detoxified in the same way. Similar problems have been found with the antioxidants BHA and BHT (126).

Establishing a salicylate tolerance level is not an easy process and it can lead to a restrictive diet which is why many doctors advice against it. Depending on your age and other factors unique to you, you may find that over a period of time you will be able to tolerate more salicylate. I suspect that at first, for some of us, our bodies are so relieved to have a reduction in the toxin that they rebel at the input of any but when the body has had time to recover it is more able to deal with eliminating salicylate and then accepts more.

Sadly, salicylates can be found in a whole range of everyday products and, depending on your sensitivity, you will have to watch out for them. Perry et al (316) have estimated that 12-20% of the salicylate in skin preparations is absorbed into the bloodstream via the skin. As some ointments can contain high proportions of salicylate the risk for a sensitive person is serious. Ensure that none of the high and very high foods, especially herbs and spices, are present. Make sure you avoid anything with the word salicylate or salicylic within it. Some of the substances you need to watch out for include:

Acetylsalicylic acid	Menthol
Almond oil	Methyl salicylate
Aspirin	Methylene disalicylic acid
Benzoic acid	Oil of wintergreen
Benzoate - any form	Ortho-hydroxybenzoic acid
Beta hydroxy	Oxylsalicylate
Birch	Salicylaldehyde
Bisabolol	Salicylanilide
Bismuth subsalicylate	Salicylic acid
Camphor	Salicylic alcohol
Castor oil	Sodium salicylate
Homosalate	Stroncylate
Hydroxybenzoate	Willow
Hydroxybenzoic	

Carefully check medications, vitamins and other supplements, herbal remedies, cosmetics, creams and ointments, deodorants, toothpaste, teething gels, soap, shampoo, household cleaning products, air fresheners, insecticides, washing powders. Beware of perfumes as salicylate is often used as a fixative. It is best to avoid using perfume and scented products. Fragrance and colour free products are increasingly available.

I suspect that some people who tried a low salicylate diet for themselves or their children have run into this problem - an improvement followed later by seemingly salicylate unrelated problems. The symptoms are the same as before but you know the tolerance level has not been exceeded. If this happens check your environment - at work, home, school, wherever you spend time.

Crinon (76) in an article on the health effects of airborne solvent exposure tell us that chemicals known as solvents are part of a broad class of chemicals called volatile organic compounds. These compounds are frequently used in a variety of settings and off-gas readily into the atmosphere. As a result of their overuse, they can be found in detectable levels in virtually all samples of both indoor and outdoor air. Once in the body they can lead to a variety of neurological, immunological, endocrinological, genitourinary, and hematopoietic problems. Some individuals also have metabolic defects that diminish the liver's clearing capacity for these compounds.

Perfumes and solvents can give you these reactions and with these it is very difficult to know if they contain salicylate or not. The only way of knowing is to trust your nose which at first can lead to many unwanted reactions. If it all sounds difficult then you're reading the situation correctly. The positive side, and it is a massive one, is the better health that follows. Salicylate causes so many problems within the nervous system that all aspects of your life are effected by it - reducing the level substantially can, for someone with a salicylate sensitivity, lead to many positive changes.

5.12

SEROTONIN

The amine 5-hydroxytryptamine is what serotonin is known as in the world of science. Because of its actions as a neurotransmitter much has been written about the mood elevating qualities of serotonin but less has been written about the difficulties that an 'excess' can cause for certain individuals. Emsley and Fell (109) cite the case of a 52 year old man who experienced 1-2 migraines a month and severe joint stiffness. After investigating his diet, which was high in meat, it was found that the cause of his problems was "a simple case of free amine overload due to a diet rich in tryptophan". Serotonin is produced from the amino acid tryptophan.

The main symptom indicators would appear to be joint inflammation with no verifiable evidence of arthritis, and migraines not responding to other solutions. Other symptoms that have been noted include abdominal cramps, breathing difficulties, burning sensation in the mouth and throat, dizziness, flushing, generalised itching, headache, nausea, urticaria, vomiting and diarrhoea. Urticaria and generalised pruritis are common.

Fish, meat, herbs and dairy products are all potentially high in tryptophan. And, chocolate, cheese, banana, kiwi fruit, plantain, plum, pickled fish, octopus, tomato, walnut, and wine are likely to contain high amounts of serotonin.

If you eat a lot of the same type of meat you may want to consider varying the sources of your protein.

Moderate amounts of serotonin have also been found in (123) aubergine, avocados, black olives broccoli, cantaloupe, cauliflower, dates, figs, grapefruit, honeydew, spinach.

To test for a problem with serotonin avoid all the above foods for at least two weeks and then reintroduce them gradually. Keep a food diary and remember that problems with serotonin are probably dose related so a single test of banana or tomato is unlikely to provide a reaction unless you are extremely sensitive. By carefully recording what you eat over a period of time, as well as any symptoms you experience, you should be able to see a pattern emerge that shows you how much food high in serotonin you can tolerate before symptoms arise.

5.13

SOLANINE

Solanine is a toxic alkaloid found in certain vegetables most notably potatoes. It probably acts as a preservative in the plants that works by making itself poisonous to fungi and bacteria and so preserving the life of the plant. It has been implicated in serious cases of food poisoning and has even resulted in death. A toxic dose will usually result in severe digestive upset and, possibly, trembling, weakness, breathing difficulties and paralysis.

McMillan et al (261) reported on 78 schoolboys who became ill after eating potato at lunch, 17 of them required admission to hospital. It was eventually found that the potatoes eaten by the boys who became ill were from an old batch and were found to be high in solanine. The symptoms were gastrointestinal, circulatory, neurological and dermatological with some boys being far more ill than others.

Vegetables containing solanine are all members of the deadly nightshade family. Everybody should know that eating potatoes that are green is dangerous and should be avoided. Always ensure that your potatoes are thoroughly peeled with all the sprouting parts removed and if the potato is green - throw it away. Solanine is not destroyed by heating. Aside from the rather serious toxic aspect of solanine there is a lesser problem of sensitivity that effects certain individuals. Ordinarily the liver will break down solanine and help us dispose of it but in some individuals this is not the case and an excess of solanine leads to inflammation.

If you have any condition involving painful joints you might like to try a solanine free diet for a while - improvements can be dramatic. Identified symptoms include arthritis, confusion, drowsiness, gastrointestinal problems, hallucination, migraine, painful joints, stomach irritation, trembling, skin problems.

Testing for a solanine problem is relatively straightforward as so few foods are involved. Simply eliminate them all from your diet for two weeks. If there is an improvement you will then have to decide on whether you wish to test or not. If there has been no change then solanine is not a problem for you.

Be cautious if you are still eating any processed food as potato starch creeps into products as diverse as soup, cakes and ice cream. The foods which contain solanine are:

Aubergine, cayenne, chilli, green and red peppers, paprika, potato, tomato.

If you have experienced an improvement but feel you cannot live without some of these foods then gradually reintroduce them and increase the amount you eat. If you keep a careful note in your food diary you should be able to find the amount you can get away with before your problems return or the discomfort becomes unacceptable to you.

5.14

SULPHUR AND SULPHITES

'Sulphur' occurs naturally in a number of foods. 'Sulphites' are sulphur based preservatives that are used to prevent or reduce discoloration of fruit and vegetables, prevent black spots on shrimp and lobster, inhibit the growth of micro-organisms in fermented foods such as wine, condition bread dough, and maintain the stability and potency of certain medications. Sulphites have been used since Roman times as preservatives in wine, sulphur dioxide was also used to sanitise wine and cider containers. Sulphites continue to be used in the wine making business in addition to their many other uses including in the wet milling of corn to soften the kernel and facilitate the removal of corn starch.

A person can develop sulphite sensitivity at any point in life and no one knows, for definite, what triggers the sensitivity. Sulphites are broken down in the body by the same detoxification system that deals with other sources of sulphur in the diet such as amino acids like methionine and cysteine. In some individuals this detoxification system may not be working well and could give rise to a sulphite problem. Some countries have now prohibited the use of sulphites on fresh fruit and vegetables and insist on clear product labelling.

Sulphites have been most frequently linked with asthma. They are not generally seen as a cause of asthma but as a substance that can seriously exacerbate the condition. It has been estimated that between 5 and 10% of asthmatics are effected in this way. The Federation of American Societies for Experimental Biology (FASEB) in 1985 estimated that more than one million asthmatics are sensitive to or allergic to the substance.

Kochen (211) in 1973 was among the first to suggest that the eating of sulphated food could cause bronchial problems. At the time he described the case of a child with mild asthma who repeatedly experienced shortness of breath, wheezing and coughing when exposed to dehydrated fruit that had been treated with sulphur dioxide.

It became more accepted after work published by Baker et al (23), and Stevenson and Simon (402), both in 1981. Stevenson and Simon showed that challenges with potassium metabisulphite could produce significant changes in pulmonary function for some asthmatics. Other reported symptoms include flushing, tingling and faintness.

Problems with sulphites can result from ingestion, inhalation and topical application. Werth (440) describes the case of an asthma sufferer who developed flushing, wheezing, and diaphoresis after inhaling vapours from a bag of dried apricots. In this case the person did not react to ingested sulphite when tested with a capsule of metabisulphite. Schwartz and Sher (368) reported on a case in which breathing problems arose after an application of potassium metabisulphite solution to the eye during treatment for glaucoma. Howland and Simon (181) demonstrated that sulphated lettuce can trigger asthmatic reactions in asthmatics with a confirmed sulphite sensitivity.

Less serious reactions can include abdominal pain and cramps, chest tightness, eczema, headache, hives, itching, localised angioedema, minor breathing problems, nausea and vomiting, stomach ache, throat irritation, urticaria.

Changes in body temperature and heart rate have also been noted (416). A typical low grade reaction would be as follows. After a meal you would suddenly find yourself a little tight chested and feeling as if you are starting with a cold. The sensation would probably disappear within a few hours and, most likely, you would forget about it. The symptoms need not all to be physical.

Randolph (327) cites cases in which individuals experienced mental symptoms including tension, nervousness, and depression. He says that "Sulfur can bring on acute mental and physical symptoms". A sulphite sensitivity could also be a hidden problem for some individuals with irritable bowel syndrome as sulphites can interfere with the process of bacterial fermentation.

If you suspect a sulphite sensitivity and have breathing problems do NOT under any circumstances take this test without medical consent and supervision. Anaphylactic shock has been recorded as a result of sulphite reactions.

Foods high in naturally occurring sulphur have given rise to a number of symptoms including abdominal pain, bloating, constipation, diarrhoea, dizziness, generally feeling unwell, headaches, lack of co-ordination, nausea and vomiting, respiratory problems, sneezing, tight sensation in the chest, tremors, visual disturbances.

It is possible to be sensitive to naturally occurring sulphur and not to added sulphites and vice versa. It has also been found that sulphites destroy vitamin B1 which can be a problem for anyone on a poor diet. In some countries it is now banned from foods high in B1 such as meat. Eberlein-Konig et al (103) also found that sulphites can contribute to UVB sensitivity.

To test for a sulphite sensitivity, check all the foods you eat very carefully and eliminate, as far as you can, all those containing any form of sulphites. At this point do not be too concerned about the foods that contain sulphur naturally - a complete elimination will probably be unnecessary and would cause you problems with eating sufficient protein.

Allow at least ten days before testing. Test by eating one of the foods you would have previously eaten that contained sulphites. If you have no reaction, gradually increase the number of foods with sulphites. If you experience any form of reaction - immediately stop the test and eliminate them from your diet once again.

If you found that you do have a sulphite sensitivity and have made some improvement but are still experiencing problems you may also need to reduce the amount of naturally occurring sulphur in your diet as well. Foods that contain natural sulphur include:

Bran, broccoli, brussels sprouts, cabbage, cauliflower, cheese, dried beans, egg yolk, fish, garlic, lentils, meat, molasses, nuts, onions, pasta, wheat germ,

You need to take great care with this type of reduction as you need to ensure that you are eating sufficient protein. If after two weeks you continue to experience problems then it is likely that you have a problem other than sulphur. Before embarking on further tests double and triple check the foods that you are eating, writing to manufacturers if need be, as residual sulphite concentrations can be found in many foods. Also ensure that you are avoiding corn products in case of sulphite contamination.

As sulphite is a product that is added to foods it is impossible to provide a full list of foods containing sulphite. The following list, based in part on the re-examination of the GRAS status of sulfiting agents (237), is intended to serve only as a guideline - you must check labels of all foods for sulphite containing ingredients.

Foods that are often **very high** in sulphites include:
Dried fruit, grape juice, lemon juice, lettuce, lime juice, molasses, sauerkraut juice, and wine.
Those that are **high** in sulphites include:
Dried potato, fruit toppings, gravies, sauces, maraschino cherries, and wine vinegar.
Foods with **moderate** amounts of sulphites include:
Corn starch, corn syrup, frozen potatoes, jams and jellies, maple syrup, mushrooms, pickles and relishes, sauerkraut, and shrimp.

Those with **low** amounts of sulphites include:
Beer, coconut, dried cod, dry soup mixes, frozen pastries, gelatin, instant tea, malt vinegar, soft drinks, sugar, tinned potatoes,

Check all processed products including biscuits, crackers, enriched milk, meat and fish pies, pastes and ready meals, pies and pizza crusts, tortillas, any baked goods, any containing dried or processed fruit or vegetables, and all tinned foods. During the testing period avoid eating away from home especially in restaurants as in some countries sulphites are added to help keep food fresh. These are the terms you need to watch out for:

E220 Sulphur dioxide
E221 Sodium sulphite
E222 Sodium hydrogen sulphite
E223 Sodium metabisulphite
E224 Potassium metabisulphite
E226 Calcium sulphite
E227 Calcium hydrogen sulphite
E150(b) Caustic Sulphite Caramel
E150 Sulphite Ammonia Caramel

Unless you are extremely sensitive you will find that you can tolerate some sulphites. Your challenge will now to be find out just what you can get away with. Whilst establishing a safe level you would be advised to avoid take out, fast food and restaurant meals. Remember that exposure to sulphites can result from ingestion, inhalation and topical application.

5.15

TANNINS

Tannins are naturally occurring chemicals found in a wide range of foods. It could be that, in similar way to salicylates, they act as a form of natural protection for plants. They are also found in processed foods, medications and supplements where they are used as binders, coatings and preservatives. The main symptom that has so far been linked with a tannin sensitivity is migraine (258). So, if you suffer from migraines and no other test has worked, consider checking your tannin tolerance level.

One of the difficulties with testing for a tannin sensitivity is that no definitive list of foods currently exists and the information that is available often does not give a clear indication of the amounts of tannin in a particular food. The easiest way of testing for a tannin sensitivity is to remove all tannin foods, listed below, for two weeks and then gradually reintroduce them. You will need to keep a food diary to be able to closely monitor how you react and you should bear in mind that reactions may be delayed and may also be the result of a cumulative effect.

Fruit: Apricot, banana, blackberry, blueberry, cherry, cranberry, currant, date, gooseberry, grape, kiwi, nectarine, peach, persimmon, raspberry, strawberry.
Nuts: Cashew, pecan, pistachio, walnut.
Legumes: Black beans, peanuts with skins, red beans.
Herbs and spices: It would appear that most herbs and spices contain tannins. As it is not currently possible to identify which are high and which are not, avoid all herbs and spices for the testing period.

Misc: Aubergine, barley (all forms), carob, cocoa, smoked foods.

Others: Avoid food dyes and gums in processed foods. Check medicines and supplements carefully.

Beverages: Apple cider, beer, coffee, fruit juices, guarana, mate, tea, wine (especially red).

If you have found yourself to be very tannin sensitive you need to know that there are non-food products which may also give you a problem. Tannins are a sub-group of phenolics which are found in fragrances, paints, solvents, cleaning materials and the like.

Do not let this concern you at this stage. Continue with a low tannin diet and if you later get a re-occurrence of migraines then consider checking on the products commonly used, by yourself and others, in your home, work and social environment. This type of delayed reaction is not uncommon (often referred to as unmasking). Do not panic or necessarily suspect other foods. Keep a diary of all products used and how you feel in different places and you should soon be able to identify the primary culprits.

5.16

TYRAMINE

Tyramine is produced from the amino acid tyrosine by enzymes produced by bacteria in both the gut and in food. In food, these bacteria increase in number, especially in ripe, fermented, some cooked, and badly stored food. Tyramine, unlike some other amines, appears to serve no useful purpose in the body. Sadly, it is present in a large number of foods and in susceptible people can lead to high blood pressure, migraines, sleepiness and mood changes. It has been particularly linked with migraines because as a vasoactive amine it affects the blood vessels in a way which leads to changes in blood pressure and produces headaches.

Smith et al (358) used double-blind placebo controlled challenges with 45 individuals with food induced migraine. Out of 94 tyramine challenges, 74 (80%) resulted in a migraine. Peatfield (309) reports on a study of 577 people attending the Princess Margaret Migraine Clinic from 1989 to 1991 who were questioned about dietary triggers of their headaches. Of the 429 who had migraines, 16.5% reported that headaches could be precipitated by cheese or chocolate, and nearly always both.

A sensitivity to alcohol, especially red wine and beer, was also found. They found that there was a definite statistical association between sensitivity to cheese/chocolate and to red wine and also to beer and concluded that cheese/chocolate and red wine sensitivity, in particular, have closely related mechanisms, in some way related more to migraine than to more chronic tension-type headache (no food sensitivities were reported in this category). They did not make the link between these food problems and tyramine but it seems likely to have been the cause.

Ghose and Turner (145) found that women may become more sensitive to the effects of vasoactive amines such as phenylethylamine and tyramine in the perimenstrum. So migraines at this point may be more likely to arise and could be misread as being caused by foods such as chocolate. The headache producing properties of tyramine are not restricted to individuals sensitive to an excess of it. Studies have shown that 100-125mg of tyramine leads to 90% of people experiencing a headache.

Tyramine sensitivity is an example of how easy it is to misread food intolerance - if your problem is tyramine and you test cheese (high in tyramine) in isolation then the migraines may abate. You will think the problem is the cheese and eliminate it from your diet. Your migraines may abate and then return leading to confusion because you thought you had identified the problem. At this point it is easy to get into a cycle of identifying and blaming other foods as well and limiting your diet unnecessarily because what has in fact happened is that your tyramine intolerance level has been exceeded. The problems caused by food chemicals has been grossly underestimated. They are difficult to ascertain because of their cumulative effect and the simple fact that we will all have different tolerance levels.

A suspected cause of the symptoms is a deficiency of diamine oxidase in the jejunum (part of the small intestine between the duodenum and ileum) which leads to diminished tyramine degradation in the gastrointestinal tract and this leads to absorption. Histamine is also metabolised by this enzyme. Tyramine can cause problems for people taking MAO (monoamine oxidase) inhibitors as monoamine oxidase in the gastrointestinal tract normally metabolises dietary monoamines such as tyramine. When this is blocked by drugs then more are absorbed into the body leading to symptoms such as palpitations, severe headaches and high blood pressure.

If you suffer from recurring migraines you may like to consider testing tyramine. Other implicating symptoms may also include high blood pressure, palpitations, agitation, nervousness and circulation problems.

The key factor in this test is to eat food as fresh as possible as the ageing, fermenting and ripening processes all increase the amount of tyramine.

To test for a tyramine sensitivity, avoid all tyramine foods listed below for at least seven days and then eat one of the foods from the list you most commonly eat but not cheese. If you immediately get a reaction then tyramine is a problem - stay of all tyramine foods for at least two weeks before trying again. On the second test try a different food from the list. Testing of cheese should only take place once you have established if you have a tyramine problem or not. The reason for this is a reaction to cheese could indicate a hidden milk intolerance problem rather than a problem with tyramine.

If on the first test there is no adverse reaction add a tyramine food each day. If you get no reactions over the next seven days then you are probably okay. If a reaction does occur then you are probably tyramine sensitive to some degree. In this case eliminate them all again and then gradually increase the number that you eat until you are able to gauge what amount you can tolerate. Full analysis of foods for tyramine has not been conducted but some information is available as it is a food chemical that must be avoided by anyone taking MAOI drugs if they are to avoid potentially serious reactions.

Food List - Tyramine
Cheese: All cheese except for cottage cheese, cream cheese and ricotta cheese. Watch out for biscuits containing cheese.
Yeast: Brewer's yeast, sour dough, yeast extracts, yeast leavened breads made with fresh yeast (those made with

bakers yeast are probably okay), yeast vitamin supplements, yeast found in processed foods.

Meat, poultry and fish: Buy fresh and eat within two days. Freshness is the key factor so be cautious in restaurants.

Avoid all tinned, smoked, aged, pickled, fermented or marinated meat, fish and poultry products. This includes bacon, caviar, ham, hot dogs, leftovers, meat extracts, offal, pepperoni, salami and sausages.

Wild game and liver pates.

Fruit: Citrus fruit especially oranges, overripe bananas (also banana skins). You would be wise to avoid any overripe or spoiling fruit.

Vegetables: Aubergine, broad beans, green beans, bean pastes, fermented bean curds, fermented soya beans, mange tout, sauerkraut

Condiments: Soy sauce, bean pastes, miso.

Beverages: Orange juice, tomato juice

Misc: Ginseng, tofu. Check the labels of any processed product to ensure avoidance of yeast and hydrolysed protein such as stock cubes, gravy, soup, sauces, stew mixes.

Alcohol: Beer including non-alcoholic brands.

Wines including non-alcoholic brands.

Whisky and liqueur.

MSG

It is probably also necessary to avoid all foods containing added MSG - check the section above for full details.

Tyramine has been identified in more than 200 foods. The foods with the higher amounts have been listed above. The following may require a limited intake - this will depend on the degree of your sensitivity:

Anchovies	Mushrooms
Avocados	Pineapple
Beetroot	Prunes
Boiled eggs	Raisins

Buttermilk	Raspberries
Caffeine	Red plums
Chocolate	Salad dressings
Colas	Sour cream
Cream and cottage cheeses	Spinach
Cucumbers	Sweet corn
Curry powder	Tomato juice
Figs	Yeast leavened bread
Fresh fish	Vanilla extracts
Lentils	Yoghurt

If you eat any of these try to eat them as fresh as possible. For the initial testing phase do not exclude these - just reducing your tyramine levels will probably be enough to provide an indication as to whether you have a problem with this amine or not. The fine tuning can come later. This method will also prevent you from you restricting your diet unnecessarily.

5.17

OTHER CHEMICALS

This chapter contains a brief outline of some of the other chemicals found in food that can cause some people problems.

Aflatoxin
Aflatoxin is a mycotoxin produced by certain moulds. It can be found in foods as varied as nuts, peanuts, corn, milk, and dried fruit. Strict regulations govern the amount of permissible aflatoxin in foods, and poisoning in 'developed' countries is rare.

Glycyrrihizic Acid
Russo et al (357) describe two cases of hypertension encephalopathy which resulted in pseudo hyperaldosteranism syndrome as a result of daily intake of low doses of liquorice. They propose that some people could be susceptible to low doses of glycyrrhizic acid because of a deficiency in a certain enzyme.

Goitrogens
Goitre, thyroid enlargement, has been linked with over consumption of naturally occurring goitrogens in vegetables. The vegetables include brussel sprouts, broccoli, cabbage, cauliflower, kale, mustard, radish, rapeseed, soy beans, and turnip. It appears that coking reduces the goitre effect of these vegetables.

Linamarin

Linamarin is found in cassava (manioc), an important vegetable in some parts of the world yet also inherently toxic. Linamarin can be converted to hydrocyanic acid and lead to toxic cyanide effects. Neurological disorders and thyroid enlargement have been found in people who eat large amounts of cassava that has not been adequately processed. To reduce toxic cyanide effects, cassava must be correctly processed by soaking, boiling, drying, and fermentation.

Nickel

Flyvholm et al (127) reviewed the nickel content of food as it is now thought that flare of hand eczema can occur after oral nickel exposure. The incidence of nickel allergy in the Danish population is thought to be 10% for women and 2% for men. Intake of nickel from the diet is estimated to be on average 150 micrograms per person per day. Anderson et al (13) found that nickel in tap water can also influence flare of hand eczema. Nielsen et al (288) found quite clear links between diet and flare of hand eczema due to nickel content.

Vegetables and grains supply the average diet with nickel. Cocoa and chocolate, soya beans, oatmeal, nuts and legumes also have a very high nickel content. Consumption of these foods in large amounts can increase the nickel intake to 900 micrograms per person per day or more. It is possible for flare of hand eczema to take place within the range of 600-5,000 micrograms. It would be necessary to establish the individual threshold.

Avoiding canned and processed foods would seem to be helpful as Smart and Sherlock (387) found high concentrations in canned vegetables, sugars and preserves (also in bread and cereals) and suggest that nickel content can increase as a result of food processing.

Myristicin

Myristicin is found in nutmeg and carrots and can cause blurred vision, chest pressure, dry mouth, flushing, hallucinations, nausea, palpitations and a sense of impending doom. It is unlikely that you will be able to consume enough carrots to cause a problem but nutmeg poisoning has been reported.

Phenols

Phenolic compounds are found in a wide range of foods. These are natural substances that colour and flavour foods. The fact that they are toxic could be nature's way of protecting itself against micro-organisms and aiding the dispersal, and germination, of the seeds. Generally our body eliminates these toxins with no difficulty but for some people they cause problems. The discovery of phenolic compounds led Dr Robert Garner to devise a neutralisation technique using dilutions of these substances to stop his own allergic reactions.

Some examples include eugenol found in almond, beef, carrot, celery, cheese, milk, orange, pea, soya bean, tomato; piperine found in beef, beet sugar, cheese, chicken, cow's milk, grape, lamb, onion, pea, potato, soya bean, tomato, yeast.

Cinnamic acid is one of the better known ones, its precursor in most plants is phenylalanine. Cinnamic acid gets its name from oil of cinnamon where it was first discovered. Its presence may reach as much as 13 mg/100 g in such foods as apples or 14 mg/100 g in sweet cherries and 14.5 mg/100g in grapes (68).

The amount and concentration of phenols varies greatly from plant to plant. How they effect health is complex as it is influenced by their interaction with each other and with other chemical compounds. As yet it is not clearly known which phenols are beneficial, which are harmful and which may lead to sensitivities.

Tin

Tin plate is commonly used in the construction of metal cans for foods. If the tins are not adequately lined when used for acidic foods such as tomato juice and fruit cocktail then tin intoxication can take place. Tin is poorly absorbed and hence the early symptoms are bloating, nausea, abdominal cramps, vomiting, diarrhoea and headache within 30 minutes to 2 hours (26).

6

FOOD PROBLEMS

Testing of individual foods does contain an element of risk which is why I advice that you carry out these tests in conjunction with your doctor. Even if you have been given the go-ahead to test a food at home I would advise that somebody is with you for at least the first hour after testing - if you have a severe reaction they can obtain medical help for you. Remember anaphylaxis can be life threatening.

The other advantage of having someone present is that we are not always very good at noticing changes within ourselves. Although you will know if you have a headache, rash or stomach ache easily enough, a change in how you are speaking or behaving is not always easy to detect. These behaviour changes are difficult to spot because if you have been reacting in the same way to a particular food for many years the change will not seem unusual to you, in fact it will feel familiar and 'safe'.

If you already avoid a food then do not test it. You are probably avoiding it for a very good reason. This of course does not apply to foods that you have never tried.

It is impossible to provide a full list of potential symptoms for each food as any food can cause any problem - it is very much an individual specific response. There are, however, some exceptions. In some instances there has been a great deal of research and common symptoms have been identified - where this is the case, as in milk, the symptoms are given.

When testing a food eat it in its most simple form. For example, testing milk by eating ice cream is not okay, nor is testing hazelnuts by eating a chocolate bar containing them. Keep it simple. In the examples given above simply drink some milk or eat some hazelnuts on their own. If at all possible use organic foods for testing, this is to avoid conflicting results due to pesticides. If you cannot find an organic version do still carry out the test and if you are uncertain of the results simply repeat the test.

6.1

CHOCOLATE

Chocolate is commonly seen as an allergenic food but very few actual 'allergies' to chocolate have been documented. It would appear that most chocolate 'allergies' are usually linked with one of the other ingredients such as milk, peanuts and eggs or with a sensitivity to a food chemical such as caffeine, tyramine or phenylethylamine.

Maslansky and Wein (257) reported on 3 patients who reacted to an allergy test for chocolate using cocoa capsules. One reacted with urticaria, another with fatigue and gastric bloating and one with nausea and cramp. Only one of the three was sensitised to cocoa as detected by allergy skin testing.

Merret et al (263) tested to see if food allergy was a major cause of migraine. Their findings were that allergies could not often be detected and concluded that the food intolerance associated with migraine headaches was not related to the conventionally defined allergic mechanism - the adverse reaction was being caused by another factor such as a food chemical intolerance.

'Allergic' reactions that have been linked with chocolate include:

Abdominal cramps	Hypotension
Abdominal pain	Itching
Angioedema	Migraine
Asthma	Nausea
Bronchial complaints	Red ears
Coughs	Rhinitis
Dermatitis	Sneezing

Diarrhoea   Urticaria
Flushing   Vomiting
Headaches

An actual intolerance or allergy to chocolate or cocoa would have to be an intolerance of either cocoa mass or cocoa butter yet these are rarely checked independently of other ingredients. Eating a chocolate bar or drinking hot chocolate is NOT the way to test for a 'chocolate' intolerance.

Intolerance problems with chocolate can be caused by any ingredient or naturally occurring chemical. In respect of ingredients it could be any of the following: Artificial sweeteners, butter, cocoa mass, cocoa butter, emulsifiers (usually lecithin - soya or egg), flavourings (usually vanilla - natural or man made), grains such as wheat, oats and rice, lactose, milk or milk powder, nuts, other vegetable oils, peanuts, sugar.

In respect of a food chemical it could be any of the following:

Caffeine and theobromine
Histamine
Phenylethylamine
Serotonin
Tyramine

Perhaps the simplest way of testing if chocolate is a problem is to eliminate chocolate in all its forms from your diet for at least seven days. Make sure that you check all confectionery for cocoa.

Test chocolate by eating some dark chocolate that contains only sugar, cocoa powder, cocoa mass, lecithin, and natural vanilla. If there is no reaction then it is unlikely that you have a problem with chocolate as such but if symptoms have abated and then begin to reappear I suggest you explore whether any other ingredients and food chemicals are a problem for you.

A detailed protocol for assessing intolerance problems with chocolate can be found in the book 'Chocolate, Cocoa, and Health' (352).

6.2

CORN

Corn is an increasing problem as it has now crept into a large number of processed foods so, although you may eat no actual corn, your diet could in fact be very high in it. Speer (392) listed corn amongst the top ten allergens. It has been linked with migraines (151, 391) and atopic dermatitis in some children (359). Symptoms that have been reported include anaphylaxis, angioedema, breathing problems, dermatitis, diarrhoea, hives, itching eyes and nose, low blood pressure, migraines, mouth swelling.

It is a problem that is now being noticed in young children as it is found in products designed for babies.

Although increasing numbers of people report having problems with corn it is still not accepted as being a major allergen problem by many doctors. If you have a sensitivity to corn it is a mute point as to whether it is an allergy or an intolerance as both effectively require the same treatment - avoidance.

There is little evidence to suggest cross reactivity between corn and other cereals (199) but it has been noted that rice and corn antigens do show some similarities (173). Because of its versatility, corn has crept into many products and, depending on your degree of sensitivity, they may all need to be avoided. You would need to avoid anything that contains the words 'corn' or 'maize'. Check all processed foods, including sweets and candies, as corn appears in products ranging from sweets to processed meats.

All of the following either do or could contain corn, always check the label carefully and if full details are not give, as in the case of 'starch' then err on the side of caution:

Baking powder
Cakes and pastries
Candies
Caramel flavour
Cereals
Chewing gums
Corn
Corn alcohol
Corn extract
Corn flakes
Corn flour
Corn meal
Corn oil
Corn starch
Corn syrup
Dextrin
Dextrates
Dextrins
Dextrose
Flavourings
Fructose
Glucose
Grits
HVP
Hydrolysed corn
Invert sugar or syrup
Maize
Maltodextrin
Malt syrup
Marshmallow
Modified food starch
Mono and di-glycerides
MSG
Polenta
Powdered sugar
Processed meats
Ready meals
Starch
Vegetable oil
Vegetable protein

The easiest way to begin testing for a corn sensitivity is to eliminate it entirely from your diet, in all its forms, for at least 5 days and then to eat some in the most natural form you can find. if you have had an improvement in your symptoms do beware of an unpleasant reaction when testing. If, on testing, you have no immediate symptoms then continue to add more corn based foods into your diet stopping immediately if there is a reaction.

It is quite possible to be able to tolerate some corn but some individuals can not tolerate any corn at all. If you fall into this group then please be aware that corn finds its way into many non-food products and that sensitivity can take place from both inhalation, ingestion and contact.

Some of the non-food products that may contain corn include:

Adhesive on stamps and envelopes
Aspirin
Bath and body powders
Cartons that are used for fruit juices and milk
Cough syrups
Ointments
Paper cups and plates
Plastic wrap
Suppositories
Toothpaste.
Vitamin C

Check all the products that you use - if need be contact the manufacturer to find out for certain. The symptoms caused by these forms of corn contact are wide ranging: For example Crippa and Pasolini (77) found allergic reactions to the corn-starch powder used as glove-lubricant-powder, symptoms included breathing difficulties, rhinitis, angioedema, and asthma.

If you find that you have improved greatly and then seem to have started to get ill again do not suspect that you have developed a new problem. Before you embark on any new tests double and triple check everything that you use, corn creeps into so many products that it can take quite some time before you have wholly identified all the sources that you come into contact with. Note also that corn can appear in alcoholic drinks including some beers and wines.

6.3

EGGS

Reactions to eggs are quite common, especially amongst children. Reported symptoms include:

Allergic rhinitis	Hives
Anaphylaxis	Migraine
Angioedema	Nausea
Asthma	Oral allergy syndrome
Catarrh	Respiratory difficulties
Dermatitis	Urticaria
Diarrhoea	Vomiting
Gastrointestinal symptoms	

Rowntree et al (351) found that 65% of children with persistent eczema and respiratory tract symptoms had a problem with eggs. Guariso (153) found that for some migraine sufferers the trigger food was eggs, as did Egger (108). Langeland (220), in a study of 84 children allergic to eggs, found that pruritis and exacerbations of atopic dermatitis were the most common symptoms.

It has also been associated with inhalation of tame bird dander and known as 'bird-egg syndrome'. Maat-bleeker et al (243) present the case of a woman who developed an egg allergy as a result of inhaled allergen sensitisation from a parrot. Mandallaz et al (249) suggest that 'bird-egg syndrome' is to do with the individual developing a sensitisation to egg-yolk livetins.

Although egg intolerance has often been associated with children, it can arise at any age. Egg allergens are well known with those in egg white often being the most common. Holen and Elsayed (177) identified ovalbumin as the most allergenic portion of egg white, followed by ovomucoid, ovotransferrin and lysozyme. Allergies are also possible to the proteins in egg yolk.

If you have always eaten eggs you will not know if they are causing you a problem. There is a much repeated story that well illustrates this point. Dr Rinkel suffered from chronic catarrh, fatigue and headaches. As his symptoms got progressively worse he began to follow advice on dietary changes and tested eggs by eating six in quick succession - rather than a worsening of symptoms he felt better.

The key factor in this case was that Dr Rinkel had been eating lots of eggs each day over a long period of time. Later he eliminated eggs completely from his diet. Within a couple of days he began to feel better. On the fifth day he ate a piece of cake and fell unconscious. The cake had, of course, contained eggs. Dr Rinkel went on to become a leading allergy specialist.

The easiest way of assessing egg intolerance is to remove egg in all its forms from the diet for at least four days and then test. Avoiding eggs means avoiding it in all its forms, as whole egg, egg white, egg yolk, powdered or dry egg, so check sauces, cakes and all processed food. The following terms may also indicate the presence of egg:

Albumin	Natural flavourings
Apovitellin	Ovalbumin
Binder	Ovomucoid
Coagulant	Ovaglobulin
Emulsifier	Ovomucin
Globulin	Ovomucoid
Lecithin	Ovotransferrin
Livetin	Ovovitellin
Lysozyme	Seasonings
Mayonnaise	Vitellin
Meringue	

Products to check carefully include:

Baked goods, baking mixes, breakfast cereals, cakes, creamy fillings, egg noodles, fat substitutes, french toast, batters, bouillon, candy, custard, ice cream, soufflés, sherbets, lemon curd, macaroni, malted drinks, marshmallows, processed meat and fish products, puddings, salad dressings, sauces, soups.

The severity of egg sensitivity varies. Some people are at serious risk from anaphylactic shock and must avoid egg in all its forms, others can eat small amounts of egg, for example, in baked goods. Should you find you only react to hard boiled eggs I suggest you read the section on the naturally occurring food chemical 'Tyramine'.

Eggs creep into a range of foods and other goods and may not always be listed. For example:

♦ In some countries, including Japan and Switzerland, lysozyme is used in medications.
♦ The egg used could have been in such small amounts that the manufacturer is not obliged to list it as an ingredient as may be the case with a glazing agent on baked goods. Freemont et al (132) found lysozyme was an unlabeled additive in cheese preparation .
♦ Egg components may also, according to Steinman (400), be found in cosmetics, shampoos and medications.

♦ Some points to note:
♦ It is possible to be intolerant of eggs in one form and not another. For example, you may be able to eat fried eggs but not boiled.
♦ You may be able to tolerate eggs in baked products such as cakes but not on their own.

♦ Reactions, particularly headaches, to hard boiled eggs could indicate a problem with tyramine rather than an egg intolerance.

♦ Intolerance can be of the whole egg, egg white or egg yolk.

♦ Some studies have found that egg is less allergenic when cooked.

♦ Many vaccines are based on egg - check with your doctor before agreeing to any injection.

♦ It is also possible to react to other bird eggs. Langeland (219) found cross reactivity between hen egg white and that of turkey, goose, duck and seagull.

♦ Many egg intolerant people can quite safely eat chicken but others experience problems.

6.4

FISH

Reactions to seafood are not uncommon and usually occur within six hours of eating. Shellfish in particular have been found to cause problems with shrimp being considered a highly allergenic food. Sicherer (378) identifies shellfish and fish as one of the most common foods that causes problems for both children and adults. The type of fish available to you will, to a large extent, be determined by where you live.

You should know that reactions have been recorded for most varieties. For example, Pascual et al (307), in a study from Spain, found that fish allergy was present in 22% of all patients with a diagnosis of food hypersensitivity. They looked at the allergenic significance of the type of fish most commonly eaten in the area which were flatfish such as sole and hake. They found hake to be the most allergenic.

Symptoms range from mild to life-threatening. Even tiny amounts of fish substances can trigger a reaction in some people. Symptoms can include:

Anaphylaxis	Bloating
Brain fogging	Breathing difficulties
Hives	Itching
Light headedness	Nasal congestion
Nausea	Wheezing
Stomach problems ranging from heartburn to diarrhoea	

Oehling et al (296) found that the most frequent skin manifestation of fish intolerance was atopic dermatitis. In a study of 48 patients (65) with crustacean allergy, the most frequent cause of symptoms was shrimp (33 cases) followed by squid (24 cases). The most frequently found symptoms were: Urticaria/angioedema (39 patients), asthma (18 patients) and rhinitis (14 patients).

It is possible to misinterpret a reaction to fish, such as tuna and mackerel, as an allergy when it might be due to a histamine sensitivity. Read the section on histamine in the food chemicals section to find out more. It is also possible to react to another ingredient in a fish product and to so misdiagnose the cause of the problem: for example, Asero (19) presented the case of a 19 year old man who experienced several episodes of angioedema of the penis and scrotum within two hours of eating canned tuna. The angioedema was in fact found to be due to tartrazine.

Some people react solely to shellfish, any fish with high levels of histamine, or any single type of fish whether it be salmon, trout, cod, hake, herring, tuna, swordfish and so on. In a study, by Bernihisee-Broadbent et al (35), of people allergic to fish a number of double blind challenges to different fish species were carried out. Most of those in this study were found to be able to safely eat a different species of fish than the one they were allergic too.

Other studies have, however, shown that cross reactivity does take place (34). Tanaka et al (409) found reactions often took place to groups of fish and they classified seafood allergens into 4 groups:

1. Salmon, sardine, horse mackerel and mackerel.
2. Cod and tuna.
3. Octopus and squid.
4. Crab and shrimp.

Hansen et al (160) set out to test cross reactivity of four species of fish, cod, mackerel, herring, and plaice, in adults with codfish allergy. Reactions were found to take place to all four types of fish and their study suggests that cross-reactivity to different fish species in adults with cod fish allergy exists, and that cod, mackerel, herring and plaice share a common antigenic structure.

DeMartino et al (91) found that some individuals with a cod-fish allergy could tolerate other species of fish but were more likely to react to the other species than those with non-fish allergies.

As fish is one of the foods that tends to provoke a very quick reaction it is unlikely that you would need to carry out any test unless you suspect histamine may be a problem or you eat fish every day. If you suspect histamine - follow the guidelines in that section. If you eat fish every day then try eliminating it from your diet for seven days to ascertain if there is a problem.

Test it by eating your chosen fish cooked by a very simple method such as poaching, avoid using a sauce at this time. At the first sign of an unwanted reaction stop eating the fish.

Avoiding fish is not too difficult as it rarely creeps into non-fish dishes but do take care in restaurants where cross contamination is possible especially if the same oil is used for frying fish as well as other products such as potatoes. If you are only allergic to one form of fish you also need to be careful when eating out in case there has been cross contamination or substitution.

Shellfish, in particular, may appear in a variety of dishes and a waiter may not always be aware of their presence - ask him to check with the chef.

Lin et al (231) gave details of a 4 year-old boy who had an anaphylactic reaction whenever he contacted food prepared with fish. His symptoms included intense itching in the throat and eyes, generalised urticaria, facial angioedema, coughing, wheezing and dyspnea. He reacted to several different types of fish including cod, tuna, salmon, trout and eel, also to chopsticks contaminated with fish preparations. They suggest that the best treatment for fish allergy is avoidance which may also have to include avoiding inhalation of cooking vapours.

6.5

FRUIT

Any fruit can cause problems. Skin rashes, as often seen with strawberries, are a common reaction but by no means the only one. Other symptoms could include itching and swelling of the mouth, tongue and lips, and breathing problems. It is possible to be sensitive to any individual fruit, to a number of fruits or to one of the chemicals found within fruit. One indicator that may help you identify a problem with fruit is seasonal fluctuation of symptoms. Do you always get rashes in the summer months? And, if yes do you at the same time eat large amounts of any of the summer fruits?

If you eat a lot of dried fruits then you could be sensitive to sulphites or salicylates - check out the respective sections in the earlier chapters. Problems with a range of fruit and vegetables is most likely to indicate a sensitivity to salicylates so if you suspect that you are reacting to a range of fruits then do please read the chapter on salicylates before testing any individual fruit. You may find it useful to know that the only fruits that are very low in salicylate are peeled pears and bananas.

Citrus fruits contain high concentrations of chlorogenic acid which has been thought to be responsible for allergic type reactions. If you know you have a problem with any one citrus fruit you might want to consider eliminating them all for a few days and then testing. You would need to avoid all the following:

Clementine
Grapefruit
Lemon

Lime
Mandarin
Orange
Pomelo
Satsumas
Tangelo
Temple

If you suspect a single fruit or summer fruits then eliminate accordingly for at least four days and test by eating them in their most natural state which means fresh not tinned, frozen or cooked. If you do have problems with some fruits and experience an improvement in symptoms and then, later, have a return of symptoms check whether your problem is in fact one of salicylate sensitivity.

All fruits have at some point been implicated in negative reactions. Two and a half hours after eating red currants a 47 year old woman had symptoms including generalised urticaria, dysphagia, dysponeia, pruritis of the palms and soles, hypotonia, and tachycardia (452l).

Oranges have been implicated in migraines (108) although this could be as a result of a tyramine sensitivity. Zhu et al (451) report that oranges are considered to be common allergenic fruits in China. They analysed the allergic histories of 26 orange-sensitive patients. Their analysis suggested that clinical symptoms of some orange-allergic subjects were different from other fruit allergies but similar to nut and other oil plant seed allergies. Interestingly they found the major allergenic components of orange reside in orange seeds instead of orange juice.

Urticaria and colitis have been noted as reactions after eating papaya (116). The oral allergy syndrome has been found to be provoked by bananas (302). Ortoloni (302) detected pear allergy in 22% of those with hay fever and oral allergy syndrome after eating fruit. Think of a fruit and someone will have had a negative reaction to it.

There have also been recorded instances of cross reactivity with pollen. Ortoloni et al found cross reactivity with almond, cherries, peaches and birch pollen in individuals with an identified birch pollen allergy. Dreborg and Foucard (99) found an association between apple, potato, carrot and birch pollen. Anderson and Dreyfus (12) found that some ragweed sensitive individuals experienced itching within the mouth when eating melons and bananas.

Kim and Hussain (206) examined the prevalence of food allergy in 137 latex allergy patients. They identified 49 potential allergic reactions to foods in 21.1% of the patients. Foods responsible for these reactions include:

Apple, apricot, avocado, banana, carrot, cherry, kiwi, loquat, peach, strawberry, tomato, and watermelon.

The reactions included:

Anaphylaxis, angioedema, asthma, diarrhoea, local mouth irritation, nausea, rhinitis, urticaria, vomiting.

They were unsure as to whether there was cross reactivity or not. Other studies have found strong links between latex allergy and certain foods most notably fruits. Brehler et al (52) noted cross reactions with avocado, banana, chestnut, fig, kiwi, mango, melon, papaya, passion fruit, peach, pineapple and tomato. These findings have been confirmed by others (31, 41). It is also possible that anyone with allergic reactions to these foods could possibly go on to develop a sensitivity to latex.

6.6

GLUTEN

Gluten has been linked with a number of conditions most notably dermatitis herpetiformis and coeliac disease. Atherton (20) states that there can be no real doubt that dietary gluten is responsible for most, if not all dermatitis herpetiformis. Feighery (119) writes in the BMJ that coeliac disease is an inflammatory disease of the upper small intestine and results from gluten ingestion in genetically susceptible individuals. Treatment consists of permanent withdrawal of gluten from the diet which results in complete remission.

The reality is that for some individuals with dermatitis herpetiformis and/or coeliac disease removal of gluten is not the answer or at least not the whole answer. However, it cannot be disputed that gluten free diets help many people.

Other conditions have also been found to be linked with gluten. Mental symptoms that respond to no other treatment may also benefit from a gluten-free diet. In the book 'Brain Allergies', Phillpot and Kalita (321) note that "After years of observing maladaptive mental reactions to foods, most orthomolecular-ecologic psychiatrists would agree that gluten is the most frequent and severe symptom reactor of all foods".

The gluten grains are barley, rye and wheat. Oats are also included and on a gluten free diet should at least in the first instance be excluded but then tested as some gluten sensitives have found them safe. There are tests available that will establish if you have a gluten sensitivity but you can also exclude gluten from your diet to see if there is any improvement. The difficulty is that if you see an improvement you will not know if it is because of a grain sensitivity (to one or more of those excluded) or a gluten intolerance. Given this difficulty you would be advised to test the grains individually over a period of time to ensure that you are clear about what it is that is causing you problems, this will help prevent you limiting your diet unnecessarily.

If you need to eat a gluten free diet you will need to avoid all foods that contain wheat (including spelt, triticale and kamut), rye, barley and possibly oats. Alternatives will need to be found for bread, cakes, pastries and biscuits. It is also essential that you check all processed foods, including meats, to avoid accidental ingestion. There are now lots of cookbooks to help people with wheat and/or gluten problems so it should not pose too many problems with finding alternatives.

Although oats are often excluded on a gluten-free diet there is increasing amounts of evidence that they are in fact tolerated by many individuals with a measurable gluten sensitivity. Janatuninen et al (187), in a study of adults with coeliac disease, compared the effects of a gluten-free diet including oats with a conventional gluten-free diet. They concluded that adults with coeliac disease can consume moderate amounts of oats without adverse imminological effects.

Hallert et al (156) carried out a review of published reports in 1999 and also presented details of their own experience at including oats in the gluten-free diets of adults. They found oats to be safe and well tolerated by adults with coeliac disease and dermatitis herpetiformis, though the risk of wheat contamination of commercial oat products was a cause of concern.

Similar findings were reported from a study of adolescents, but no such studies have been made of small children. They conclude that that the inclusion of oats would broaden the range of foodstuffs tolerable to coeliac patients, though they should be used only by adults until more information is available.

Reunala et al (337) carried out a study to ascertain the tolerance to oats by individuals with dermatitis herpetiformis. Eleven individuals on gluten-free diets with the condition were challenged daily with 50g oats for six months. A control group comprised of 11 people with dermatitis herpetiformis on a conventional gluten-free diet were also studied.

Eight of those challenged with oats remained symptom free, two developed a transient rash, and one withdrew because of the appearance of a more persistent but mild rash. It should be noted that 3 of the 11 controls also developed a transient rash. Various tests were conducted to measure the impact, if any, of the oats, and the conclusions were that oats do not affect gluten sensitive small bowel mucosa and indicate that dermatitis herpetiformis is not activated by eating oats.

Given this evidence the wisest course may be to, at first, exclude oats along with the other grains and then, once the condition has been stabilised, to test oats.

In respect of coeliac disease it is important that you know that some people continue to have problems on a gluten free diet. Although gluten is now seen as the cause of coeliac disease this was not always the case. As Gottschall (150) tells us, prior to 1952, coeliac disease was being treated as a carbohydrate intolerance problem by a specific carbohydrate avoidance diet. She argues that the gluten free diet does not work for all sufferers because of the continued use of carbohydrates. It is certainly the case that straightforward avoidance of gluten does not work for everyone.

An Australian study (118) set out to explore why some people with coeliac disease continue to have symptoms even when following a gluten free diet. Thirty nine adults who had persistent gastrointestinal symptoms despite adhering to a gluten free diet were evaluated. They discovered that 22 (56%) were consuming a gluten free diet as defined by the WHO/FAO Codex Alimentarius (Codex-GFD) in which foods containing up to 0.3% of protein from gluten-containing grains can be labelled as 'gluten free'. The remaining 17 were following a 'no detectable gluten diet' as defined by Food Standards, Australia.

All 39 followed the 'no detectable gluten diet' during the study. For 5 of the 22 who made the change in diet, symptoms disappeared and were reduced for a further ten. Food elimination diets were then tried with 31 of the participants leading to further improvement for 24 (77%). Three common problems were soya, amines and salicylates. They argue that if symptoms persist after following a 'no detectable gluten diet' then other food sensitivities should be explored.

6.7

GRAINS

The grain most likely to cause food intolerance depends on where you live. For example, in Europe wheat is a common problem and buckwheat is often recommended as an alternative, whereas in Japan buckwheat is a major food intolerance problem. These population based problems arise as a result of the frequency with which any one food is eaten.

Any symptom could be related to a grain sensitivity. Aside from diagnosed coeliac conditions, grains have been particularly linked with digestive system problems (bloating, abdominal pain, diarrhoea, constipation) and skin complaints.

Rasanen et al (330) explored the role of cereal allergy or intolerance in children with atopic dermatitis. On oral provocation, 18 children exhibited a positive response to wheat, three to rye, one to barley, and one to oats. Cereal-induced symptoms were dermatologic, gastrointestinal, or oropharyngeal, and their onset after provocation was immediate in eight cases and delayed in 14 cases with one experiencing both immediate and delayed reactions. They also concluded that there was little direct link between cereal allergy and coeliac disease. Other symptoms that have been reported include:

Angioedema	Behaviour changes
Cloudy thinking	Depression.
Fatigue	Irritability
Joint pain	Muscle cramps
Skin rashes	
Tingling numbness in the legs	

Anaphylaxis to millet has been reported (300).

Please note that It is a common misconception that an intolerance to cereals is always indicative of coeliac disease. In their study, Kaukinen et al (203) found that intolerance to cereals is not a specific sign of overt or latent coeliac disease.

Links between alcoholism and food intolerance, especially grains, have also been found. The difficulties in giving up alcohol for some people have been misread as a problem with alcohol when in fact the problem is with a grain. Intolerance of any food can lead to overwhelming cravings and when a product, like an alcoholic drink, contains a number of ingredients then it is not always possible to know, without thorough testing, which ingredient it is that is causing the problems. Wheat and corn have been particularly implicated in this way.

There are some that argue our bodies have never adapted to grains and that we should as a matter of course exclude them from our diet. The theory behind this argument is that our bodies were never designed to deal with cereals. The diet of our stone-age ancestors certainly did not include grains, they did consume carbohydrates but obtained these from fruits and vegetables rather than from grains. Our dependence on grains arose when settled agriculture developed and they are now an accepted part of our diet and even appear very high on the list of 'healthy' foods that we should be eating.

Sadly, for some people this type of reliance on grains leads to a host of unwanted symptoms that can go undetected throughout their life time. A condition known as carbohydrate intolerance has also been noted (150) and a diet excluding these used to be the main treatment for coeliac disease before the discovery of the role of gluten.

If you find that you are reacting to a number of grains you may like to try a grain free diet for a few weeks and see if that helps. Certainly a spell on a grain free diet will be an education for anyone willing to try it. For some people the changes have been dramatic, others find they can not manage on this type of diet. Remember that you are unique so don't expect something that works for some people to necessarily work for you. If you are a vegetarian you would not be advised to try this type of diet as you are unlikely to be able to obtain sufficient protein for your body's needs.

The biggest hurdle to living a grain sensitivity is that we live in societies that place so much focus on carbohydrate but, as many are discovering, a diet low in carbohydrates can be extremely beneficial. If you suspect a grain sensitivity you need to eliminate that grain in all its forms from your diet for at least 5 days before testing. You may find a reduction in some of your symptoms or a general sense of well being.

How you react on testing the grain will probably determine whether you then continue to include it in your diet or not.

Buckwheat is often substituted for grains as it is not taxonomically related to wheat and other cereal grains but it is not without problems. Occupational exposure to buckwheat flour has been associated with rhinitis, conjunctivitis, contact urticaria, and occupational asthma. Davidson et al (86) present a case of an individual developing urticaria and hypotension after eating buckwheat. Like all foods, it can cause problems for some individuals. They did find that appeared to be no cross-reactivity between buckwheat and wheat.

It is often thought that if you have a reaction to one grain then others are often also a problem, this is not necessarily the case.

Jones et al (190) explored the degree of intra botanical cross-reactivity among cereal grains and related grasses with the aim of better defining the prevalence of multiple grain hypersensitivity. One hundred and forty-five patients with cereal and/or grass allergies were involved in the study, 80% had reactivity to only one grain so don't assume that just because one grain is a problem for you that all the others will also be a problem.

Rice has often been seen as one of the least allergenic foods but it can nevertheless cause some people serious problems. A study in France (15) found that 17% of 580 patients with adverse reactions to food were sensitive to rice. A study in Finland of 16 wheat sensitive children with atopic dermatitis found that 67% were also sensitive to rice (423).

Lezan et al (230) reported on the case of a woman with rhinoconjuctivitis, asthma and urticaria as reactions to rice. Symptoms have included asthma, atopic dermatitis, contact urticaria, diarrhoea, eczema, and vomiting. Adults are 6 times more likely than children to be sensitive to rice (229). If you have a problem with rice then do try it in various forms - you may find that whilst white rice is okay you cannot eat brown rice, can tolerate rice noodles but not rice cakes and so on.

To test for a grain sensitivity, exclude all foods containing the grain you are testing for at least seven days and then eat it in it's most natural form. Testing of grains should always be in their simplest forms - make something at home.

Don't eliminate a food without thorough testing. Wheat and other cereals are at their most nutritious in whole grain form but it is possible to be intolerant of whole grains and yet be quite comfortable with their more refined counterparts. So, if you find yourself unable to eat, for example, whole-wheat then test an organic white flour. I am suggesting an organic flour used in a simple product such as a pancake as this will eliminate the risk of miss reading a test - a white loaf will contain preservatives, raising agents and have been treated with bleaching agents all of which can give rise to problems. It is also possible to be intolerant of too much fibre.

More details on corn, gluten, and wheat can be found in separate chapters.

6.8

HERBS AND SPICES

It is easy to forget about herbs and spices when assessing food intolerance but given their frequent use and the fact they each is chemically complex and different they cannot be ignored. It is possible to be intolerant of any herb or spice or even a group of them. Spices in particular can cause respiratory problems when inhaled.

Virtually all herbs and spices have, at some time, caused someone problems. A few examples follow:

♦ Reider et al (335) report on instances of allergic reactions, including anaphylactic shock, to camomile and suggest that the incidence and risk of camomile allergy has been underestimated. Some individuals with a sensitivity to camomile were also sensitive to mugwort and birch pollen.

♦ Gonzalez-Guitiernez et al (149) presented the case of a patient allergic to the spice anis.

♦ Chiu and Zacharisen (70) give details of what they believe to be the first case of confirmed dill allergy. The patient developed oral pruritis, tongue and throat swelling, urticaria, vomiting and diarrhoea after eating foods cooked with dill. The person concerned also experienced reactions after smelling food prepared with dill.

If you use a lot of herbs and spices in your cooking and, after having tried other tests, are still experiencing problems then consider trying a week free of them all. Then introduce them one at a time to see if there is any noticeable reaction. It would be impossible to list all the components of each herb and spice, even if they were all identified, so we are left with an 'eliminate it and see' approach.

Should you find that you react to a number of herbs and spices then I suggest you try the low salicylate diet just in case you are in fact salicylate intolerant.

Some of the more common herbs and spices are listed below:

Anise	Ginger
Basil	Marjoram
Bay	Mustard
Borage	Nutmeg
Cardamom	Oregano
Caraway	Paprika
Camomile	Parsley
Chilli	Pepper
Cinnamon	Peppermint
Clove	Rosemary
Coriander	Sage
Cumin	Tarragon
Curry powder	Thyme
Dill	Turmeric
Fennel	Vanilla
Fenugreek	

If you do find yourself sensitive to any herb or spice check labels of all processed foods and beware those that use the terms 'spices' or 'seasonings' as these two terms could indicate the presence of the herb or spice you are trying to avoid. It may also be necessary to check products such as toothpaste, medications, supplements and toiletries - it is surprising how many herbs and spices crop up in somewhat unusual places.

6.9

LEGUMES

All members of the legume family have been found to cause food intolerance symptoms. However, it is not the case that because you cannot tolerate, say, butter beans, that all the others will also be a problem. The two main types of legumes are:

1. Those that we know as common foods such as peas, beans, soya and peanuts.
2. Those whose seeds or gum are used as thickeners and stabilisers in prepared foods such as locust bean gum from the carob tree.

Peanut and soya, two of the most commonly known allergens, are members of this food family and they are given chapters of their own.

Legumes are an important source of proteins and their consumption is very frequent in the Mediterranean region and in some Asian and African countries. In some of these regions, lentils and chickpeas are one of the main food allergens. In India legumes are the most important allergy (289). Lentils seem to be the most common legume implicated in paediatric allergic patients in the Mediterranean area (360).

Darco et al (85) tell us about 3 individuals who developed asthma and rhinitis after exposure to raw but not cooked green beans. Ewan (114) describes the case of an individual so sensitive to peas that even sitting at a table with people who were eating peas induced periorbital oedema.

Legumes are also used as food additives due to their emulsifying properties and can be present in many manufactured foods. These hidden food allergens have the potential of causing adverse reactions in anyone with a legume sensitivity.

There is a significant degree of cross-reactivity among legumes, the clinical relevance of which seems to be dependent on the dietary habits in different communities. In Spain, the consumption of several legumes is frequent and, therefore, clinical allergy to more than one species in children is common. Clinical manifestations include skin, digestive and respiratory symptoms (256).

The list of legumes is quite lengthy:

Acacia gum	Haricot bean
Aduki bean	Lentils - all forms
Alfalfa	Lima bean
Black eyed bean	Liquorice
Black turtle bean	Locust bean gum
Borlotti bean	Masur bean
Broad bean	Mung bean
Butter bean	Navy bean
Cannellini bean	Pea
Carob	Peanut
Chick pea	Pinto bean
Fava bean	Red kidney bean
Fenugreek	Snap bean
Flageolet bean	Soya bean
Garbonzo bean	String bean
Green bean	Tragacanth gum
Guar gum	Wax bean
Gum arabic	White bean

Gums also cause problems and can not be ignored. Lagier et al (216) found occupational rhinitis and asthma to guar gum amongst workers in pharmaceuticals and carpet manufacturing. One of these individuals, after eating ice cream and salad dressing containing guar gum experienced angioedema. Danoff et al (83) reported on a case of anaphylaxis after eating a hamburger containing tragacanth gum.

One clear way of knowing if you have a problem with legumes is if you have ever changed to a vegetarian or vegan diet and at the same time seen an increase in health problems. The occasional attack of wind does not count! One of the reasons that legumes seem to cause problems is because of their high lectin content. Lectins are carbohydrate binding proteins present in many plants. One of the legumes with a very high concentration of these is the red kidney bean. If you are going to eat beans please make sure you follow the guidelines for soaking and cooking very carefully. This could minimise your risk. See the chapter on lectins for further details.

The only way of checking a legume sensitivity is to eliminate them all from your diet and then test them individually. It could be that you eat very few so the test will not take very long but if you are a vegan or vegetarian the process could be lengthy and the results could have serious repercussions for your diet. Vegetarians and vegans may prefer to test legumes individually to avoid a too restrictive diet and, in the case of vegetarians, an over reliance on cheese. This is not the ideal way of testing but it should be sufficient to help you identify if there is a problem.

Eliminate the chosen legume for at least five days and then test it in a simple meal - not a processed food.

Anybody needing to avoid all legumes will also need to check foods for the following gums:

E410 Locust bean gum
E412 Guar gum
E413 Tragacnth gum
E414 Gum arabic

6.10

MARGARINE

Margarine is not a natural food product yet, over the last few decades, has come to be seen as healthier than butter. If you are intolerant of butter then this may very well be the case but if you are not then take a close look at margarine before continuing using it. Margarine is a complex processed product. Not only does it contain a number of ingredients, the natural oils that are used have been chemically changed by the process that converts the oil to an acceptable spreadable product.

The process of hydrogenation changes not only the physical form of the oils, but also alters the way they are metabolised by the body. The structure of the fatty acids is altered, or destroyed, and you are often left with trans fatty acids which are definitely not good for the body. So if you want to eat margarine avoid one that uses hydrogenated oils. This, however, is not the end of the potential problems.

Despite popular belief, margarines vary enormously in content from each other in the following ways: the types of oil used (some now do declare which oils are used but many don't), the type and number of preservatives used, the use of artificial and, so called, 'natural' colours, and the quality and source of the added vitamins.

It is possible to be intolerant of one of the oils being used or of one of the preservatives the oil was treated with before being converted into margarine. You could have a problem with one of the added preservatives. Do not be lulled into assuming that a natural colour is necessarily any safer than any other - if you are sensitive to it then it will cause you a problem. The added vitamins may have been treated with preservatives and you will not know which ones.

A further difficulty with some margarines is that some contain milk products which, of course, could cause problems for anyone with a milk intolerance.

It is quite likely that during other tests you have already either excluded margarine or changed brands. If this is the case and you are symptom free then no further testing will be necessary. However, if you can tolerate butter do consider changing to it as it is a far simpler product. If you are still having problems quite simply remove margarine from your diet and do not replace it with butter for at least seven days. If there is improvement but it is slow in taking place then do not test it for at least another seven days. (It can take time for the accumulated preservatives to diminish in their impact on your body.)

Testing is straightforward - use some of your usual brand and wait and see. If no immediate reaction takes place then use it more regularly and closely monitor your health. If the brand you have been testing is a problem then choose another brand but make your choice carefully - go for the most natural and the one with least number of ingredients.

Whether you change brands, switch to butter or stop using any form of spread will depend on how you have responded to the tests.

If you find yourself intolerant of them all then don't despair - alternative spreads such as nut butters are available and oil can be substituted for butter and margarine in at least some forms of baking.

6.11

MEAT AND POULTRY

Meat has become the main source of protein for many of us but it is not without it's problems. Like any food, it is possible to be intolerant of any one meat but it is also possible to misinterpret meat problems due to naturally occurring food chemicals and additives in processed meats. There is little point in testing meats you have an aversion to or never eat unless your diet is so restrictive that you need to find foods you can incorporate.

If there is a single meat that you eat every day then consider testing it as it may be masking an intolerance problem. Also if your diet is very high in meat products and you have health problems then you may want to consider a period without meat or with a lot less meat. Although high protein/low carbohydrate diets work for some, others need low protein/high carbohydrate diets.

It is possible to react to all forms of meat from a single animal or just to certain parts. It is possible to have a sensitivity to one meat only or to more than one. As always, it depends on the individual.

Llatser et al (234) tell us of a woman who reacted with anaphylaxis to pork gut and kidney but was able to tolerate pork meat. Hjorth and Roed-Peterson (172) found a range of symptoms in people sensitive to beef including contact urticaria in people handling beef; and chronic diarrhoea, migraine and stomach ache after ingestion.

Kelso et al (204) found that some individuals who are allergic to one form of bird meat, such as chicken, turkey, dove or quail, may also be allergic to others including game birds. Ayuso et al (22) found cross reactivity between beef, venison, lamb and milk and they suggest that pork rather than lamb should be included in hypoallergenic diets. It is not always the case that if you are allergic to beef that you will also have problems with milk or vice versa.

To test for a meat intolerance remove all products containing the meat you are testing from your diet for at least five days. Then eat some of the meat in it's most simplest form - if there is no reaction then try it in a different form. For example: if you test beef as roast beef, then try it as steak and then try it as mince.

Monitor your reactions - the method of cooking alters the chemical make-up and you may be able to eat it in one form but not another. It is not an uncommon mistake to assume that you have a problem with meat when in fact the problem lies more in the form you are eating it in. Processed meats are far higher in natural (and man made chemicals) than, say, a joint roasted in it's own juices. Grilling, stewing, barbecuing and frying all increase the amine content of meat If you suspect a problem with meat first check the sections on amines, histamine and tyramine.

The complexity of processed foods can give rise to misleading diagnoses. For example, sausages will contain many ingredients other than meat. A negative reaction does not necessarily mean a problem with the meat, the reaction could be caused by any one of the ingredients.

Continuing with the above example, caseinates are often found in sausages which, if you are milk intolerant, could cause problems. The spices in sauces and some processed meat products such as salamis can also lead to a wrong diagnosis. A reaction to these foods could indicate a salicylate sensitivity.

Nitrates and nitrites also often cause problems leading to stomach upsets and bloating. They have also been linked with cancer. Most processed meat contains added nitrates. The additives you would need to watch out for are:

E249 Potassium nitrite
E250 Sodium nitrite
E251 Sodium nitrate
E252 Potassium nitrate

If you eat meat choose to eat it in its simplest form.

6.12

MILK

Problems with milk are extremely common. Milk contains a number of proteins, such as casein, that can lead to allergies. Milk also contains lactose which many of us cannot digest and this also leads to problems. Lactose is the sugar in milk and it requires the enzyme lactase to digest it. Lactose intolerance is quite common and some have suggested that it arises because we were never intended to consume milk after infancy. There are tests available to identify both milk protein allergy and lactose intolerance - your doctor will be able to advise on these if you wish to find out more.

For many the relief obtained from a milk free diet is so extensive that they simply give up all forms of milk. Milk is in fact not a natural food. It is produced by females for their young and was never intended as a food for those beyond infancy. Do you know of any animal that habitually drinks the milk of another animal especially when it is grown up?

The main symptoms linked with milk problems are:

Recurring digestive problems such as excessive gas, bloating, cramps, pain, diarrhoea, constipation, and recurring catarrhal problems.

It has also been linked with:

Arthritis	Hyperactivity
Asthma	Irritability
Chest complaints	Learning difficulties
Colds,	Migraine
Dermatitis	Sinusitis

Ear problems   Sleep disorders

Rousquet et al (345) reported that between 7 and 29% of asthma sufferers have a milk sensitivity. They also found it was often a cause of rhinoconjuctivitis in young children and may be implicated in serious otitis media. Elimination diets worked for migraine sufferers in a study by Mylek (284) and the food most usually implicated was cow's milk.

Kahn et al (198) in a study of 146 children referred for sleep disturbance identified 15 whose sleep problems were resolved within 5 weeks of starting a diet free from cow's milk. In a subsequent challenge, the sleep disturbances returned within 4 days of reintroducing the cow's milk.

In children the two major symptoms that appear early on are gastrointestinal upsets and dermatitis. Some children appear to grow out of a milk allergy but some don't. James and Sampson (186) found that those who retain a milk sensitivity often have a decrease in skin disorders but an increase in gastrointestinal and respiratory symptoms.

To test for a milk sensitivity, avoid all milk, foods made from milk and foods that contain milk products. Give yourself at least five milk free days before testing. If you can manage it, live without milk for two weeks and experience the effects fully.

Milk causes many people problems solely because it is consumed many times every day. Giving yourself a holiday from it will be a interesting, and hopefully, beneficial experience.

If milk has been causing you problems, the good news is that you should notice an improvement quite quickly. If your symptoms disappear or if you test and have a negative reaction then decide on a strategy: As some people are sensitive to the chemicals the cow has ingested or been treated with, it is always safest to start your test with an organic milk.

If you find you have a problem, your options are to give up milk completely, test various products to see what you can tolerate (for example, you may be able to eat yoghurt and cheese but not drink milk; milk in baked products may be okay but not on its own; evaporated milk may be okay but not whole milk) or find out if your problem is lactose intolerance and take digestive enzymes to help if you wish to continue with milk.

What you decide to do will depend in part on how addicted to milk you are, not so much physically but by habit. At the outset giving up milk seems very strange and awkward because it seems to be everywhere and even your daily tea and coffee has to taste different. All of these problems can be overcome but it does take time to make the adjustment. There is nothing wrong with testing out how much milk in its different forms you can tolerate. If your unpleasant symptoms return this will provide you with the motivation you need to give it up completely.

You can try alternative milks such as goat and sheep - some people can tolerate these others can't. There are also soy, rice and oat milks now available. Initially you may find these unpalatable (your taste buds are still expecting cow's milk) but you will soon adapt or learn to do without. Life without milk is possible!

Soya milk is often used as a substitute for cow's milk and was considered safe for children intolerant of milk. This is no longer thought to be the case. Lee and Heiner (225) found that about one-fourth of those sensitive to cow's milk went on to become allergic to soy protein.

Reactions to cheese only may indicate a sensitivity to food chemicals such as tyramine and histamine rather than to milk.

The foods and ingredients you need to avoid are:

> Milk in any form including dried milk
>
> | | |
> |---|---|
> | Butter | Lactalbumin |
> | Buttermilk | Lactose |
> | Casein | Milk chocolate |
> | Caseinate (all forms) | Natural flavouring |

Cheese including cottage cheese
Cream   Rennet
Curds   Sour cream
Custard   Whey
Ghee   White chocolate
Hydrolsates   Yoghurt
Ice cream

Gern et al (143) reported casein as a cause of allergic reactions for some individuals who had been eating so called 'non-dairy' products. Casein and caseinates appear in a wide range of processed foods as they are used as extenders and tenderisers and, also, to nutritionally fortify certain foods so check labels carefully. They can be found in foods ranging from meat and fish products, coffee whiteners, salad dressings and bakery glazes.

Meats purchased from deli counters can pose a problem arising from cross contamination if cheese and other milk products are stored and/or sliced nearby.

You will need to carefully check any processed food including:

Meats and breads, desserts, and margarine.
Non-dairy products.
Sweets and any snack foods.
Beware also of the terms 'emulsifier' and 'protein' as these may be milk based.
Brown sugar flavouring, caramel flavours, and high protein flour may all indicate the presence of milk protein.

Many people are very concerned about a milk free diet for fear of not getting sufficient amounts of calcium. It is quite possible, as vegans have proved, that the body's calcium requirements can be met from other foods. Foods that are high in calcium include canned salmon with bones, sardines, greens, broccoli, and tofu. You can also ask your doctor if you should take a calcium supplement.

If you are lactose intolerant and want to continue using milk you may have some options to total avoidance although this will depend on the degree of your sensitivity.

♦ Digestive enzymes could help.

♦ Some people can tolerate small amounts of lactose such as that found in 1/2 cup of milk or other high-lactose food at one time.

♦ Foods containing lactose are sometimes better tolerated if eaten with other foods.

♦ It is possible that you can tolerate cooked milk products but not, for example, milk on your cereal.

♦ Eating smaller amounts of lactose food over a day rather than one single large amount may be easier for you.

♦ You may be able to eat some products like yoghurt without difficulty.

It will be a case of experimentation till you find the level that is acceptable to you - balancing any occurrence of symptoms with the amount and type of milk that you eat.

6.13

PEANUT

Peanut allergy is a serious and life-long allergy affecting both children and adults. Sicherer (379) identifies peanuts as one of the most common foods that causes problems for both children and adults. It is essential that individuals with peanut allergy avoid even the slightest exposure to peanuts to prevent life threatening reactions. The commonest manifestation of peanut allergy is with acute hives (or urticaria) following exposure.

Some people develop severe swelling and breathing problems leading to anaphylaxis. Deaths from peanuts have been reported. Some individuals are so sensitive that they will develop symptoms if they kiss someone who has eaten peanuts or eat out of a food utensil which has been in contact with peanuts. This is why many products now carry the warning that there may be traces of peanut - this means that the same machinery has been used to make the product you are buying as well as for one containing peanuts.

It had been thought that peanut oil was safe for those allergic to peanuts but some studies (175, 273) have identified the allergen within these oils and hence it could pose a serious problem for some individuals.

The majority of peanut sensitive individuals are not allergic to tree nuts such as pecans, walnuts or almonds but some will have multiple sensitivities that may include nuts. A 1995 study by Loza and Brostoff (236) found that 50% of individuals allergic to peanuts reported allergic reactions to other nuts as well. Ewan's (114) study of 62 people varying in age from 11 months to 53 years found peanuts to be the commonest cause of allergy (47 cases), brazil nuts came in second (18 cases), followed by almond (14 cases) and hazelnut (13 cases).

Multiple allergies appeared progressively with age with the commonest symptom being angioedema. Ewan concluded that children with peanut allergy are at increased risk of developing allergy to tree nuts. Interestingly only 4 of the 62 reacted to other legumes (peas, lentils, beans and soya) and one of these did not react to peanuts.

Peanut allergy has rather over shadowed lesser problems. It is quite possible to be intolerant of peanuts without being allergic or at risk of anaphylaxis. However because of the potential risks I am an not advocating a peanut test at home. If you suspect peanuts as a problem please discuss testing with an allergist or doctor. If an allergy test is negative and you still believe that peanuts are a problem then eliminate them from your diet and test them but still ensure that someone is present who understands what needs to be done in case of anaphylaxis (this advice is based on the fact that allergy tests are not always 100% reliable).

Avoiding peanuts is not totally straightforward as the oil, in particular, is used in a variety of oriental dishes. It is essential that you check labels extremely carefully. Peanuts and peanut derivatives can also be found in biscuits, breakfast cereals, ice cream, soups, and sweets. Beware the terms 'flavouring' and 'vegetable oil'. Restaurant meals and take out meals also need to be treated with extreme caution. Remember that staff when checking ingredients may make assumptions that ingredients such as 'vegetable oil' are safe.

Non-food hazards can also present themselves especially in the form of body and massage oils; watch out for the terms peanut or arachis oil.

Words to look out for include:

Groundnuts, mixed nuts, peanut, peanut butter, peanut extracts, peanut flour, peanut oil, vegetable oil.

Also, be suspicious of natural flavouring and hydrolysed vegetable protein (HVP).

The types of food that peanuts appear in include:

Baked goods, cereals, chilli, chocolate bars, crackers, egg rolls, frozen deserts, Indian food and other 'ethnic' dishes, kebabs, marzipan, spaghetti sauces, soups, sweets.

6.14

SEEDS AND NUTS

Nuts and seeds present a hidden danger for many. Because of their versatility they are found in a wide range of processed foods and restaurant meals including meat dishes, breakfast cereals, sweets, spreads, sauces and desserts. Sicherer (378) identifies tree nuts as one of the most common foods that causes problems for both children and adults.

Nut and seed allergies usually present in childhood but intolerance can develop at any time especially as they are now, often inadvertently, consumed in greater and more regular quantities.

A sensitivity to more than one could indicate a more general problem with salicylates and/or amines.

All varieties of seeds and nuts have at some time been implicated in a food intolerance or allergy problem. Reactions to nuts and seeds have included:

Abdominal cramps	Facial swelling
Anaphylaxis	Gastrointestinal upsets
Angioedema	Hypotension
Breathing difficulties	Rhinoconjuctivitis
Coughing	Tingling in the mouth
Dermatitis	Urticaria
Diarrhoea	Vomiting
Eczema	

Guariso (153) found that some young people's migraines were triggered by hazelnuts. Ewan's (114) study found allergies to brazil nut alone, brazil nut plus other nuts, almond, almond plus other nuts, hazelnut, hazelnut plus other nuts, walnut, cashew nut.

Sicherer et al (379) in a study of those with peanut and tree nut allergies found that out of 122 people:

> 68 had reactions only to peanut
> 20 only to tree nuts
> 34 to both

Of those reacting to tree nuts, 34 had reactions to one nut, 12 to two nuts, and 8 to three or more nuts.

The most common tree nuts to cause reactions were walnut, pecan and almond. Eighty-nine percent of the reactions involved the skin (urticaria, angioedema), 52% the respiratory tract (wheezing, throat tightness, repetitive coughing, dyspnea), and 32% the gastrointestinal tract (vomiting, diarrhoea).

Coconut has been implicated in skin problems (406).

Like the pistachio nut, the cashew nut contains oleoresins similar to those found in poison ivy and oak which can lead to contact dermatitis, stomach problems and other allergy type symptoms. The problems seem to manifest more in adults than in children.

Cross reactivity between tree nuts and other foods and pollens have been recorded. Eriksson et al (113) found coconut hypersensitivity in 22 (out of 380) birch-pollen allergic individuals and 26% reported reactions to walnut. In respect of hazelnuts, they found those with birch-pollen allergy more often reported hypersensitivity to hazelnuts (53%) than those without pollen allergy (7%).

Vocks et al (433) found the degree of cross-reactivity among kiwi, sesame seeds, poppy seeds, hazelnuts, and rye grain was found to be very high in the patients studied but the degree and exact type of cross reactivity varied.

Eating large amounts of hazelnuts can lead to an increase in nickel intake which potentially could lead to aggravating symptoms usually identified by the individual as being caused by nickel (127).

I don't know whether nuts and seeds are more potentially allergenic than other foods but, because of the large number of reported cases of anaphylactic shock, I do not recommend testing nuts and seeds when on your own. You can eliminate them form your diet but when you are actually testing please ensure that somebody is with you for at least the first hour after eating the test nut or seed. A list of nuts and seeds follows:

Almond	Pine
Brazil	Pistachio
Butternut	Poppy seed
Cashew	Pumpkin seed
Coconut	Sesame seed
Hazelnut (or filbert)	Sunflower seed
Macadamia	Sweet chestnut
Pecan	Walnut

You can eliminate and test each nut and seed separately or eliminate them all and then introduce them one by one during the testing phase. Remember that reactions to more than one of those high in amines or salicylate could indicate a much more general problem. Those that are particularly high in these are noted below (full details can be found in the relevant chapters).

Those high in salicylate are almonds, brazil nuts, desiccated coconut, macadamia nuts, pine nuts, pistachio, sesame seeds, walnuts, (peanuts with skins on and peanut butter).

Those high in amines are brazil, hazelnut, pecan, and walnut.

Sicherer et al (379) found that accidental ingestions are common and occur most frequently outside of the home. Some of the ways in which accidental ingestion took place were as a result of sharing food, hidden ingredients, cross contamination, and school crafts projects using peanut butter.

Particular attention needs to be drawn to sesame seeds as allergic reactions to sesame seeds in the west have become increasingly commonplace since their introduction into processed food including burgers at many fast food outlets and the increase in the number of 'exotic' meals now being eaten both in restaurants and as ready made meals.

Anaphylaxis, angioedema, atopic dermatitis, allergic rhinitis, and bronchial asthma have all been caused by sesame seeds. Other reactions are possible and, even, likely. Remember that these vary from individual to individual. My husband, on testing sesame seeds experienced a total high which a few hours later had changed into overwhelming feelings of depression, fuddled thinking, tiredness and overall ill health. Until that time he had not known that sesame seeds caused any problems. It took more than three days for the symptoms to abate.

If sesame seeds are a problem, extreme vigilance is needed with processed and restaurant food as sesame can often be a hidden ingredient. Kagi and Wuthrich (197) reported on a case of anaphylaxis that was caused by sesame seed in a falafel burger. Food cooked in oil must always be suspected as reactions including anaphylaxis have been reported from sesame oil (71, 200).

Sesame oil finds its way into other products such as ointments and absorption through the skin can also lead to problems. Sesame oil, as a constituent of a zinc oxide liniment, was found to be the cause of contact dermatitis in 15 out of 98 people with leg ulcers who had been using the liniment (420, 421). Malten (248) found in 100 cases of leg ulcers, 11 people showed positive patch test reactions to a paste containing 40% sesame oil and a higher proportion showed positive reactions to 100% sesame oil.

6.15

SOYA

Reactions to soya have become more widespread mainly due to the increasing use of soya. If you are shaking your head and saying you never eat any - check the foods you most commonly buy that are pre-prepared especially bread. Soya, and the emulsifier lecithin, are commonly used in processed foods ranging from soups to chocolate, and most mass produced bread contains soya. For many it truly is a hidden problem.

The symptoms experienced will vary from individual to individual but all of the following have been noted:

Abdominal pain	Eczema
Acne	Heart palpitations
Anaphylaxis	Hives
Angioedema	Hypotension
Anxiety	Itching
Asthma	Lethargy
Bloating	Mouth sores
Breathing difficulties	Rhinitis
Colitis	Urticaria
Conjunctivitis	Vomiting
Dermatitis	Wheezing
Diarrhoea	

In the last few years there has been much publicity about the health benefits of soya. You should know that some researchers now believe that soya products increase the risk of thyroid disease and suggest that only small amounts are eaten.

To test for a soya sensitivity you need to eliminate it from your diet in all its forms for at least 5 days and then test it in its most natural form. You need to avoid foods made directly from soya including HVP, miso, soy bean sprouts, soya flakes, soya protein, soy sauce, soya flour, tamari, tempeh, tofu and of course the beans themselves. You also need to avoid foods containing vegetable oil that do not state which oils are used.

Some people can tolerate soya oil but as cases of anaphylaxis have been reported it is best avoided. Watch out for hidden soya, including lecithin, in processed foods. This requires very diligent label checking as it is found in so many foods - never assume something is safe. The following terms may also indicate the presence of soya:

> Bulking agent
> Emulsifier
> Flavourings
> Hydrolysed vegetable protein (HVP)
> Protein
> Protein extender
> Stabiliser
> Starch
> Textured vegetable protein (TVP)
> Thickener
> Vegetable broth/stock
> Vegetable starch
> Vegetable gum.

If you find you only react to fermented soya products you may in fact have an amine sensitivity rather than one to soya (see earlier chapter).

One of the hardest aspects of a soya sensitivity is avoiding the hidden soya so if you find you are very sensitive you will need to check and double check all foods not prepared by yourself - do not trust anyone else to check for you.

Like many other foods, soya is also present in many non-food items. If you are very sensitive to soya these may also cause you a problem.

Steinman (400) lists some possible non-food sources of soya including:

Adhesives	Fertilisers
Blankets	Flooring materials
Body lotions and creams	Lubricants
Dog food	Nitroglycerine
Enamel paints	Paper
Fabric finishes	Printing inks
Fabrics	Soap

Falleroni and Zeiss (115) report on a case of a 6 year old boy who reacted to soy bean dust from a bean bag.

6.16

SUGARS AND SWEETENERS

Sugar is primarily used as a sweetening agent in the form of sucrose. It is probably the most overused food in the Western world. Not only does it appear in soft drinks and sweets but is now commonly found in sauces, yoghurts, low-fat meals, tinned vegetables and processed meat products. The amount we consume without realising it is frightening.

Blood-sugar problems have frequently been linked with the over consumption of refined cereals and sugar. Other problems are also quite possible. Sugar intolerance can lead to:

> Anxiety
> Depression
> Food cravings and over eating
> Hyperactivity
> Irritability
> Migraines
> Mood swings
> Nervous tension
> Pre Menstrual Syndrome

If you have any of the above symptoms and fuel your energy needs with sugary foods then try a sugar free diet for a couple of weeks and see what happens - the changes can be dramatic. Sugar has been blamed for a lot of ills which may not be justified. It is quite possible that problems that seem to have been caused by sugar have in fact been caused by other ingredients.

It is rare that we eat sugar in its most natural form and if you look at the ingredients in shop bought candies, sweets and confectionery you will invariably find a number of food additives especially colours which have been linked with problems such as hyperactivity.

To test for a sugar problem eliminate it in all its forms. Don't be tempted to replace it with other sweeteners as these can also cause problems - avoid all sweeteners such as syrups, treacles and artificial sweeteners. You can expect to experience cravings. Make sure you plan ahead and have substitutes that you can eat such as plain crackers, crisps or fruit.

This planning aspect is vital especially if you suffer from depression as you may find the symptoms increase for a while. Treat yourself gently, rest as much as you can, take light exercise (more if able) and eat wholesome food.

Test sugar in it's most natural form - simply as sugar. If you can find an organic brand choose that for preference. Avoid testing a complex product as this will not be helpful in clearly identifying a sugar problem. If you experience a sudden high and then have a change in mood for the worse - you probably have a sugar problem. It is possible that you can tolerate some sugar but you will have to experiment until you find a level that is acceptable to you. If any sugar gives you problems don't despair - life without sugar is possible.

Artificial Sweeteners

In respect of artificial sweeteners, I am tempted to say don't test these just eliminate them but that is a decision you must make for yourself.

Artificial sweeteners are manufactured products to help give you the illusion of sweetness without the calories. In many countries they have been passed as safe to eat but evidence is continually emerging of potential health problems. The most common one used is 'Aspartame' which has been found to cause a diverse and bewildering array of symptoms.

Much of this evidence is anecdotal and not accepted by many but if you recognise your symptoms and know you consume large amounts of aspartame on a regular basis then you would be well advised to take the test. It is usually suggested that you eliminate all products with artificial sweeteners for a period of sixty days and monitor your health. If there is a dramatic improvement then you have probably identified the culprit. If there is no change then the choice is yours - to continue or not.

Maher and Wurtman (247) write that aspartame is consumed, primarily in beverages, by a very large number of Americans, causing significant elevations in plasma and, probably, brain phenylalanine levels. Anecdotal reports suggest that some people suffer neurologic or behavioural reactions in association with aspartame consumption. Since phenylalanine can be neurotoxic and can affect the synthesis of inhibitory monoamine neurotransmitters, the phenylalanine in aspartame could conceivably mediate neurologic effects.

The reported symptoms include both physical and emotional and behavioural symptoms and these are listed below.

Aspartame reported emotional/ behavioural symptoms:

Anxiety attacks	Irritability
Brain fog	Memory loss
Can't think straight	Panic attacks
Confusion	Personality changes
Depression	Phobias
Feeling unreal	Poor memory
Inability to concentrate	Stammering

Aspartame reported physical symptoms:

Abdominal Pain	Heart palpitations
Bloating	Hives (Urticaria)

Blood Sugar Problems
Breathing difficulties
Burning eyes or throat
Burning Urination
Chest Pains
Chronic cough
Chronic Fatigue
Diarrhoea
Dizziness
Excessive Thirst or Hunger
Flushing of face
Frequent infections
Hair Loss or thinning
Headaches/Migraines
Hearing Loss

Hypertension
Impotency
Insomnia
Itching
Joint pains
Menstrual problems
Muscle spasms
Nausea
Palpitations
Seizures
Tingling limbs
Tinnitus
Vision problems
Weight gain

Aspartame intolerance has also been found to mimic symptoms or worsen a number of conditions including:

Alzheimer's Disease
Arthritis
Asthma
Attention Deficit Disorder
Birth Defects
Chronic Fatigue Syndrome
Depression and other Psychological Disorders
Diabetes
Epilepsy

Fibromyalgia
Lupus
Lyme Disease
Lymphoma
Multiple Sclerosis
MCS

Panic Disorder
Parkinson's Disease

No artificial sweetener currently on the market is without drawbacks or potential health hazards. If you decide to use them then reduce the amount you consume. If you have any problems with them, or are concerned about the problems they may cause, then give them up - your body and mind will thank-you.

6.17

VEGETABLES

Reactions to vegetables are not as well documented as, for example, reactions, to milk or nuts. This does not mean that they are 'safe'. The complexity of a single vegetable is immense and unwanted reactions can occur to any single vegetable or group of vegetables or naturally occurring chemical such as salicylate, solanine, sulphur and MSG found within them.

Adverse reactions to single vegetables is usually noticed early on in infancy and the vegetable is simply avoided. If you always avoid a particular vegetable then do not bother to test it unless you really feel you want to run the risk of an adverse reaction.

If you can think of a symptom then someone somewhere will probably have experienced it as a result of a sensitivity to a vegetable. Muhlemann and Wuthrich (279) in a study of 229 people with allergies found the most common food allergens to be amongst vegetables with 44.5% reacting to celery, 14.4% to carrots and 16.6% reacting to spices. Quirce et al (324) found various symptoms including bronchial asthma, urticaria and Quinckes oedema associated with a reaction to potatoes.

Hoffman et al (173) found that 10 out of the 25 eczema patients in their study reacted to avocado. Lybarger (242) identified respiratory, nasal and skin reactions to garlic. Garlic has been linked with causing contact dermatitis and asthma (315). Celery has been found to cause anaphylaxis, angioedema, and urticaria (303). In a study by Mylek (284) migraines for some individuals were triggered by cabbage.

The biggest problem with vegetables is that we are told they are good for us and so many of us make ourselves eat them against our own intuitive wisdom. If you have ever tried to eat a diet high in vegetables and have felt worse then you could have a food chemical problem. There is no easy way of suggesting where you start. Read the food chemical sections especially the symptoms and see if any spring out at you.

For example, if you have a lot of joint pain then it may be useful to try the solanine test. Or, if you dislike or feel ill after eating aubergine, then the histamine test may be useful. If you have a problem with a large number of vegetables, and fruit, then consider checking for a salicylate sensitivity.

Reactions to individual vegetables, as shown above, have been reported. If you suspect a vegetable (and are sure it is not a food chemical problem) then remove it from your diet for four days and then test it. Make sure the test vegetable is fresh not frozen or tinned and preferably organic. Don't add a sauce to it.

Some people have tried eating diets high in raw vegetables and have often after an initial improvement felt much worse. This is not necessarily indicative of a sensitivity. It could be, quite simply, that your body cannot handle raw vegetables - try cooking them. The cooking process changes the vegetable and, in many cases, removes or reduces the allerginicity.

The high chemical content of vegetables can also lead to problems of mis-diagnosis. It is quite possible to test a vegetable, react badly to it, eliminate it totally, feel better and a few days or weeks later experience a return of all the symptoms. If this happens it is indicating that it was not the individual vegetable but one of the chemicals - read the lists and see if you need to do a further test.

A further problem is the one-off reactions that can occur often leading to quite strong adverse reactions after eating a vegetable you are usually okay with. This is more likely to be caused by pesticide contamination. It is safer when testing vegetables to at first eat them in their organic form.

6.18

WHEAT

Wheat frequently causes problems mainly because we eat so much of it. It is not unusual to eat some wheat at every meal - in cereal at breakfast, sandwiches at lunch, biscuits as a snack, and pasta or bread with the evening meal. Reactions to wheat tend to fall into three groups:

1. A sensitivity to gluten.
2. Intolerance of or allergy to wheat more generally.
3. Problems with whole-wheat.

Speer (392) has wheat listed in the top ten most allergenic foods and Andre et al (15) found wheat to be one of the most common allergenic foods.

If you have any stomach problems, skin problems, and/or arthritis you should consider testing wheat. Blood sugar problems, especially if your main snack foods contain wheat, could be another indicator. Wheat has also been found to cause migraines for some people (108,151) and even asthma (362, 442). Twelve per cent of 102 children who were allergic to pollen were also allergic to wheat (90).

If you have a problem with wheat do not assume that you have a gluten sensitivity. Not all problems with wheat are related to gluten. Test each of the gluten grains individually to see if you can tolerate them - there is no point in limiting your diet unnecessarily. There are now lots of cookbooks to help people with wheat and/or gluten problems so it should not pose too many problems with finding alternatives.

To test for a wheat sensitivity exclude all foods containing wheat for at least seven days and then eat it in it's most natural form. Testing of grains should always be in their simplest forms - make something at home like a very simple pancake. If you test wheat in the form of bread and experience a reaction you will not know whether you are reacting to the wheat, a preservative, raising or bleaching agent.

It is possible that although wheat combined with yeast or other raising agent will be a problem, wheat in other recipes may be okay.

Don't eliminate wheat without thorough testing. Although wheat, and other cereals, are at their most nutritious in whole grain form it is possible to be intolerant of whole grains and yet be quite comfortable with their more refined counterparts. So, if you find yourself unable to eat whole-wheat, test an organic white flour. I am suggesting an organic flour used in a simple product such as a pancake as this will eliminate the risk of miss reading a test - a white loaf will contain preservatives, raising agents and have been treated with bleaching agents all of which can give rise to problems. It is also quite possible to be intolerant of too much fibre.

Symptoms, even with wheat, can be dose related. Hanakawa et al (157) reported on the case of a 24-year-old Japanese woman who had suffered for 2 years from attacks of urticaria, breathing irregularities, and temporary loss of consciousness due to a sudden fall in blood pressure - all of which were associated with exercise after the ingestion of wheat. On testing with varying amounts of wheat in different forms they were able to identify the amounts at which reactions took place: for example, exercise following ingestion of 64g, but not 45g, of bread induced generalised urticaria for this individual.

Wheat can be found in most of these ingredients:

Bread crumbs, bran, bulgar, cereal extract, coffee substitutes, couscous, crackers, durum wheat, enriched flour, farina, flour, gluten, gluten flour, gram flours, high protein flour, HVP, modified food starch, natural

flavouring, pasta, semolina, spelt, starch, vinegar made from grain, wheat bran, wheat germ, wheat starch, white flour, whole wheat.
Alcoholic beverages such as beer and whiskey.

Check all processed food very carefully.

You may find that you are only sensitive to wheat but if you find that after some respite from symptoms they begin to re-emerge you may want to consider testing other grains as some degree of cross reactivity has been noted. For example, some individuals with wheat induced asthma also reacted to rye, barley and soya flours (362).

If you find you are very sensitive to wheat, it is also important to check that you are not using non-food products that contain some wheat. Varjonen et al (423) report on a case of contact urticaria caused by hydrolysed wheat in a body cream.

7

THE NEXT STAGE

How easily you adapt to your new diet will depend on a number of factors including:

♦ The degree of improvement you've experienced.
♦ How motivated you are
♦ Whether you have identified all your food intolerance problems.
♦ How long you were ill for and how severe your problems were.
♦ How restricted your diet has become.
♦ The amount of support you have.

If there has been any improvement please do not give up on yourself - keep going. One of the things that quite commonly happens is that there is some major improvement and then things seem to get a little sluggish and you start to doubt the wisdom of your new diet. Give it a chance.

The older you are the longer you have been putting your body under stress. Your body's first reaction is likely to have been one of celebration and joy and now, after the party is over, it is taking time to recover. Trust it and let it heal in it's own time. If you return to your old diet you will simply set yourself back. It is possible, and very useful, to re-test foods but if you had an adverse reaction do not re-test for at least six months. And if the reaction was very severe leave it at least twelve months. As your body recovers it will be able to tolerate more foods over time.

There are cases where people find they have become intolerant of virtually all foods. I suspect that this is more to do with an undiagnosed food chemical intolerance rather than a problem with the foods themselves. However, if you find that this is happening then rotate the foods that you can eat and gradually introduce others. You rotate foods by never eating the same food on more than one day in any four day cycle.

If you have been carrying large amounts of excess weight you will have found this diminishing. If this is the case you will probably experience times of extreme hunger - do not starve your body, feed it. This seems to be part of an adjustment process and I doubt you will gain any weight. After a few days the need for extra food will subside and if you still need to lose weight it will once again begin to diminish. Avoid the temptation to speed up this process - you will only place extra stress on your body. It doesn't need it. Feed it the right foods for it and your mind and your weight will adjust quite naturally.

When you have identified a food intolerance problem you may want to find out more about your condition. The internet is a wonderful place for accessing this information but what you need to try avoid doing is overwhelming yourself with information. At first limit yourself to a couple of sites and gradually build up your store of information. If you want to explore the medical literature you will probably, at some point, find conflicting articles. Personally I am very wary of any articles or research, regardless of who is responsible for it, that categorically states that a particular food is not a problem or that a specific condition is never caused, or at least made worse, by food intolerance.

Remember that:

- The individual doctor or researcher may have specific interests that 'colour' their work.
- Research is often funded by large corporations including pharmaceutical companies and food manufacturers.

- ♦ The research may have been limited to a very small number of cases.
- ♦ Food intolerance is often simply not accepted.
- ♦ The overall evidence is clear - any food can lead to any symptom.

So search, read and discuss - information is liberating. But, in the final analysis, trust your own results from your own eliminating/testing.

The only person who can help you stick to your diet is you. You can help yourself in a number of ways: Plan your meals - get really organised, eat regularly and so avoid getting hungry and being tempted to eat the wrong foods, buy cookbooks that provide you with recipes you can use and experiment with, congratulate yourself on having done so well, build in treats that you know you can tolerate, make contact with others with a similar problem.

Be extremely cautious about any processed food or food prepared by others. The easiest way of getting caught out is by trusting someone who says "It's safe - I checked". Ask for a list of the ingredients and check for yourself. If this seems like overkill take note of the following case reported by Schwartz (369) in 1993. A child with a known milk allergy was given chicken soup in a hospital and the result was a nearly fatal case of anaphylaxis. The sodium caseinate that was in the soup had not been recognised by the staff as being a milk protein. More worryingly, they had also perceived reactions to milk as relatively harmless. Don't assume that because you understand your problems that everyone else will - they won't.

You will have setbacks - accidental ingestion of the food or substance you can't tolerate. The best advice I can give is treat yourself *gently*. The reaction will pass so don't give in to any cravings that might come. Eat the foods that are safe, rest and learn from the experience.

You've simplified your diet, carried out food tests using the elimination diet and are feeling better. You're quite confident that you know what causes your problem and are careful to avoid the problem foods. Then, inexplicably you have a reaction and find that, no matter how hard you think back and check the food you've eaten, there is no way in which you could have eaten one of your problems foods. You have introduced some new foods but all the ingredients listed are ones you know you are okay with. Have you found a new food problem?

It's possible but, before you put yourself through the rigors of further eliminating and testing, re-check the foods you have introduced. If any of these are processed products remove them from your diet for at least seven days and then try again. If you have a reaction again then the likely culprit is a hidden ingredient that is probably on your NO list. How did this happen? Quite simply legislation may permit a manufacturer not to list an ingredient constituting less than a specific percentage of the total product. You can, if you so choose, write to the manufacturer to verify your own results.

This was demonstrated very clearly in a report by Enrique et al (111) in respect of eggs. They cite the instance of a 25 year old woman who had been diagnosed with an egg allergy and told to avoid all forms of egg protein. Two months later she experienced a further reaction after eating a strawberry and cream candy. No egg compound was stated on the candy label. Tests confirmed that it was the candy she was reacting to and also identified the presence of ovalbumin, which is added to candies as a binder, and this was confirmed by the manufacturers.

Cantani (63) reported on similar problems with milk. Other possible forms of contamination are listed by Steinman (400) including:

- Manufacturing plants using the same equipment to make different products such as milk ice cream and dairy free ice cream.
- The use of the same oil to cook different foods.
- 'Natural' flavours.
- Ingredient switching that involves use of a different oil, nut, sugar, herb or spice.
- Binders and emulsifiers which are not defined.

The move towards wanting to eat organic food seems to arise naturally as part of wanting a healthier diet. Certainly when one reads about the potential health problems that can be caused by pesticides it seems like the only logical step to take but is it always the right way to go? I ask this question because when no pesticides are used the plant produces more of its own natural toxins so some vegetables and fruit will at times have a higher salicylate content than those grown with the use of pesticides. I am not advocating eating non-organic food but I am raising this issue especially for anyone with a salicylate sensitivity. If you are salicylate sensitive and have found that some of your problems have become worse after switching to organic food this could be the reason why.

One of the areas I have not covered in this book is that of botanical families and the reason for this is I tend to find these mislead people. As Barnes Koerner and Sampson (27) say "Although it is often helpful to think of foods in certain botanical families, no clinical evidence supports consistent broad intra-botanical or intra-species cross reactivity". Some times the problem is misread and the true problem is in fact a food chemical one. I think the safest approach is never to assume that you will react to all members of a botanical family rather to test of each of the foods individually and if you find you react to them all then first check that you do not have a salicylate or other food chemical sensitivity.

Biochemical individuality is about far more than the foods you can tolerate. It very much deals with the amount of each nutrient that your body needs. For example, some people need far more B6 than others. To assess your individual needs on this level you would need medical help and it may not be forthcoming. Many doctors still believe that RDA (recommended daily allowance) for vitamins and minerals is more than adequate for all and that we all need the same amounts. Others disagree strongly saying that the RDAs will simply stop the occurrence of diseases such as scurvy (lack of vitamin C) or pellagra (lack of B3).

In 1969 Linus Pauling introduced us to 'Orthomolecular Medicine' which focuses on using naturally occurring substances like vitamins, minerals, trace elements, enzymes and amino acids to treat illness and maintain health. Doctors embracing this approach had some startling successes including the treatment of schizophrenia with B vitamins by Dr Hoffer and others. But, sadly this approach has never been embraced more generally by the medical profession. This is not because it does not work or is in some way flawed.

There is a great deal of evidence to indicate that existing diets do not provide adequate amounts of vitamins and minerals even by RDA standards. Werbach's (438) survey of nutritional influences on illness includes a section on nutritional deficiencies. To give you an overview of the type of problems that exist, I will summarise a selection of the findings:

♦ An American study found that the majority of the US population, especially adult women, were obtaining levels of calcium below the Recommended Dietary Allowance.
♦ Chromium deficiency is common in western diets relying on high intake of refined foods.
♦ Iodine deficiency is common in many countries.
♦ Magnesium intake is often low. Vitamin B3 is often deficient in elderly people.
♦ Selenium is frequently inadequate in Western diets.

- Thousands of people develop vitamin A deficiency each year.
- Vitamin C intake is often below recommended daily amounts.
- Zinc is commonly inadequate in Western diets.

There are also vitamins and minerals that can help people with food related problems. Some examples follow:

- Vitamin C can help reduce a reaction which raises the blood histamine level and may also reduce MSG sensitivity.
- Vitamin B12 may help reduce sulphite sensitivity.
- A magnesium deficiency may increase allergic reactions and lead to symptoms similar to chronic fatigue syndrome.
- Calcium supplementation may reduce allergic reactions.
- Vitamin B6 may reduce MSG sensitivity.
- A molybdenum deficiency may lead to sulphite sensitivity.
- Vitamin B3 may slow down the release of histamine.
- Vitamin B5 may reduce allergic reactions particularly those involving the nasal passages and help in cases of chronic fatigue.

Getting adequate vitamins and minerals is essential not just to maintain health but also to reduce the impact of allergic reactions on the body. Philpott (321) says that vitamins C, B6 and B3 "have the most important value in preventing such maladaptive reactions". A poor diet that doesn't provide us with the full range of vitamins and minerals that we need can also lead to illness both physical and mental. Some examples follow:

- Vitamin B1 deficiency can lead to irritability, depression, confusion, and an acute sensitivity to noise.

- Diets low in pantothenic acid can make some people depressed, withdrawn and irritable.
- Low potassium levels can lead to fatigue.
- A good quality multi vitamin and mineral supplement with additional vitamin C would seem to be essential for all of us especially if we have been ill or are getting older.
- Older readers should note that studies have shown that many older people do not absorb adequate amounts of many essential nutrients. Supplementation may be the way to remedy this.

Some links between an excess of iron and the development of cancer cells has been found which is why some vitamin companies now produce multi vitamin and mineral supplements that exclude iron. Supplements of individual vitamins and minerals should be taken with great care as many of them rely on other vitamins and minerals to be of any benefit and some in large doses can be toxic. Some examples of problems follow:

- Evening primrose oil can exacerbate temporal lobe epilepsy and may exacerbate mania.
- High doses of folic acid may decrease levels of B12.
- High doses of iron can lead to stomach problems.
- Manganese intoxication can lead to irreversible movement and other neurological disorders. It can also lead to high blood pressure in some people over 40.
- Too much selenium has been associated with hair loss, thickened, fragile nails, nausea and fatigue.
- Exceptionally high doses of Vitamin A can lead to birth defects.
- Large doses of vitamin B6 can lead to neurological symptoms.
- Very large doses of vitamin C can lead to diarrhoea.

Find out as much as you can before you supplement with single vitamins and minerals and it is generally the safest option to only take individual vitamins and minerals along side a multi. Pregnant women should seek medical advice as some supplements can be of harm to the foetus.

Be very cautious about the preparations you buy - you really do need to look for quality and you do need to be sure that any supplement you buy is safe for you. If the label is confusing then check with the manufacturer. And if you start to feel worse after taking any supplement - stop taking it immediately. Never start taking more than one supplement at a time - if you have a reaction you will not know which supplement is to blame.

Beware of hypo-allergenic supplements as these may not be safe for you. If you feel unsure of how to go about boosting your system with vitamins and minerals consult a nutritionist and/ or read some of the very good books on the market.

Ideas for other ways in which you can boost your system follow. By making sure that you eat as much fruit and vegetables as you can you will help keep your system balanced towards alkalinity which will also help you feel better. Increase the amount of exercise you take, relax more and do things that interest you. Ill health effects all aspects of our lives and we need to start to put the balance back.

Having said that - don't go mad and try to do too much! This will over tire you and then frustrate you if you find yourself ill again. Gently build up your activities and take lots of rest. Some people have found great help from taking digestive enzymes - find out if these could help you. Various herbs, such as echinacea, can help boost the system but take them with care (reactions to herbs are not unusual) especially if you are salicylate sensitive. You may also like to consider using a water filter to reduce the amount of chlorine and other water contaminants being ingested.

In an article on the detoxification enzyme systems, Liska (233) explores the complex process involved in the body's ongoing battle to deal with toxins. "These mechanisms exhibit significant individual variability, and are effected by environment, lifestyle, and genetic influences". Impairment of these systems could lead to the development of conditions such as Parkinsons Disease, Fibromyalgia, Chronic Fatigue Syndrome, and other immune system disorders.

It has been suggested that the difficulties some individuals experience with food chemicals and food additives is due to some impairment in this detoxification system that predominantly takes place in the liver. Some individuals have seen improvement in their sensitivities as a result of using supplements to help the liver. Amongst these 'cysteine', a sulfur amino acid is used by the body to manufacture glutathione which plays a vital role in the body's ability to eliminate toxins.

Also, ensure your diet is as high as it can be with fruit and vegetables as many of these, including cabbage and brussel sprouts, encourage enzyme activity. This effect of vegetables and fruits could in part explain why they seem to protect against certain cancers. And look after your gut. The gastrointestinal tract provides a physical barrier to many unwanted products and, after the liver, is the second major site in the body for detoxification. You need to have a healthy gut so eat well and ensure that you have a good supply of healthy bacteria. If you have had gastrointestinal problems, or still have them, you may find some of the acidophilus supplements useful.

Carl Pfeiffer (320) says that "Every thought and feeling we have can alter, and is altered by, the chemistry of our body". If you have been ill for a long time and are now experiencing better health do not be surprised if, after the initial relief and joy, you experience some feelings of anger and grief about the time you have lost and that you may have been misdiagnosed for many years. By all means look at these feelings, write them out, talk them through with a friend or counsellor but do not get stuck in them

The simple truth is that although improvement in your condition may have been a long time in coming it has arrived. For many people the answer may never appear. Consider yourself lucky, focus on the positive feelings and look to the future. The past, no matter how right or wrong elements in it may have been, has now gone. As you recover, focus on the present and when you feel stronger turn your attention to the future remembering that now you are free of chronic ill health there are many things you can once again dream of doing and actually begin to do.

But please don't make the mistake of rushing into a whole range of new activities. If you were ill for a long time you need to allow yourself time to recover. Release your imagination, explore ideas, rest and try to take pleasure from the moment, the here and now. Getting healthier is an amazing experience, take the time to savour it and the fact that you have been the one to bring it about.

When you feel ready to embark on your new life be gentle with yourself. List all the things you want to do and prioritise them. Don't try do them all at once - you'll exhaust yourself. By being clear about your goals you'll achieve them more easily and with less effort. As you throw yourself into new activities do remember to take the time to monitor your diet and health. As your body and mind changes you may need to make adjustments in your diet.

You may have found yourself, rather than feeling inspired, feeling lost, cast adrift with little idea of what to do next, as if everything that seemed real and solid before has changed. This is most likely to arise if you had been having many psychological symptoms that have now improved or disappeared. The best advice I can give you is to take some time to get to know yourself.

Enjoy the process. Don't assume that just because you did something before in a certain way that you have to continue doing so. You have changed and you can now choose what you do and how you respond. You may find it useful to take some time to explore what your dreams are. A couple of brain storming exercises might help. Firstly write out 50 things you enjoy doing and then write out 50 things you really want to do. Let your imagination fly.

Remember, it was not your fault you were ill. You have always tried to do the best for yourself. Celebrate your achievement. You may find it useful to make contact with others with a similar problem. How you do this will depend on you as an individual and also where you live. Some options include:

- ◆ Support groups - check in your area or with a national organisation that deals with your condition.
- ◆ On-line through discussion lists and chat groups.
- ◆ Reading books and articles. If books are out of print then ask at your library.
- ◆ One to one - if you know someone else with similar problem arrange to meet regularly.

Support can also come from family, friends and work colleagues but don't expect them to understand if you don't explain it to them. Anybody who has seen you have a reaction will probably be understanding but some of those who haven't may be very sceptical and may even hinder you.

Have patience with others and do try to avoid evangelising - rather than helping this often has the effect of putting people off. I always try to remember what I was like before I knew about my food intolerance problems - basically I knew nothing about allergy or food intolerance and really wasn't very interested. You can't change others so don't be hurt if people don't follow your advice or don't believe you.

Your biggest source of support is always going to be yourself. Nobody else can control what you eat but you. Become your own best friend and stop worrying about what anybody else thinks.

8

TIPS AND TRICKS

1. Plan your meals ahead so that you always have food available that you can eat.

2. Use your freezer - make up extra batches of meals for the days when you just can't be bothered.

3. Never trust food given to you by others unless you know for definite that they understand what your problems are. Even then you would be better to check by asking for details of the ingredients.

4. Prepare a list of foods that you can eat (rather than ones you can't) that you can give to others or restaurants to help them in preparing a meal for you.

5. If you are making a long journey always take more food with than you think you will need - unexpected delays can turn into nightmares if you don't have food and drinks with you that are safe for you.

6. Take time out to invent or discover new recipes - this will help you stop getting bored with the food you eat.

7. If you buy any processed food - ALWAYS check the ingredients as these do change.

8. Use the word 'allergic' rather than 'food intolerant' with people you don't know - allergy is more accepted and most people will understand that this means you have a problem.

9. Don't assume that anybody cooking for you will know what foods contain salicylates, MSG, sulphur, additives, milk, wheat etc... Spell it out for them (see tip 4).

10. Eat as balanced and varied diet as you can.

11. Avoid defining yourself as allergic or food intolerant (or any other label) Remain the person who you are. You are not your condition or illness but rather a unique individual.

12. Never forget that what works for you may not work for anyone else - avoid converting and being converted to particular diets and/or supplements.

13. Take advice but then check it out for yourself - nobody has all the answers. The best expert on you is always you.

14. If reactions effect your mind prepare to deal with them. Have strategies in place for avoiding contact, explaining your behaviour, making yourself feel safe. You may also find it useful, when well, to write yourself a note which you can read when a reaction takes hold - it should explain what is happening and reassure you that it will pass. If you have someone who understands what is happening talk to them as sometimes this helps minimise the effects of the anxiety.

15. Be gentle with yourself.

9

FINAL WORD

We have reached the end of 'Change Your Diet and Change Your Life'. I hope you have found the information useful and that you are well on the way to finding the ideal diet for you.

Health, after life itself, is our most precious possession. Without it we are limited and restricted in what we do and even in how we think.

Never give in on finding the answers to your health problems. Work with your doctors but remember they do not know everything and do not have all the answers.

Always do the very best you can for yourself and remember you are a unique individual.

I wish you well.

Sharla

APPENDIX

FOOD ADDITIVES

Food additives are substances added to food for a *technological* purpose - that is, to help the manufacturer in the preparation, production and distribution of the product. Additives are generally not a substance you would add to a dish if you were if preparing it a home. They are not food.

Since 1986, the law in the UK requires that most foods carry a list of virtually all their ingredients including additives. Additives are identified either by their name or number: for example, E326 or Potassium lactate; 621 or Monosodium Glutamate. The main categories of additives are:

- ♦ COLOURS - added to enhance or change the existing colour of the food. Some have been linked with hyperactivity in children.
- ♦ PRESERVATIVES - added to prevent or delay food spoiling and so increase the shelf life of the product. Problems with hyperactivity and asthma have been found.
- ♦ ANTIOXIDANTS - added to fats to prevent them becoming rancid and also to prevent discoloration in non-fat foods. One of these, E320 Butylated Hydroxyanisole (BHA), has been linked with allergies and stomach problems. An antioxidant more well known to us all is lemon juice.

The other main groups of additives are:

- ♦ Emulsifiers, which bind oil and water together.
- ♦ Thickeners.

- Sweeteners.
- Stabilisers, to maintain the product texture.
- Yeast nutrients.

The following lists of additives that have been identified as sometimes causing problems are intended solely as a guide. Both the E number and name have been given. Please note that additives are not universally deemed to be safe - what is allowed in one country may be banned in another. It is advisable that you get hold of a book on additives in food and familiarise yourself more closely.

Aspirin sensitivity

E102 Tartrazine	E110 Sunset yellow FCF
E122 Carmoisine	E124 Ponceau
155 Brown HT	E212 Potassium Benzoate
E213 Calcium Benzoate	E214 Ethyl 4-hydroxybenzoate
E310 Propyl gallate	E311 Octyl gallate
E312 Dodecyl gallate	E321 Butylated Hydroxytoluene (BHT)

Asthma

E102 Tartrazine	E122 Carmoisine
E124 Ponceau	155 Brown HT
E163 Anthocyanines	E210 Benzoic acid
E211 Sodium benzoate	E212 Potassium benzoate
E213 Calcium Benzoate	E214 Ethyl 4-hydroxybenzoate
E220 Sulphur dioxide	E221 Sodium sulphite
E222 Sodium hydrogen sulphite	
E223 Sodium metabisulphite	
E224 Potassium metabisulphite	
E226 Calcium sulphite	
E227 Calcium hydrogen sulphite	
E310 Propyl gallate	E311 Octyl gallate
E312 Dodecyl gallate	

BHA and BHT

BHA and BHT are added to oil containing foods to prevent oxidation and retard rancidity. The International Agency for Research on Cancer, part of the World Health Organisation, has linked BHA with the possible development of cancer in humans and the State of California has listed it as a carcinogen. Other studies have shown similar links for BHT.

E320 Butylated Hydroxyanisole (BHA)
E321 Butylated Hydroxytoluene (BHT)

Many vegetable oils may have been treated with BHA and BHT - check labels carefully. Both additives also frequently appear in lotions and creams.

Hyperactivity

E102 Tartrazine	E104 Quinoline yellow
E107 Yellow 2G	E110 Sunset yellow FCF
E120 Cochineal	E122 Carmoisine
E123 Amaranth	E124 Ponceau 4R
E127 Erythrosine	E128 Red 2G
E131 Patent Blue V	E132 Indigo Carmine
133 Brilliant blue FCF	E151 Black PN
154 Brown FK	155 Brown HT

E160b Annatto, bixin, norbixin

E180 Pigment rubine	E210 Benzoic acid
E211 Sodium benzoate	E212 potassium benzoate

E215 Ethyl 4-hydroxybenzoate sodium salt
E216 Propyl 4-hydroxybenzoate
E217 Propyl 4-hydroxybenzoate sodium salt
E218 Methyl 4-hydroxybenzoate
E219 Methyl 4-hydroxybenzoate sodium salt
Probably advisable to avoid all sulphites and nitrates (see below)

E310 Propyl gallate	E311 Octyl gallate

E312 Dodecyl gallate   E320 Butylated Hydroxyanisole
(BHA)
E321 Butylated Hydroxytoluene (BHT)

Flavour enhancers with known problems
620 L-Glutamic acid   621 Monosodium glutamate
622 Potassium hydrogen L-glutamate
623 Calcium dihydrogen di-L-glutamate
627 Guanosine 5   631 Inosine 5
635 Sodium 5 ribonucleotide

Lactose intolerance
E270 Lactic acid   E325 Sodium lactate
E326 Potassium lactate   E327 Calcium lactate
E472(b) Lactic acid esters of mono- and di-glycerides of fatty
acids
478 Lactylated fatty acid esters of glycerol and propane-1, 2-
diol
E481 Sodium stearoyl-2 lactylate
E482 Calcium stearoyl-2 lactylate

Migraine
E102 Tartrazine   E281 Sodium Propionate
E282 Calcium Propionate   E282 Potassium Propionate

Nitrates
Nitrates and nitrites have been used for centuries to preserve
meat. The problem with them occurs when nitrate combines
with certain other compounds in the digestive system it forms
nitrosamines which are powerful cancer causing chemicals.
Most processed meat contains added nitrates and should be
avoided.

    E249 Potassium nitrite   E250 Sodium nitrite
    E251 Sodium nitrate   E252 Potassium nitrate

Purines, If avoiding

    627 Guanosine 5   631 Inosine 5
    635 Sodium 5 ribonucleotide

Salicylate risk (See also Aspirin Sensitivity and Hyperactivity - all listed additives should be avoided). The following may also cause problems.

E100 Curcumin

E160a Alpha-carotene, beta-carotene, gamma-carotene

E160c Capsanthin   E160d Lycopene

E161   Xanthophylls (also E160c-g)

E162 Beetroot Red   E163 Anthocyanines

E210 Benzoic acid   E211 Sodium benzoate

E212 Potassium benzoate   E213 Calcium Benzoate

E214 and E215 Ethyl 4-hydroxybenzoate

E216 Propyl 4-hydroxybenzoate

E217 Propyl 4-hydroxybenzoate sodium salt

E218 Methyl 4-hydroxybenzoate

E219 Methyl 4-hydroxybenzoate sodium salt

Probably advisable to avoid all sulphites (see below)

Citric acid links E330-E333 and 380-381, may be tolerated in small amounts depending on the degree of sensitivity:

E330 Citric Acid   E331 Sodium citrates

E332 triPotassium citrate

E333 mono-, di-, and triCalcium citrate

  380 triAmmonium citrate   381 Ammonium ferric citrate

E472(c) Citric acid esters of mono- and di-glycerides of fatty acids

E334 Tartaric acid

E335 mono and diSodium tartrate

E336 mono and diPotassium tartrate (Cream of tartar)

E337 Potassium sodium tartrate

  355 Adipic acid   E440 Pectin

May not be tolerated if extremely sensitive:

E460 Microcrystalline cellulose

E461 Methylcellulose
E463 Hydroxypropylcellulose
E464 Hydroxypropylmethylcellulose
E465 Ethylmethylcellulose
E466 Carboxymethylcellulose sodium salt

Sulphites
E220 Sulphur dioxide   E221 Sodium sulphite
E222 Sodium hydro sulphite
E223 Sodium metabisulphite
E224 Potassium metabisulphite
E226 Calcium sulphite
E227 Calcium hydrogen sulphite
E150(b) Caustic Sulphite Caramel
E150 Sulphite Ammonia Caramel

Urticaria or skin sensitivity
E102 Tartrazine   155 Brown HT
E210 Benzoic acid   E211 Sodium benzoate
E212 potassium benzoate   E213 Calcium Benzoate
E214 Ethyl 4-hydroxybenzoate
Possibly the sulphites E220 - E227.
E320 Butylated Hydroxyanisole (BHA) and E321 Butylated
Hydroxytoluene (BHT)
  430 Polyoxyethylene (8) stearate
Possibly the other colours made from azo dyes:
E107 Yellow 2G   E110 Sunset yellow FCF
E122 Carmoisine   E123 Amaranth
E124 Ponceau 4RR   E127 Erythrosine
E128 Red 2G   E131 Patent Blue
E132 Indigo Carmine   133 Brilliant blue FCF
E151 Black PN   154 Brown FK
 155 Brown HT

REFERENCES

1. Abraham G E . Nutritional factors in the etiology of the pre-menstrual tension syndrome. Journal Reprod Med 1983;28(7):446-64.
2. Abraham G E. Management of the pre-menstrual tension syndromes: Rationale for a nutritional approach. In: Blond J (ed). 1986 A Year in Nutritional medicine. Keats 1986.
3. Alexander P. It could be ALLERGY and it can be CURED. Ethicare Pty Ltd 1990.
4. Allen DH, Baker GJ. Chinese restaurant asthma. N Eng J Med 1981;278:796.
5. Allen DH, Delohery J, Baker G. Monosodium L-glutamate-induced asthma. J Allergy Clin Immunol 1987;80(4):530-7.
6. Allergen Data Collection. Hazelnut (Corylus avellana) Internet Symposium on Food Allergens 1999;1(4):161-75.
7. Allison SP. The management of malnutrition in hospital. Proc Nutr Soc 1996;55(3):855-62.
8. Allsop KA, Brand Miller J. Honey revisited: the role of honey in preindustrial diets. Br J Nutr 1996;75:513-20.
9. American Academy of Allergy and Immunology Committee on Adverse Reactions to Foods. US Dep H&HS, NIH Publications; 1984:84-2442.
10. Amlot PL, Kemeny DM, Zachary C, Parks P, Lessof MH. Oral allergy syndrome (OAS): symptoms of IgE mediated hypersensitivity to foods. Clin Allergy 1987;17:33-8.
11. Andersen AFR. Ulcerative colitis: an allergic phenomenon. Am J Dig Dis 1942;9:91-98.
12. Anderson BL, Dreyfuss EM, Logan J, Johnstone DE, Glaser J. Melon and banana sensitivity coincident with ragweed pollinosis. J Allergy 1970;45:310-18.
13. Anderson KE, Nielsen GD, Flyvholm MA, Fregert S, Gruvberg B. Nickel in tap water. Contact dermatitis. 1983;9(2):140-3.
14. Anderson CM, French JM et al. Coeliac disease: gastrointestinal studies and the effect of dietary wheat flour. Lancet 1952;1:836-842.
15. Andre F, Andre C, Colin L, Cacaraci F, Cavagna S. Role of new allergens and of allergen consumption in the increased incidence of food sensitivity in France. Toxicology 1994;93(1):77-83.
16. Antico A, Soana R, Clivio L, Baioni R. Irritable colon syndrome in intolerance to food additives. Minerva Dietol Gastroenterol 1989;35(4):219-24.

17. Antico A, Di Berardino L. The role of additives in chronic pseudo-allergic dermatopathies from food intolerance. Allerg Immunol (Paris) 1995;27(5):157-60.
18. Armanini D, Bonanni G, Palmero M. Reduction of serum testosterone in men by licorice. N Eng J Med 1999;341(15):1158.
19. Asero R. A strange case of "tuna allergy". Allergy 1998;53(8):816-7.
20. Atherton DJ. Diagnosis and management of skin disorders caused by food allergy. Ann Allergy 1984;53(6Pt2):623-8.
21. August PJ. Successful treatment of urticaria due to food additives with sodium cromoglycate and exclusion diet. In: Pepys J, Edward AM (eds). The Mast Cell: its role in health and disease. Pitman Medical 1979;584-590.
22. Ayuso R, Lehrer SB, Lopez M, Reese G, Ibanez MD, Esteban MM, Ownby DR, Schwartz H. Identification of bovine IgG as a major cross-reactive vertebrate meat allergen. Allergy 2000;55(4):348-54.
23. Baker GJ, Collet P, Allen DH. Bronchospasm induced by metabisulfite-containing foods and drugs. Med J Aust 1981;2:614-16.
24. Baldwin JL. Pharmacologic food reactions. In: Metcalfe DD, Sampson HA, Simon RA. Food Allergy: Adverse reactions to foods and food additives, 2nd ed. Blackwell Science 1997, 419-29.
25. Balyeat RM, Brittain FL. Allergic migraine. Based on the study of fifty-five cases. Am J Med Sci 1930;180:212-221.
26. Barker WH Jr, Runte V. Tomato juice associated gastroenteritis, Washington and Oregon, 1969. Am J Epidemiol 1972;96:219-26.
27. Barnes Koerner C, Sampson HA. Diets and Nutrition. In: Metcalfe DD, Sampson HA, Simon RA. Food Allergy: Adverse reactions to foods and food additives, 2nd ed. Blackwell Science 1997.
28. Bartholomew LG, Carlson HC. An unusual case of acute gastroenteritis. Mayo Clin Proc 1994;69:675-6.
29. Batey J, Cozzo M, Marin A, Eseverri JL. Monosodium glutamate and skin pathology in pediatric allergology. Allergol Immunopath 1988;16:425-8.
30. BBC News 18 Nov 1999. Autism link to food intolerance. http://news.bbc.co.uk/hi/english/health/newsid_526000/526044.stm
31. Beezhold DH, Sussman GL, Liss GM, Chang NS. Latex allergy can induce clinical reactions to specific foods. Clin Exp Allergy 1996;26:416-22.
32. Benton D. Lipids and cognitive functioning. In: Hillbrand M and Spitz R T (eds). Lipids and Human Beahvior. American Psychological Assoc 1996.
33. Beri D, Malaviya AN, Shandilya R, Singh RR. Effect of dietary restrictions on disease activity in rheumatoid arthritis. Ann Rheum Dis 1988;47:69-72.

34. Bernihisel-Broadbent J, Sampson HA. Oral challenge and in vitro study results in fish hypersensitive patients. J Allergy Clin Immunol 1990;85:270.

35. Bernihisel-Broadbent J, Scanlon SM, Sampson HA. Fish hypersensitivity.1. In vitro and oral challenge results in fish-allergic patients. J Allergy Clin Immunol 1992; 89:730-7.

36. Bernstein JM, Lee J, Conboy K, Ellis E, Li P. Further observations on the role of IgE-mediated hypersensitivity in recurrent otitis media with effusion. Otolaryngol Head Neck Surg 1985;93(5):611-5.

37. Bethune C A, Gompels M M, Spickett G P. Physiological effects of starvation interpreted as food allergy. BMJ 1999;319:304-305.

38. Bibby BG. Food and teeth. Vantage Press, 1990.

39. Bircher AJ, Van Melle G, Haller E, Curty B, Frei PC. IgE to food allergens are highly prevalent in patients allergic to pollens, with and without symptoms of food allergy. Clin Exp Allergy 1994;24:367-74.

40. Bishop JM, Hill DJ, Hoskins CS. Natural history of cow milk allergy - clinical outcome. J Pediatrt 1990;116:862-67.

41. Blanco C, Carrillo T, Castillo R, Quiralte J, Cuevas M. Latex allergy: clinical features and cross-reactivity with fruits. Ann Allergy 1994;73:309-14.

42. Blauss MS, McCants M, Lehrer S. Anaphylaxis to cabbage: detection of allergens. Ann Allergy 1987;58:248-50.

43. BMJ News. Very low fat diets may harm some people. BMJ 1998;316:517.

44. Bolton S, Feldman M, Null G, Revici E, Stumper L. A pilot study of some physiological and psychological effects of caffeine. J Orthomolecular Psych 1985;13(1).

45. Bolton S, Null G. Caffeine: Psychological Effects, Use and Abuse; Ortho Psych 1981;10(2):202-211.

46. Borg AA, Dawes PT, Swan CH, Hothersall T E. Persistent monoarthritis and occult coeliac disease. Postgrad Med J 1994;70(819):51-3E.

47. Boris M. Food and chemical intolerance: Placebo-controlled studies in attention deficit disorders. In: Bellanti JA, Crook WG, Layton RE, eds. Attention Deficit Hyperactivity Disorder: Causes and Possible Solutions (Proceedings of a Conference). Jackson, TN: International Health Foundation; 1999.

48. Boris M, Mandel FS. Foods and additives are common causes of the attention deficit hyperactive disorder in children. Ann Allergy 1994;72:462-468.

49. Braverman ER. The Healing Nutrients Within. Keats 1987.

50. Bray GA, Macdiarmid J. The epidemic of obesity. West J Med 2000;17:78-9.

51. Breakey J. The role of diet and behaviour in childhood. J Paediatr Child Health 1997;33(3):190-4.

52. Brehler-R; Theissen-U; Mohr-C; Luger-T. Latex-fruit syndrome: frequency of cross-reacting IgE antibodies. Allergy. 1997; 52(4): 404-10.

53. Breneman J. Allergy elimination diet as the most effective gall bladder diet. Ann Allergy 1968;26:83.

54. Breneman J. Basics of Food Allergy. Charles C Thomas 1978.

55. Brien J A, Sigma. Ototoxicity associated with salicylates: A brief review. Drug Saf 1993;9(2):143-8.

56. Brostoff J. BBC News on-line Tuesday October 13 1998. http:\\www.bbc.co.uk.

57. Bruun LI, Bosaeus I, Bergstad I, Nygaard K. Prevalence of malnutrition in surgical patients: evaluation of nutritional support and documentation. Clin Nutr 1999;18(3):141-7.

58. Burks AW, James JM, Hiegel A, Wilson G, Wheeler JG, Jones SM, Zuerlein N. Atopic dermatitis and food hypersensitivity reactions. J Pediatr 1998;132(1):132-6.

59. Burks AW, Mallory SB, Williams LW, Shirrell MA. Atopic dermatitis: clinical relevance of food hypersensitivity reactions. J Pediatr 1988;113(3):447-51.

60. Burks AW, Williams LW, Helm RM, Thresher W, Brooks JR, Sampson HA. Identification of soy protein allergens in patients with atopic dermatitis and positive soy challenges; determination of change in allergenicity after heating or enzyme digestion. Adv Exp Med Biol 1991;289: 295-307.

61. Bush RK, Taylor SL, Nordlee JA, Busse WW . Soybean oil is not allergenic to soybean-sensitive individuals. 1985 J Allergy Clin Immunol 76(2 Pt 1):242-5.

62. Businco L, Falconieri P, Giampietro P, Bellioni B. Food allergy and asthma. Pediatr Pulmonol Suppl 1995;11:59-60.

63. Cantani A. Hidden presence of cow's milk proteins in foods. J Investig Allergol Clin Immunol 1999;9(3):141-5.

64. Carter CM, Urbanowicz M, Hemsley R, Mantilla L, Strobel S, Graham PJ, Taylor E. Effects of a few food diet in attention defect disorder. Arch Dis Child 1993;69(5):564-8.

65. Castillo R, Carrilo T, Blanco C, Quiralte J, Cuevas M. Shellfish hypersensitivity: clinical and immunological characteristics. Allergol Immunopathol (Madr) 1994;22(2):83-7.

66. Cazals Y. Auditory sensori-neural alterations induced by salicylate. Prog Neurobiol 2000;(6):583-631.

67. Chafee RH, Settipane GA. Asthma caused by FD&C approved dyes. J Allergy 1967;40:65-72.

68. Charambous I, ed. The Quality of Foods And Beverages, Vol. 1. Academic Press, page 394, 1981.

69. Charney DS, Heninger GR, Jatlow PI. Increased anxiogenic effects of caffeine in panic disorders. Arch Gen psychiatry 1985;42:233-43.

70. Chiu AM, Zacharisen MC. Anaphylaxis to dill. Ann Allergy Asthma Immunol 2000;84(5):559-60.

71. Chiu, JT; Haydik, IB. Sesame seed oil anaphylaxis. J Allergy Clin Immunol 1991;88:414-415.

72. Clarke TW. The relation of allergy to character problems in children; A survey. Ann Allergy 1950;8:75-87.

73. Coca AF. Familial Nonreaginic Food Allergy. Charles C Thomas 1945.

74. Cooke RA. Allergic neuropathies. In: Cooke RA ed. Allergy in theory and practice. WB Saunders, 1947, 325-36.

75. Crayton JW. Adverse reactions to foods: relevance to psychiatric disorders. J Allergy Clin Immunol 1986;78 (1Pt 2):243-50.

76. Crinnion W J. Environmental Medicine, Part 2 - Health Effects of and Protection from Ubiquitous Airborne Solvent Exposure. Altern Med Rev 2000;5(2):133-143.

77. Crippa M, Pasolini G. Allergic reactions due to glove-lubricant-powder in health-care workers. Int Arch Occup Environ Health 1997;70(6):399-402.

78. Crook WG. Can what a child eats make him dull, stupid or hyperactive? J Learn Dis, 1980;13:53-8.

79. Crook WG. Sugar, yeast and ADHD: fact or fiction? In: Bellanti JA, Crook WG, Layton RE, eds. Attention Deficit Hyperactivity Disorder: Causes and Possible Solutions (Proceedings of a Conference). Jackson, TN: International Health Foundation; 1999.

80. CSPI (Center for Science in the Public Interest) 1999. Jacobson M F, Schardt M S. Diet, ADHD and Behaviour: A Quarter-Century Review.

81. CSPI (Center for Science in the Public Interest). Chemical Cuisine: CSPI's Guide to Food Additives. http://www.cspinet.org/reports/chemcuisine.htm.

82. D'Adamo PJ. Eat Right 4 Your Type: The Individualized Diet Solution to Staying Healthy, Living Longer & Achieving Your Ideal Weight. 1997 G. P. Putnam's Sons.

83. Danoff D, Linoln L, Thomson DMP, Gold P. Big Mac Attack. N Eng J Med 1978;298:1095-96.

84. Darlington LG. Dietary therapy for arthritis. Rheum Dis Clin North Am 1991;7:273-285.

85. Daroca P, Crespo JF, Reano M, James JM, Lopez-Rubio A, Rodriguez J. Asthma and rhinitis induced by exposure to raw green beans and chards. Ann Allergy Asthma Immunol 2000;85(3):215-8.

86. Davidson AE, Passero MA, Settipane GA. Buckwheat-induced anaphylaxis: a case report. Ann Allergy 1992; 69(5):439-40.
87. Davis RE, Osorio I. Childhood caffeine tic syndrome. Pediatrics 1998;101(6):E4.
88. deBartolo H M Jr. Zinc and diet for tinnitus. Am Journal Otol 1989;10(3):256.
89. de Diego Lorenzo A, Robles Fornieles J, Herrero Lopez T, Cos Arregui E. Acute pancreatitis associated with milk allergy. Int J Pancreatol 1992 Dec;12(3):319-21.
90. De Martino M, Novembre E, Cozza G, deMarco A, Bonazza P, Vierucci A. Sensitivity to tomato and peanut allergies in children monosensitized to grass pollen. Allergy 1988;43:206-13.
91. de Martino M, Novembre E, Galli L, de Marco A, Botarelli P, Marano E, Vierucci A. Allergy to different fish species in cod-allergic children: in vivo and in vitro studies. J Allergy Clin Immunol 1990 Dec;86(6,Pt1):909-14.
92. Derebery MJ. Otolaryngic allergy. Otolaryngol Clin North Am 1993;26(4):593-611.
93. Derebery M J. Allergic management of Meniere's disease: an outcome study. Otolaryngol Head Neck Surg 2000;122(2):174-82.
94. Derebery MJ, Berliner KI.. Prevalence of allergy in Meniere's disease. Otolaryngol Head Neck Surg 2000;123(1Pt1):69-75.
95. Derebery MJ, Valenzuela S House. Meniere's syndrome and allergy. Otolaryngol Clin North Am 1992, 25 (1): 213-24.
96. Dimick PS, Hoskin JC. Review of apple flavor-state of the art. Crit Rev Food Sci Nutr. 1983;18(4):387-409.
97. Doeglas HMG, Huisman J, Nater J P. Histamine intoxication after cheese. Lancet 2;1967:1361-2.
98. Douglas JM. Psoriasis and diet. Calif Med 1980;133:5.
99. Dreborg S, Foucard T. Allergy to apple, carrot and potato in children with birch pollen allergy. Allergy 1983; 38:167-72.
100. Duke WW. Meniere's syndrome caused by allergy. JAMA 1923;34:645-47.
101. Dunn DW, Snyder CH. Benign paroxysmal vertigo of childhood. Am J Dis Child 1976;130:1099-100.
102. Eades M and Eades M D. Protein Power: The high protein, low carbohydrate way to lose weight, feel fit, and boost your health. Thorsons 2000.
103. Eberlein-Konig B, Bergner T, Diemer S, Przybilla B. Evaluation of phototoxic properties of some food additives: sulfites exhibit prominent phototoxicity. Acta Derm Venereol 1993;73(5):362-4.
104. Edwards SL. Malnutrition in hospital patients: where does it come from? Br J Nurs 1998;7(16):954-8,971-4.

105. Egger J, Carter CM, Graham PJ, et al. Controlled trial of oligoantigenic treatment in the hyperkinetic syndrome. Lancet 1985;i:540-545.

106. Egger J, Carter CM, Soothill JF, Wilson J. Oligoantigenic diet treatment of children with epilepsy and migraine. J Pediatr 114: 51-58, 1989.

107. Egger J, Stolla A, McEwen LM, et al. Controlled trial of hyposensitisation in children with food-induced hyperkinetic syndrome. Lancet 1992;339:1150-1153.

108. Egger J, Wilson J, Carter CM, Tuner MW, Soothill JF. Is migraine food allergy? A double-blind controlled trial of oligoantigenic diet treatment. Lancet 1983;2:865-869.

109. Emsley J, Fell P. Was it something you ate? Food Intolerance: what causes it and how to avoid it. O.U.P. 1999.

110. Endicott JN, Stucker FJ. Allergy in Meniere's disease related fluctuating hearing loss preliminary findings in a double-blind crossover clinical study. Laryngoscope 1977;87(10Pt1):1650-7.

111. Enrique E, Cistero-Bahima A, Alonso R, San Miguel MM. Egg protein: a hidden allergen in candies. Ann Allergy Asthma Immunol. 2000;84(6):636.

112. Eriksson NE. Food sensitivity reported by patients with asthma and hay fever. A relationship between food sensitivity and birch pollen-allergy and between food sensitivity and acetylsalicylic acid intolerance. Allergy 1978;33(4):189-96.

113. Eriksson NR, Formgren H, Svenonius E. Food Hypersensitivy in patients with pollen allergy. Allergy,1982;62:186-189.

114. Ewan PW. Clinical study of peanut and nut allergy in 62 consecutive patients: new features and association. BMJ 1996;312:1074-78.

115. Falleroni AE, Zeiss CR. Bean bag allergy revisited: a case of allergy to inhaled soybean dust. Ann Allergy Asthma Immunol 1996;77(4):298-302.

116. Falliers CJ. Anaphylaxis to kiwi fruit and related 'exotic' items. J Asthma 1983;20:193-6.

117. Farah DA, Calder I, Benson L, MacKenzie JF. Specific food intolerance: its place as a cause of gastrointestinal symptoms. Gut 1985;26(2):164-8.

118. Faulkner-Hogg KB, Selby WS, Loblay RH, Morrow AW. . Dietary analysis in symptomatic patients with coeliac disease on a gluten-free diet: the role of trace amounts of gluten and non-gluten food intolerances. Scand J Gastroenterol 1999;34(8):784-9.

119. Feighery C. Coeliac Disease. BMJ 1999;319:236-39.

120. Feingold B. Introduction to Clinical Allergy. Charles C. Thomas, 1973.

121. Feingold B. Why your child is hyperactive. Random House 1985.

122. Feingold B, Feingold H. The Feingold cookbook for hyperactive children and others with problems associated with food additives and salicylates. Random House, 1979.

123. Feldman JM, Lee EM. Serotonin content of foods: effect on urinary excretion of 5-hydroxyindoleacetic acid. Am J Clin Nutr 1985;42:639-43.

124. Fell PJ, Brostoff J, O'Donnell H, et al. ALCAT - "a new test for food induced problems in medicine?" Presented at the Annual Meeting of the American Academy of Otolaryngic Allergy, October 1, 1988, Washington, D.C.

125. Fiocchi A, Restani P, Riva E. Beef allergy in children. Nutrition 2000;16(6):454-7.

126. Fisherman EW, Cohen GN. Aspirin and other crossreacting small chemicals in known aspirin intolerant patients. Ann Allergy 1973;31:476-84.

127. Flyvholm MA, Nielsen GD, Andersen A. Nickel content of food and estimation of dietary intake Z Lebensm Unters Forsch 1984;179:427-31.

128. Food interacting with MAO inhibitors. Med Lett Drugs Ther 1989;31:11-12.

129. Freed D L J. Do dietary lectins cause disease? BMJ 1999;318:1023-24.

130. Freedman B J. A diet free from additives in the management of allergic disease. Clin Allergy 1977;7:417-21.

131. Freedman BJ. Asthma induced by sulphur dioxide, benzoate and tartrazine contained in orange drinks. Clin Allergy 1977;7:407-415.

132. Fremont S, Kanny G, Nicolas JP, Moneret-Vautrin DA. Prevalence of lysozyme sensitization in an egg-allergic population Allergy 1997;52(2):224-8.

133. Friedman R B. Food diets: Evaluation of five common types. Postgrad Med 1986;89(1):249-58.

134. Fry L. Dermatitis herpetiformis. Baillieres Clin Gastroenterol 1995; 9(2):371-93.

135. Gaboardi F, Perletti L, Cambie M, Mihatsch MJ. Dermatitis herpetiformis and nephrotic syndrome. Clin Nephrol 1983, 20: 49-51.

136. Gaby AR. The role of hidden food allergy/intolerance in chronic disease. Altern Med Rev 1998;3(2):90-100.

137. Gaby AR. Alternative treatments for rheumatoid arthritis. Altern Med Rev 1999;4(6):392-402.

138. Gancedo SQ, Freire P, Rivas MF, Davila I, Losada E. Urticaria from caffeine. J Allergy Clin Immunol 1991;88:680-81.

139. Garioch JJ, Lewis HM, Sargent SA, Leonard JN, Fry L. 25 years' experience of a gluten-free diet in the treatment of dermatitis herpetiformis. Br J Dermatol 1994;131(4):541-5.

140. Gastaminza G, Bernaola G, Camino ME. Acute pancreatitis caused by allergy to kiwi fruit. Allergy 1998 Nov;53(11):1104-5.

141. Gawkrodger DJ, Blackwell JN, Gilmour HM, Rifkind EA, Heading RC, Barnetson RS. Dermatitis herpetiformis: diagnosis, diet and demography. Gut, 1984;25(2):151-7.

142. Genton C, Frei PC, Pecoud A. Value of oral provocation tests to aspirin and food additives in the routine investigation of asthma and chronic urticaria. J Allergy Clin Immunol 1985;76(1):40-5.

143. Gern JE, Young E, Evrard HM, Sampson HA. Allergic reactions to milk-contaminated "nondairy" products. New Eng J Med 1991;324:976-79.

144. Gerrard JW, Richardson JS, Donat J. Neuropharmacological evaluation of movement disorders that are adverse reactions to specific foods. Int J Neurosci 1994;76(1-2):61-9.

145. Ghose K, Turner P. The menstrual cycle and the tyramine pressor response test. Br J Clin Pharmacol 1977;4:500-02.

146. Gibson A, Clancy R. Management of chronic idiopathic urticaria by the identification and exclusion of dietary factors. Clin Allergy 1980;10:699-704.

147. Gilbert RJ. Healthy eating day. Communicable Disease Report 1988;33:3-4.

148. Golding DN. Is there an allergic synovitis? J R Soc Med 1990;83(5):312-4.

149. Gonzalez-Gutierrez ML, Sanchez-Fernandez C, Esteban-Lopez MI, Sempere-Ortells JM, Diaz-Alperi P. Allergy to anis. Allergy 2000;55(2):195-6.

150. Gottschall E. Whatever happened to the cure for coeliac disease? Nutritional Therapy Today. 1997:7(1):8-11.

151. Grant EC. Food allergies and migraine. Lancet 1979;1(8123):966-9.

152. Greden JF. Anxiety or caffeinism - a diagnostic dilemma. Am J Psychiatry 1974;131:1089-92.

153. Guariso G, Bertoli S, Cernetti R, Battistella PA, Setari M, Zacchello F. Migraine and food intolerance: a controlled study in pediatric patients. Pediatr Med Chir 1993;15(1):57-61.

154. Haid CT, Watermeier D, Wolf SR, Berg M. Clinical survey of Meniere's disease: 574 cases. Acta Otolaryngol Suppl 1995;520 Pt 2:251-5.

155. Hall K. Allergy of the nervous system: a review. Ann Allergy 1976;36(1):49-64.

156. Hallert C, Olsson M, Storsrud S, Lenner RA, Kilander A, Stenhammar L. Oats can be included in gluten-free diet. Lakartidningen 1999;96(30-31):3339-40.

157. Hanakawa Y, Tohyama M, Shirakata Y, Murakami S, Hashimoto K. Food-dependent exercise-induced anaphylaxis: a case related to the amount of food allergen ingested. Br J Dermatol 1998;138(5):898-900.

158. Hanifin J M et al. Diet and atopic dermatitis. Western J of Med 1989;151:6.

159. Hannuksela M, Haahtela T. Hypersensitivity reactions to food additives. Allergy 1987;42(80:561-75.

160. Hansen TK, Bindslev-Jensen C, Skov PS, Poulsen LK. Codfish allergy in adults: IgE cross-reactivity among fish species. Ann Allergy Asthma Immunol 1997;78(2):187-94.

161. Hanssen M. E for additives. Thorsons 1991.

162. Hay KD, Reade PC. The use of an elimination diet in the treatment of recurrent aphthous ulceration of the oral cavity. Oral Surg 1984;57:504-507.

163. Health Which. Health Food Allergy Tests Condemned. BBC News on-line Thurs 10 Dec 1998.

164. Heller RF and Heller RF. The Carbohydrate Addict's Lifespan Program: A personalized plan for becoming slim, fit and healthy in your 40s, 50s, 60s and beyond. Plume 1998.

165. Henz BM, Zuberbier T. Most chronic urticaria is food-dependent, and not idiopathic. Exp Dermatol 1998;7(4):139-42.

166. Heyden S, Muhlbaier LH. Prospective study of "fibrocystic breast disease" and caffeine consumption. Surgery 1984;96(3):479-84.

167. Heymann H. Migraine and food allergy. S Afr Med J 1952;26:949-950.

168. Hicklin JA, McEwen LM, Morgan JE. The effect of diet in rheumatoid arthritis. Clin Allergy 1980;10:463.

169. Hill DJ, Hoskins CS. Infantile colic and food hypersensitivity. In: Metcalfe DD, Sampson HA, Simon RA. (eds) Food Allergy: Adverse reactions to foods and food additives, 2nd ed. Blackwell Science 1997.

170. Hill SM et al. Colitis caused by food allergy in infants. Archives of Disease in Childhood 1990;65:1.

171. Hill DJ, Hudson IL, Sheffield LJ, Shelton MJ, Menahem S, Hosking CS. A low allergen diet is a significant intervention in infantile colic: results of a community-based study. J Allergy Clin Immunol 1995;96(6 Pt 1):886-92.

172. Hjorth N, Roed-Peterson. Occupational protein contact dermatitis in food handlers. J Contact Derm 1976;2:28-42.

173. Hoffman D, Yamamato F, Ceiler B, Haddad Z. Specific IgE antibodies in atopic eczema. J Allergy Clin Immunol 1975;(55)256-67.

174. Hoffman DR. The specificities of human IgE antibodies combining with cereal grains. Immunochem 1975;12:535-38.

175. Hoffman DR, Collins-Williams C. Cold pressed peanut oils may contain peanut allergen. J Clin Allergy Immunol 1994;93(4):801-02.

176. Hoj L. Diagnostic value of ALCAT test in intolerance to food additives compared with double-blind placebo-controlled (DBPC) oral challenges. Presented at the 52nd Annual Meeting of the American Academy of Allergy, Asthma and Immunology, March 15-20, 1996, New Orleans.

177. Holen E, Elsayed S. Characterisation of four major allergens of hen egg-white by IEF/SDS-PAGE combined with electrophoretic transfer and IgE immunoautoradiography. Int Arch Allery Appl Immunol 1990;9:136-41.

178. Hollander DH. Beef allergy and the Persian Gulf syndrome. Med Hypotheses 1995;45(3):221-2.

179. Host A. Mechanisms in adverse reactions to food. The sinuses. Allergy 1995;50(20Suppl):60-3.

180. Howanietz H, Lubec G. Idiopathic nephrotic syndrome, treated with steroids for five years, found to be allergic reaction to pork. Lancet 1985;2:450.

181. Howland WA, Simon RA. Restaurant-provoked asthma: sulfite sensitivity? J Allergy Clin Immunol 1985;75:145.

182. Iancono G, Carroccio A, Mantalto G et al. Severe infantile colic and food intolerance; a long term prospective study. J Pediatr Gastr Nutr 1991;12:332-35.

183. Ignys I, Bartkowiak M, Baczyk I, Targonska B, Krawczynski M IV. Food allergy in pathogenesis of chronic abdominal pain in children. Pediatr Pol 1995;70(4):307-11.

184. Jacobson DW. Adverse reactions to benzoates and parabens. In: Metcalfe DD, Sampson HA, Simon RA. (eds) Food Allergy: Adverse reactions to foods and food additives, 2nd ed. Blackwell Science 1997, 375-386.

185. James JM, Burks AW. Food-associated gastrointestinal disease. Curr Opin Pediatr 1996;8(5):471-5.

186. James JM, Sampson HA. Immunolgic changes associated with the development of tolerance in children with cow milk allergy. J Pediatr 1992;121:371-77.

187. Janatuinen E K, Kemppainen T A, Pikkarainen P H, Holm K H, Kosma V-M, Uusitupa M I J, Maki M, Julkunen R J K. Lack of cellular and humoral immunological responses to oats in adults with coeliac disease. Gut 2000;46:327-31.

188. Jenkins HR, Pincott JR, Soothill JF, Milla PJ, Harries JT. Food allergy: the major cause of infantile colitis. Arch Dis Child 1984 Apr;59(4):326-9.

189. Joneja JMV, Ehmann S. Stress profile of clients referred for investigation of food allergy. J Nut Env Med 2000;10:289-96.

190. Jones SM, Magnolfi CF, Cooke SK, Sampson HA. Immunologic cross-reactivity among cereal grains and grasses in children with food hypersensitivity. J Allergy Clin Immunol 1995;96(3):341-51.

191. Jones VA, Dickinson RJ, Workman E, Wilson AJ, Freeman AH, Hunter JO. Crohn's disease: maintenance of remission by diet. Lancet 1985,27;2(8448):177-80.

192. Jones VA, McGlaughlan P, Shorthouse M, et al. Food intolerance: a major factor in the pathogenesis of irritable bowel syndrome. Lancet 1982;2:1115-1117.

193. Jones VA, Workman E, Freeman AH, et al. Crohn's disease: maintenance of remission by diet. Lancet 1985;2:177-180.

194. Juhlin L. Additives and chronic urticaria. Ann Allergy 1987;59(5/2):119-23.

195. Juhlin L, Michaelsson G, Zetterstrom O. Urticaria and asthma induced by food-and-drug additives in patients with aspirin hypersensitivity. J Allergy Clin Immunol 1972;50:92-98.

196. Kadunce DP, McMurry MP, Avots-Avotins A, Chandler JP, Meyer LJ, Zone JJ. The effect of an elemental diet with and without gluten on disease activity in dermatitis herpetiformis. J Invest Dermatol 1991;97(2):175-82.

197. Kagi, MK; Wuthrich, B. Falafel-burger anaphylaxis due to sesame seed allergy. Lancet 1991;338: 582.

198. Kahn A, Mozin MJ, Rebuffat E et al. Milk intolerance in children with persistent sleeplessness: a prospective double blind crossover evaluation. Pediatrics 1989;84:595-603.

199. Kalverman M, Forck G. Crossreactivity between grass and corn pollen antigens. Int Arch Allergy Appl Immunol 1978;57:549-53.

200. Kanny G, De Hauteclocque C, Moneret-Vautrin DA Sesame seed and sesame seed oil contain masked allergens of growing importance. Allergy 1996;51(12):952-7.

201. Kaplan BJ, McNicol J, Conte RA, Moghadam HK. Dietary replacement in preschool-aged hyperactive boys. Pediatrics 1989;83(1):7-17.

202. Kaufman W. Food-induced, allergic musculoskeletal syndromes. Ann Allergy 1953;11:179-184.

203. Kaukinen K, Turjanmaa K, Maki M, Partanen J, Venalainen R, Reunala T, Collin P. Intolerance to cereals is not specific for coeliac disease. Scand J Gastroenterol 2000;35(9):942-6.

204. Kelso JM, Cockrell GE, Helm RM, Burks AW. Common allergens in avian meats. J Allergy Clin Immunol 1999;104(1):202-4.

205. Kidd PM. Attention Deficit/Hyperactivity Disorder (ADHD) in Children: Rationale for Its Integrative Management Altern Med Rev 2000;5(5):402-428.

206. Kim KT, Hussain H. Prevalence of food allergy in 137 latex-allergic patients. Allergy Asthma Proc 1999;20(2):95-7.

207. King DS. Can allergic exposure provoke psychological symptoms? A double-blind test. Biol Psychiatry 1981;16(1):3-19.

208. Kinsman SL, Vining EPG, Quaskey SA, Mellitis D, Freeman JM. Efficacy of the ketogenic diet for intractable seizure disorders: review of 58 cases. Epilepsia 1992;33:1132-36.

209. Kivity S, Dunner K, Marian Y. The pattern of food hypersensitivity in patients with onset after 10 years of age. Clin exp Allergy 1994;24:19-22.

210. Kjeldsen-Kragh J, Haugen M, Borchgrevink CF, et al. Controlled trial of fasting and one-year vegetarian diet in rheumatoid arthritis. Lancet 1991;338:899-902.

211. Kochen J. Sulfur dioxide, a respiratory tract irritant, even if ingested. Letter. Pediatrics 1973;52:145-6.

212. Kokkonen J, Karttunen TJ, Niinimaki A. Lymphonodular hyperplasia as a sign of food allergy in children. J Pediatr Gastroenterol Nutr 1999;29(1):57-62.

213. Kondo N, Shinoda S, Agata H, Nishida T, Miwa Y, Fujii H, Orii T. Lymphocyte responses to food antigens in food sensitive patients with allergic tension-fatigue syndrome. Biotherapy 1992;5(4):281-4.

214. Kruger PG, Nyland HI. The role of mast cells and diet in the onset and maintenance of multiple sclerosis: a hypothesis. Med Hypothesis 1995;44(1):66-69.

215. Kumar A, Freeman S. Protein contact dermatitis in food workers. Case report of a meat sorter and summary of seven other cases. Australas J Dermatol 1999;40(3):138-40.

216. Lagier F, Cartier A, Somer J, olovich J, Malo J-L. Occupational asthma caused by guar gum. J Allergy Clin Immunol 1990;85:785-90.

217. Lagrue G, Heslan JM, Belghiti D, Sainte-Laudy J, Laurent J. Basophil sensitization for food allergens in idiopathic nephrotic syndrome. Nephron 1986;42(2):123-7.

218. Lagrue G, Laurent J, Rostoker G. Food allergy and idiopathic nephrotic syndrome. Kidney Int Suppl 1989;27:S147-51.

219. Langeland T. A clinical and immunological study of allergy to hen's egg white. Allergy 1983;38:399-412.

220. Langeland T. Allergy to hen's egg white in atopic dermatitis. Acta Derm Verereol: 1985;114(Suppl):109-12.

221. Langseth L, Dowd J. Glucose tolerance and hyperkinesis. Fd Cosmet Toxicol 1978;16:129-133.

222. Laurent J, Lagrue G. Dietary manipulation for idiopathic nephrotic syndrome. A new approach to therapy. Allergy 1989;44(8):599-603.

223. Laurent J, Rostoker G, Robeva R, et al. Is adult idiopathic nephrotic syndrome food allergy? Value of oligoantigenic diets. Nephron 1987;47:7-11.

224. Laurent J, Wierzbicki N, Rostoker G, Lang P, Lagrue G. Idiopathic nephrotic syndrome and food hypersensitivity. Value of an exclusion diet. Arch Fr Pediatr 1988;45(10):815-9.

225. Lee EJ, Heiner DC. Allergy to cow's milk 1985. Pediatrics in review 1986;7(7):195-203.

226. Lee I-M, Paffenberger RS. Life is sweet: candy consumption and longevity. BMJ 1998;317:1683-84.

227. Lehman CW. A double-blind study of sublingual provocative food testing: a study of its efficacy. Ann Allergy 1980;45:144-149.

228. Leira R, Rodriguez R. Diet and migraine. Rev Neurol 1996;24(129):534-8.

229. Lewis WH, Imber WE. Allergy epidemiology in the St Louis, Missouri, area.V. Cereal ingestants. Ann Allergy 1975;35:251-4.

230. Lezan A, Igea J, Davila I, Martin JA, Alonso MD et al. Occupational asthma and contact urticaria to rice in a housewife. Schweiz me Wschr 1991;121(p2):296.

231. Lin HY, Shyur SD, Fu JL, Lai YC, Lin JS. Fish induced anaphylactic reaction: report of one case. Zhonghua Min Guo Xiao Er Ke Yi Xue Hui Za Zhi 1998;39(3):200-2.

232. Lindemayr H, Schmidt J. Intolerance to acetylsalicylic acid and food additives in patients suffering from recurrent urticaria. Wien Klin Wochenschr 1979;91(24):817-22.

233. Liska DJ. The detoxification enzyme systems. Altern Med Rev 1998: 3(3), 197-98.

234. Llaster R, Polo F, De La Hoz F, Guillaumet B. Alimentary allergy to pork. Crossreactivity among pork and kidney and lamb gut. Clin Exp Allergy 198;28(8):1021-5.

235. Lothe L, Lindverg T, Jakobsson I. Cow's milk formula as a cause of infantile colic: a double blind study. Pediatrics 1982;70:7-10.

236. Loza C, Brostoff J. Peanut Allergy (review). Clin Exp Allergy 1995;25:493-502.

237. LSRO (Life science research office). The re-examination of the GRAS status of sulfiting agents. Fed Am Socs for Exp Biology, Jan 1985.

238. Lucarelli S, Frediani T, Zingoni AM, Ferruzzi F, Giardini O, Quintieri F, Barbato M, D'Eufemia P, Cardi E. Food allergy and infantile autism. Panminerva Med 1995;37(3):137-41.

239. Lucarelli S, Lendvai D, Frediani T, Finamore G, Grossi R, Barbato M, Zingoni AM, Cardi E II. Hemicrania and food allergy in children. Minerva Pediatr 1990;42(6):215-8.

240. Lust KD, Brown JE, Thomas W. Maternal intake of cruciferous vegetables and other foods and colic symptoms in exclusively breast-fed infants. J Am Diet Assoc 1996;96(1):46-8.

241. Lutz E G. Restless legs, anxiety and caffeinism. J Clin Psyciatry 1978; 693-8.

242. Lybarger JA, Callagher JS, Pulver DW, Litwin A, Brooks A, Bernstein IL. Occupational asthma induced by inhalation and ingestion of garlic. J Allergy Clin Immunol 1982;69:448-54.

243. Maat-Bleeker de F, Van Dijik A G, Berrens L. Allergy to egg yolk possibly induced by a sensitisation to bird serum antigens. Ann Allergy 1985;54:245-48.

244. Mackarness R. Not All In The Mind. Pan 1976.

245. MAFF (Ministry of Agriculture, Fisheries and Food). About food additives. Booklet 2 in food sense ser, 1997.

246. MAFF Survey of caffeine and other methylxanthines in energy drinks and other caffeine-containing products (updated). Food Surveillance Information Sheet, (144): 26pp, March 1998 (No 103 revised).

247. Maher TJ, Wurtman RJ. Possible neurologic effects of aspartame, a widely used food additive. Environ Health Perspect 1987;75:53-7.

248. Malten, K.E. Sesame oil contact hypersensitivity in leg-ulcer-patients. Contact Dermatitis Newsletter 1972;(11):251.

249. Mandallaz M, de Weck AL, Dahinden CA. Bird egg syndrome. Int Arch Allergy Appl Imm 1988;87:143-50.

250. Mandell M, Scanlon L W. Dr Mandell's 5-Day Allergy Relief System. Thomas Y Crowell 1979.

251. Mansfield J. Arthritis, Allergy, Nutrition and the Environment. Thorsons 1995.

252. Mansfield LE. Food allergy and headache. Whom to evaluate and how to treat. Postgrad Med 1988;83(7):46-51,55.

253. Manu P, Matthews DA, Lane TJ. Food intolerance in patients with chronic fatigue. Int J Eat Disord 1993;13(2):203-9.

254. Marchbanks CR. Drug-drug interactions with fluoroquinolines. Pharacotherapy 1993,13(pt2):23S-28S.

255. Martin P. The Sickening Mind: Brain Behaviour, Immunity and Disease. Harper Collins 1997.

256. Martinez San Ireneo M, Ibanez Sandin MD, Fernandez-Caldas E Hypersensitivity to members of the botanical order Fabales. J Investig Allergol Clin Immunol 2000;10(4):187-99.

257. Maslansky L, Wein G. Chocolate allergy: a double-blind study. Conn Med J 1971;35:5-9.

258. Mather M. Migraines and tannins-any relationship? Headache 1997;37(8):529

259. Matteo A, Sarles H. Is food allergy a cause of acute pancreatitis? Pancreas 1990 Mar;5(2):234-7.

260. McKenna KE, Walsh MY, Burrows D. The Melkersoon-Rosenthal syndrome and food additive hypersensitivity. Br J Dermatol 194;131:921-22.

261. McMillan M, Thompson JC. An outbreak of suspected solanine poisoning in schoolboys: Examinations of criteria of solanine poisoning. Q J Med 1979;48(190):227-43.

262. Mela DJ, Rogers PJ, Shepherd R, Mackie HJH. Real people, real foods, real eating solutions. Appetite 1993;19:69-73.

263. Merrett J, Peatfield RC, Rose FC, Merrett TG. Food related antibodies in headache patients. J Neurol Neurosurg Psychiatry 1983;46(8):738-42.

264. Merry P et al. Modifications of rheumatic symptoms by diet and drugs. Proc Nutr Soc 1989;48:363-69.

265. Metcalfe DD, Sampson HA, Simon RA. (eds) Food Allergy: Adverse reactions to foods and food additives, 2nd ed. Blackwell Science 1997.

266. Michaelsson G, Gerden B, Hagforsen E, Nilsson B, Pihl-Lundin I, Kraaz W, Hjelmquist G, Loof L. Psoriasis patients with antibodies to gliadin can be improved by a gluten-free diet. Br J Dermatol 2000;142(1):44-51.

267. Michaelsson G, Juhlin L. Urticaria induced by preservatives and dye additives in foods and drugs. Br J Dermatol 1973;88:525-32.

268. Miller JB. A double-blind study of food extract injection therapy: a preliminary report. Ann Allergy 1977;38:185-191.

269. Millichap JC, Jones JC, Rudis BP. Mechanisms of anti-convulsant action of ketogenic diet. Am J Disorders Childhood, 1964;107:593-604.

270. Mills N. Depression and food intolerance: a single case study. Hum Nutr Appl Nutr 1986;40(2):141-5.

271. Mindell EL, Hopkins V. Prescription Alternatives: Hundreds of safe, natural, prescription-free remedies to restore and maintain your health. Keats 1999.

272. Moneret-Vautrin DA, Hatahet R, Kanny G, Ait-Djafer Z. Allergenic peanut oil in milk formulas. Lancet 1991;338(8775):1149.

273. Moneret-Vautrin DA, Hatahet R, Kanny G. Risks of milk formulas containing peanut oil contaminated with peanut allergens in infants with atopic dermatitis. Pediatr Allergy Immunol 1994;5:184-8.

274. Moneret-Vautrin DA et al. The multifood allergy syndrome. Allerg Immunol (Paris) 2000;32(1):12-5.

275. Montano Garcia ML, Orea M. Frequency of urticaria and angioedema induced by food additives. Rev Alerg Mex 1989;36(1):15-8.
276. Morrow JD, Margolies GR, Rowland BS, Roberts LJ. Evidence that histamine is the causative toxin of scombroid-fish poisoning. N Eng J Med 1991; 324:716-20.
277. Moss M. Purines, Alcohol and Boron in the Diets of People with Chronic Digestive Problems. J Nutrit Env Med 11(1):23-32.
278. Motil KJ, Scrimshaw NS. The role of histamine in scombroid poisoning. Toxicity Lett 1979;2:219.
279. Muhlemann RJ, Wuthrich B. Food allergies 1983-1987. Schweiz Med Wochenschr 1991;121(46):1696-700.
280. Mullen G E. Questions and Answers: Food allergy and irritable bowel syndrome. JAMA 1991;265(13):1736.
281. Mumby K. Food Allergies and Environmental Illness: the complete guide to. 1993 Thorsons.
282. Murray MT, Pizzorno JT. Encyclopaedia of Natural Medicine. Rocklin, CA: Prima Publishing; 1998.
283. Myers BM, Smith L, Graham DY. Effect of red pepper and black pepper on the stomach. Am J Gastronterol 1987;82:211-14.
284. Mylek D. Migraine as one of the symptoms of food allergy. Pol Tyg Lek 1992;20-27;47(3-4):89-91.
285. Nanda R, James R, Smith H, et al. Food intolerance and the irritable bowel syndrome. Gut 1989;30:1099-1104.
286. Nenonen MT, Helve TA, Rauma AL, Hanninen OO. Uncooked, lactobacilli-rich, vegan food and rheumatoid arthritis. Br J Rheumatol 1998;37(3):274-81.
287. Nevett G. Malnutrition of the hospitalised patient-assessment of provision of diet and dietary intake. EDTNA ERCA J 1997;23(4):22-4.
288. Nielsen GD, Jepsen LV, Jorgensen PJ, Grandjean P, Bradnrup Y. Nickel-sensitive patients with vesicular hand eczema: oral challenge with a diet naturally high in nickel. Br J Dermatol 1990;122(3) 299-308.
289. Niphadker PV, Patil SP, Bapat MM. Legumes, the most important food allergen in India. Allergy 1992;47:318.
290. Nolan A, Lamey P-J, Milligan KA, Forsyth A. Recurrent aphthous ulceration and food sensitivity. J Oral Pathol Med 1991;20:473-475.
291. Novembre E, Dini L, Bernardini R, Resti M, Vierucci A . Unusual reactions to food additives. Pediatr Med Chir 1992;14(1): 39-42.
292. Nsouli TM, Nsouli SM, Linde RE, et al. Role of food allergy in serious otitis media. Ann Allergy 1994;73:215-219.
293. Nuffield Trust Report. Managing Nutrition in Hospital. Davis AM, Bristow A.1999.

294. O'Banion D, Armstrong B, Cummings RA, Stange J. Disruptive behavior: a dietary approach. J Autism Child Schizophr 1978 ;8(3):325-37.

295. O'Banion DR. Dietary control of rheumatoid arthritis pain: three case studies. J Holistic Med 1982;4(1):49-57.

296. Oehling A, Fernandez M, Cordoba H, Sanz ML. Skin manifestations and immunological parameters in childhood food allergy. J Investig Allergol Clin Immunol 1997;7(3):155-9.

297. Ogle KA, Bullock JD. Children with allergic rhinitis and/or bronchial asthma treated with elimination diet. Ann Allergy 1977;39:8-11.

298. Okudaira, H; Ito, K; Miyamoto, T et al. Evaluation of new system for the detection of IgE antibodies (ImmunoCAP®) in atopic disease. Arerugi; 1991;40(5):544-545.

299. Okudaira N, Kripke DF, Mullaney DJ. Theophylline delays human sleep phase. Life Sci 1984;34(10):933-8.

300. Olivieri J, Hauser C. Anaphylaxis to millet. Allergy 1998;53(1):109-10.

301. Onorato J, Merland N, Terral C, et al. Placebo-controlled double-blind food challenge in asthma. J Allergy Clin Immunol 1986;78:1139-1146.

302. Ortoloni C, Ispano M, Pastorello E, Bisi A, Ansaloni R. The oral allergy syndrome. Ann Allergy 1988;61:47-52.

303. Ortoloni C, Pastorello E, Luraghi MT, Della Torre F, Bellani M, Zanussi C. Diagnosis of intolerance to food additives. Ann Allergy 1984;53:587-91.

304. Panush RS. Food induced ("allergic") arthritis: clinical and serologic studies. J Rheumatol 1990;17(3):291-4.

305. Panush RS, Carter RL, Katz P, et al. Diet therapy for rheumatoid arthritis. Arthritis Rheum 1983;26:462-471.

306. Panush RS, Stroud RM, Webster EM. Food-induced (allergic) arthritis. Inflammatory arthritis exacerbated by milk. Arthritis Rheum 1986;29(2):220-6.

307. Pascual C, Martin Esteban M, Crespo JF. Fish allergy: evaluation of the importance of cross-reactivity. J Pediatr 1992;121(5 Pt 2):S29-34.

308. Pastorello E et al. Evaluation of allergic etiology in perennial rhinitis. Ann Allergy 1985;55:854-56.

309. Peatfield RC. Relationships between food, wine, and beer-precipitated migrainous headaches. Headache 1995;35(6):355-7.

310. Peatfield RC, Glover V, Littlewood JT, Sandler M, Clifford Rose F The prevalence of diet-induced migraine. Cephalalgia 1984;4(3):179-83.

311. Pelikan Z. Nasal response to food ingestion challenge. Arch Otolaryngol Head Neck Surg 1988;14(5):525-30.

312. Pelikan Z, Pelikan-Filipek M. Bronchial response to the food ingestion challenge. Ann Allergy 1987;58:164-172.
313. Pelliccia A, Lucarelli S, Frediani T, D'Ambrini G, Cerminara C, Barbato M, Vagnucci B, Cardi E. Partial cryptogenetic epilepsy and food allergy/intolerance. A causal or a chance relationship? Reflections on three clinical cases. Minerva Pediatr 1999;51(5):153-7.
314. Pelto L, Salminen S, Lilius EM, Nuutila J, Isolauri E. Milk hypersensitivity-key to poorly defined gastrointestinal symptoms in adults0. Allergy 1998;53(3):307-10.
315. Perez-Pimiento AJ, Moneo I, Santaolalla M, de Paz S, Fernandez-Parra B, Dominguez-Lazaro AR . Anaphylactic reaction to young garlic. Allergy 1999;54(6):626-9.
316. Perry CA et al. Health effects of salicylates in foods and drugs. Nutrition reviews 1996;54(8):225-240.
317. Petitpierre M, Gumowski P, Girard JP. Irritable bowel syndrome and hypersensitivity to food. Ann Allergy 1985;54(6):538-40.
318. Petrus M, Bonaz S, Causse E, Rhabbor M, Moulie N, Netter JC, Bilstein G. Asthma and intolerance to benzoates. Arch Pediatr 1996;3(10):984-9.
319. Pfaffenbach B, Adamek RJ, Bethke B, Stolte M, Wegener M Z. Eosinophilic gastroenteritis in food allergy. Gastroenterol 1996;34(8):490-3.
320. Pfeiffer CC. Mental and Elemental Nutrients. Keats 1975.
321. Philpott W H, Kalita D H. Brain Allergies: The Psychonutrient and Magnetic Connections. Keats 2000.
322. Pola J, Subiza J, Armentia A, Zapata C, Hinjosa M, Losada E, Valdivieso R. Urticaria caused by caffeine. Ann Allergy 1988;60:207-8.
323. Prinz RJ, Roberts WA, Hantman E, et al. Dietary correlates of hyperactive behavior in children. J Consult Clin Psychol 1980;48:760-769.
324. Quirce S, Diet Gomez ML, Hinjosa M Cuevas, Rivas MF, Pujana J et al. Housewives with raw potato-induced bronchial asthma. Allergy 1989;44:532-36.
325. Race S. Chocolate Cocoa, and Health. 2001 Tigmor Press. E-book version, see http://www.foodcanmakeyouill.co.uk
326. Randolph TG. Fatigue and weakness of allergic origin to be differentiated from "nervous fatigue" or neurasthenia. Ann Allergy 1945;3:418-30, 460.
327. Randolph TG, Moss R W. An Alternative Approach to Allergies: The new field of clinical ecology unravels the environmental causes of

mental and physical ills (revised edition). Perennial Library, Harper & Row 1990.

328. Rapaport HG. The Complete Allergy Guide. Simon and Schuster, 1970.

329. Raphael G, Raphael MH, Kaliner M. Gustatory rhinitis: a syndrome of food-induced rhinorrhea. J Allergy Clin Immunol 1989;83(1):110-5.

330. Rasanen L, Lehto M, Turjanmaa K, Savolainen J, Reunala T. Allergy to ingested cereals in atopic children. Allergy 1994;49(10):871-6.

331. Ratner D, Eshel E, Schneeyour A, Teitler A. Does milk intolerance affect seronegative arthritis in lactase-deficient women? Isr J Med Sci 1985;21:532-534.

332. Ratner D, Eshel E, Vigder K. Juvenile rheumatoid arthritis and milk allergy. J R Soc Med 1985;78:410-413.

333. Rea WJ, Peters DW, Smiley RE, Edgar R, Greenberg M, Fenyves E. Recurrent environmentally triggered thrombophlebitis: a five year follow-up. Ann Allergy 1981;(5Pt1):338-44.

334. Read NW, Krejs GJ, Read MG, Santa Ana CA, Morawski SG, Fordtran JS. Chronic diarrhea of unknown origin. Gastroenterology 1980;78(2):264-71.

335. Reider N, Sepp N, Fritsch P, Weinlich G, Jensen-Jarolim E. Anaphylaxis to camomile: clinical features and allergen cross-reactivity. Clin Exp Allergy 2000;30(10):1436-43.

336. Reunala T. Dermatitis herpetiformis: coeliac disease of the skin. Ann Med 1998;30(5):416-8.

337. Reunala T, Collin P, Holm K, Pikkarainen P, Miettinen A, Vuolteenaho N, Maki M. Tolerance to oats in dermatitis herpetiformis. Gut 1998;43(4):490-3.

338. Richards DG, Somers S, Issenman RM, Stevenson GW. Cow's milk protein/soy protein allergy: gastrointestinal imaging. Radiology 1988;167(3):721-3.

339. Rider JA, Moeller HC. Food hypersensitivity in ulcerative colitis: further experience with an intramucosal test. Am J Gastroenterol 1962;37:497-507.

340. Reichelt R. Gluten, Milk Proteins and Autism: Dietary Intervention Effects on Behaviour and Peptide Secretion. J App Nutr 1990;42(1).

341. Rinkel H J, Randolph TG, Zeller M. Food Allergy. Thomas 1951.

342. Riordan AM, Hunter JO, Cowan RE, et al. Treatment of active Crohn's disease by exclusion diet: East Anglian Multicentre Controlled Trial. Lancet 1993;342:1131-1134.

343. Rippere V. Placebo-controlled tests of chemical food additives: Are they valid? Med Hypotheses 1981;7:819-823.

344. Rippere V. Food additives and hyperactive children: a critique of Conners. Br J Clin Psychiatry 1983;22:19-32.

345. Rousquet J, Chanez P, Michel F-B. The respiratory tract and food hypersensitivity. In: Metcalfe DD, Sampson HA, Simon RA. (eds) Food Allergy: Adverse reactions to foods and food additives, 2nd ed. Blackwell Science 1997.

346. Rowe AH. Allergic fatigue and toxemia. Ann Allergy 1959;17:9-18.

347. Rowe AH, Rowe A Jr. Chronic ulcerative colitis: atopic allergy in its etiology. Am J Gastroenterol 1960;34:49-60.

348. Rowe AH, Young EJ. Bronchial asthma due to food allergy alone in ninety-five patients. JAMA 1959;169:1158-1162.

349. Rowe KS. Synthetic food colourings and 'hyperactivity': a double-blind crossover study. Aust Paediatr J 1988;24(2):143-7.

350. Rowe KS, Rowe KJ. Synthetic food coloring and behavior: a dose response effect in a double-blind, placebo-controlled, repeated-measures study. J Pediatr 1994;125(5Pt1):691-8.

351. Rowntree S et al. Development of IgE and IgG antibodies to food and inhalant allergens in children at risk of allergic disease. Arch Dis Childh 1985;60: 727-735.

352. Rozin P, Leveine E, Stoess C. Chocolate craving and liking. Appetite 1991;17:199-212.

353. Rudzki E, Czubalski K, Grzywa Z. Detection of urticaria with food additives intolerance by means of diet. Dermatologica 1980;161(1):57-62.

354. Rudman D, Galambos JT, Wenger J, Achord JL. Adverse effects of dietary gluten in four patients with regional enteritis. Am J Clin Nutr 1971;24:1068-1073.

355. Ruokonen J, Paganus A, Lehti H. Elimination diets in the treatment of secretory otitis media. J Pediatr Otorhinolaryngol 1982;4(1):39-46.

356. Russell L C. Caffeine restriction as initial treatment for breast pain. Nurse Pract 1989;14(2):36-37,40.

357. Russo S, Mastropasqua M, Mosetti MA, Persegani C, Paggi A. Low doses of liquorice can induce hypertension encephalopathy. Am J Nephrol 2000, 20(2):145-8.

358. Sampson H, Eigenmann PA. Allergic and non-allergic rhinitis: Food allergy and intolerance. In: Mygind N, Naclerio R, eds. Allergic and non-allergic rhinitis. Copenhagen: Munksgaard, 1997.

359. Sampson HA, McCaskill CC. Food hypersensitivity and atopic dermatitis: evaluation of 113 patients. J Pediatr 1985;107(5):669-75.

360. Sanchez-Monge R, Pascual CY, Diaz-Perales A, Fernandez-Crespo J, Martin-Esteban M, Salcedo G. Isolation and characterization of relevant allergens from boiled lentils. J Allergy Clin Immunol 2000;106(5/1):955-961.

361. Sandberg DH, McIntosh RM, Bernstein CW, et al. Severe steroid-responsive nephrosis associated with hypersensitivity. Lancet 1977;1:388-391.

362. Sandiford CP, Tee RD, Newman-Taylor AJ. Identification of crossreacting wheat, rye, barley and soya flour allergens using sera from individuals with wheat-induced asthma. Clin Exp Allergy 1995;25(4):340-9.

363. Sandler M, Youdin MBH, Hannington E. A phenylethylamine oxidising defect in migraine. Nature 1974;350:335-7.

364. Schardt D. Diet and behavior in children. Nutrition Action Healthletter 2000;27:10-11. Washington, DC: Center for Science in the Public Interest.

365. Schauss AG. Nutrition and antisocial behaviour. Int Clin Nutr Review 1984;4(4):172-7.

366. Scheife RT, Hills JR. Migraine headache: signs and symptoms, biochemistry, and current therapy. Am J Hosp Pharm 1980;37(3):365-74.

367. Schwartz GR. Aspartame and breast and other cancers. West J Med 1999;171:300-301.

368. Schwartz H, Sher TH. Bisulfite intolerance manifest as bronchospasm following topical dipirefrin hydrochloride therapy for glaucoma. Letter. Arch opthalmol 1985;103:14-15.

369. Schwartz, RH. Near-fatal anaphylaxis to chicken soup and near-anaphylactic events to cow's milk occurring in the hospital. J Allergy Clinical Immunol; 1993;91(1pt2):152.

370. Seltzer S. Foods, and food and drug combinations, responsible for head and neck pain. Cephalalgia 1982 Jun;2(2):111-24.

371. Selye H. The Stress of Life. McGraw-Hill rev ed, 1984 .

372. Serio FG, Siegal MA, Slade BE. Plasma cell gingivitis of unusual origin. J Periodon 1991;62:390-3.

373. Settipane GA. The restaurant syndrome. N Eng Reg Allergy Proc 1987;8(1):39-46.

374. Settipane GA, Pudupakkam RK. Aspirin intolerance III: sub-types, familial occurence and cross reactivity with tartrazine. J Allergy Clin Immunol 1975;56:215-21.

375. Shannon WR. Neuropathic manifestations in infants and children as a result of anaphylactic reactions to foods contained in their diet. Am J Child Dis 1922;24:89-94.

376. Sheldon JM, Randolph TG. Allergy in migraine-like headaches. Am J Med Sci 1935;190:232-236.

377. Shulman, A. Tinnitus: Diagnosis/Treatment. Lea & Febiger, 1991.

378. Sicherer SH. Manifestations of food allergy: evaluation and management. Am Fam Physician 199915;59(2):415-24,429-30.

379. Sicherer SH, Burks AW, Sampson HA. Clinical features of acute allergic reactions to peanut and tree nuts in children. Pediatrics 1998;102(1):e6.

380. Silverman K, Evans SM, Strain EC, Griffiths RR. Withdrawal syndrome after the double-blind cessation of caffeine consumption. New Eng J Med 1992;327:1109-14.

381. Simon R A. Adverse reactions to food and drug additives. J Imm All Clinic NA 1996;16(1):137-76.

382. Skoldstam L, Larsson L, Lindstrom FD. Effect of fasting and lactovegetarian diet on rheumatoid arthritis. Scand J Rheumatol 1979;8(4):249-55.

383. Skoldstam L, Magnusson KE. Fasting, intestinal permeability, and rheumatoid arthritis. Rheum Dis Clin North Am 1991;17(2):363-71.

384. Sloper KS, Wadsworth J, Brostoff J. Children with atopic eczema. I: Clinical response to food elimination and subsequent double-blind food challenge. Q J Med 1991;80(292):677-93.

385. Sloper KS, Wadsworth J, Brostoff J. Children with atopic eczema. II: Immunological findings associated with dietary manipulations. Q J Med 1991;80(292):695-705.

386. Slot O, Locht. Arthritis as presenting symptom in silent adult coeliac disease. Two cases and review of the literature. Scand J Rheumatol 2000;29(4):260-3.

387. Smart GA, Sherlock JC. Nickel in foods and the diet. Food Addit Contam 1987;4(1):61-71.

388. Smith I, Kellow AH, Hannington E. A clinical and biochemical correlation between tyramine and migraine headache. Headache 1970;10:43-51.

389. Soutter V, Swain A, Loblay, R. Food allergy and food intolerance in young children. Asia Pacific Journal of Clinical Nutrition 1995;4(3):329.

390. Spector S. The role of allergy in sinusitis in adults. J Allergy Clin Immunol. 1992;90:518-520.

391. Speer F. Allergy and migraine: a clinical study. Headache 1971;11:63-67.

392. Speer F. Multiple food allergy. Ann Allergy 1975;34:71-6.

393. Speer F et al. Aspirin allergy. Ann Allergy 1981 46(3):123-6.

394. Speer G. Allergy of the Nervous System. Thomas 1970.

395. Spiller GA. The methylxanthine beverages and foods: chemistry, consumption and health effects. Prog Clin Biol Res 1984;1: 854-6.

396. Spring B et al. Psychobiological effects of carbohydrates. Journal of Clinical Psychiatry 50 Supplement, 1989.

397. Squire EN. Angioedema and MSG. Lancet 1987;24:167-72.

398. Staffieri D, Bentolila L, Leuit L. Hemiplegia and allergic symptoms following ingestion of certain foods. Ann Allergy 1951;10:38-39.

399. Stager J, Wuthrich B, Johanssen SGO. Spice allergy in celery-sensitive patients. Allergy 1991;41:475-78.

400. Steinman HA. Hidden allergens in foods. J Allergy Clin Immuno 1996;98(2):241-50.

401. Stenius BSM, Lemola M. Hypersensitivity to acetylsalicylic acid (ASA) and tartrazine in patients with asthma. Clin Allergy 1976;6:119-129.

402. Stevenson DD, Simon RA. Sensitivity to ingested metabisulfites in asthmatic subjects. J Allergy Clin Immunol 1981;68:26-32.

403. Stewart A. Tired all the time. Optima 1993.

404. Stoff JA, Pellegrino CR. Chronic fatigue Syndrome: The Hidden epidemic. Harper-Collins 1992.

405. Straus SE, Dale JK, Wright R, Metcalfe DD. Allergy and the chronic fatigue syndrome. J Allergy Clin Immunol 1988; 81(5 Pt 1):791-5.

406. Stricker WE, Anorve-Lopez E, Reed CE. Food skin testing in patients with idiopathic anaphylaxis. J Allergy Clin Immunol 1986;77:516-519.

407. Swain A , Dutten SP, Truswell AS. Salicylates in Food. J Am Dietetic Assoc 1985;85(8).

408. Swain A, Soutter V, Loblay R, et al. Salicylates, oligoantigenic diets, and behaviour. Lancet 1985;2 :41-42.

409. Tanaka R, Ichikawa K, Hamano K. Clinical characteristics of seafood allergy and classification of 10 seafood allergens by cluster analysis. Arerugi 2000;49(6):479-86.

410. Taylor SL. Chemical intoxications. In: Chiver DO (ed). Foodborne disease. S D Ac Press 1990:171-82.

411. Taylor SL, Byron B. Probable case of sorbitol-induced diarrhea. J Food Prot 1984;47:249.

412. Tettenborn M. Health Doctors "allergic to truth about food". BBC News on-line Tue Oct 13 1998.

413. Teuber SS, Brown RL, Haapanen LA. Allergenicity of gourmet nut oils processed by different methods. J Allergy Clin Immunol 1997;99(4):502-7.

414. Thune P, Granholt A. Provocation tests with antiphologistica and food additives in recurrent urticaria. Dermatogica 1975;151:360-64.

415. Todd E A et al. What do patients eat in hospital. Human Nutr Ampi Nutr 1984;38A:294-97.

416. Tollefson L. Quarterly report on consumer complaints on sulfiting agents. US Dept H&H Services, memo, April 2 1986:1-7.

417. Trotsky MB. Neurogenic vascular headaches, food and chemical triggers. EarNoseThroat J 94;73(4):228-36.

418. Van Bever HP, Docx M, Stevens WJ. Food and food additives in severe atopic dermatitis. Allergy 1989;44(8):588-94.

419. Van de Laar/van der Korst. Food intolerance in rheumatoid arthritis. A double blind, controlled trial of the clinical effects of elimination of milk allergens and azo dyes. Ann Rheum Dis 1992;51(3):298-302.
420. Van Dijk E, Neering H, Vitányi BE. Contact hypersensitivity to sesame oil in zinc oxide ointment. Ned. Tijdschr. Geneeskd. 1972,116:2255.
421. Van Dijk E, Neering H, Vitányi BE. Contact hypersensitivity to sesame oil in patients with leg ulcers and eczema. Acta Derm.-Vener. 1973;53:133.
422. Van Ketel WG. Immediate type allergy to malt in beer. Contact Derm 1980;6:297-8.
423. Varjonen E, Petman L, Makinen-Kiljunen S. Immediate contact allergy from hydrolyzed wheat in a cosmetic cream. Allergy 2000;55(3):294-6.
424. Varjonen E, Vanio E, Kalimo K, Junten-Backman K, Savolainen J. Skin-prick test and RAST responses to cereals in children with atopic dermatitis. Clin Exp Allergy 1995;25:1100-7.
425. Vatn MH. Food intolerance and psychosomatic experience. Scand J Work Environ Health 1997;23 Suppl 3:75-8.
426. Veien NK, Hattel T, Justesen O, Norholm A. Oral challenge with food additives. Contact Dermatitis 1987;17(2):100-3.
427. Veien NK, Hattel T, Justesen O, Norholm A. Dietary restrictions in the treatment of adult patients with eczema. Contact Dermatitis 1987;17(4):223-8.
428. Veien NK, Krogdahl A. Cutaneous vasculitis induced by food additives. Acta Derm Venereol 1991;71(1):73-4.
429. Verschave A, Stevens E, Degreef H. Pseudo-allergen-free diet in chronic urticaria. Derma 1983;167(5):256-9.
430. Vickers A, Zollman C. ABC of complementary medicine: Unconventional approaches to nutritional medicine. BMJ 1999;319:1419-1422.
431. Viscomi GJ. Allergic secretory otitis media: an approach to management. Laryngoscope 1975;85:751-758.
432. Vlissides DN, Venulet A, Jenner FA 2. A double-blind gluten-free/gluten-load controlled trial in a secure ward population. Br J Psychiatry 1986;148:447-5.
433. Vocks E, Borga A, Szliska C, Seifert HU, Seifert B, Burow G, Borelli S. Common allergenic structures in hazelnut, rye grain, sesame seeds, kiwi, and poppy seeds. Allergy 1993;48(3):168-72.
434. Wantke F, Gotz M, Jarisch R. The histamine-free diet. Hautarzt 1993;44(8):512-6.
435. Waring RH, Klovrza LV. Sulphur Metabolism in Autism. J Nut Env Med 2000;10:25-32.

436. Weber RW. Adverse reactions to the antioxidants BHA and BHT. In: Metcalfe DD, Sampson HA, Simon RA. (eds) Food Allergy: Adverse reactions to foods and food additives, 2nd ed. Blackwell Science 1997:387-95.

437. Weiss B, Williams JH, Margen S, Abrams B, Caan B, Citron LJ, Cox C, McKibben J, Ogar D, Schultz S. Behavioral responses to artificial food colors. Science 1980;28,207(4438):1487-9

438. Werbach M R. Nutritional Influences on Illness: A sourcebook of clinical research . Third Line Press 1996.

439. Werfel SJ, et al. Clinical reactivity to beef in children allergic to cow's milk. J Allergy Clin Immunol 1997;99(3):293-300.

440. Werth GR. Inhaled metabisulfite sensitivity. Letter. J Allergy Clin Immunol 1982;70:143.

441. WHO/FAO. Dietary carbohydrate and disease. In: Carbohydrates in human nutrition 1998. FAO F/N 66:19-23.

442. Williams AJ, Church SE, Finn R. An unsuspected case of wheat induced asthma. Thorax. 1987;42(3):205-6.

443. Williams R. Biochemical Individuality: The Basis for the Genetotrophic Concept. Keats 1998.

444. Williams WR et al. Aspirin-like effects of selected food additives and industrial sensitising agents. Clin Exp Allergy 1989;19(5):533-37.

445. Wolraich M, et al. The effects of sugar on behavior and cognition in children: a meta-analysis. J Am Med Assoc 1995;274:1617-1621.

446. Wray D. Gluten-sensitive recurrent aphthous stomatitis. Dig Dis Sci 1981;26:737-740.

447. Wright A, Ryan FP, Willingham SE, et al. Food allergy or intolerance in severe recurrent aphthous ulceration of the mouth. Br Med J 1986;292:1237-1238.

448. Wright R, Truelove SC. A controlled therapeutic trial of various diets in ulcerative colitis. BMJ 65;2:138-141.

449. Wurtman JJ, Brzezinski A, Wurtman RJ, Laferrere. Effect of nutrient intake on premenstrual depression. Am J Obst & Gyn 1989;161:1228-34

450. Wuthrich B, Fabro L. Acetylsalicylic acid and food additive intolerance in urticaria, bronchial asthma and rhinopathy. Schweiz Med Wochenschar 1981;111(39):1445-50.

451. Zhu SL, Ye ST, Yu Y. Allergenicity of orange juice and orange seeds: a clinical study. Asian Pac J Allergy Immunol 1989;7(1):5-8.

452. Zollner TM, Schmidt P, Kalveram CM, Emman AC, Boehncke WH. Allergy 2000;55(5):511.

453. Zuberbier T, et al. Pseudoallergen-free diet in the treatment of chronic urticaria. Acta Derm Venereol 1995 ;75(6):484-7.

454. Zuberbier T, Czarnetzki BM. High response rate to additive-free diet in chronic urticaria. Br J Dermatol 1996;134(6):1159.